ON SUNDAYS WE WORE WHITE

Eileen Elias re-creates family life between the years 1910 and 1920, a life that today seems like a different world. It is the story of a home bound by conventions of its time, when father knew best and on Sundays little girls wore white, a time when people believed that there would be peace forever. Of course, the Great War changed everything, especially the private world of a child.

EILEEN ELIAS

◆

ON SUNDAYS WE WORE WHITE

Complete and Unabridged

ULVERSCROFT
Leicester

First published in Great Britain in 1978 by
W. H. Allen & Co. Limited
London

First Large Print Edition
published August 1992

British Library CIP Data

Elias, Eileen
    On Sundays we wore white: childhood
reminiscences.—Large print ed.—
Ulverscroft large print series: non fiction
I. Title
942.163

    ISBN 0–7089–2692–4

Published by
F. A. Thorpe (Publishing) Ltd.
Anstey, Leicestershire
Set by Words & Graphics Ltd.
Anstey, Leicestershire
Printed and bound in Great Britain by
T. J. Press (Padstow) Ltd., Padstow, Cornwall

To my husband

To my husband

Introduction:

'Get Off at the Fire Station'

I GOT off the bus at the Fire Station — the familiar red Fire Station that we all knew when we were young. 'Get off at the Fire Station,' we used to tell our visitors. 'You can't miss it.' Only it was the tram that took you there in those days, lurching and groaning along the busy South London streets. Slowly I walked up the quiet tree-lined road; any road, in any suburb, houses all alike of yellow brick, bay windows, trim front gardens, seven white steps up to each front door.

At first sight it hadn't changed a bit. There were gaps between the houses, certainly, here and there; and a new block of flats where one of the flying bombs had landed. But the acacia trees still bordered the road, one outside every fifth house, though the little verge of green grass of which we used to be so

1

proud — 'just like the country' — had given way to hard grey asphalt, easier to maintain.

And yet it wasn't the same. Little things were subtly different. Some of the houses were divided into two, if not three. Gone for ever were the days of the large family, the daily 'girl', the tradesmen's entrance. Cars and motor-bikes stood outside, TV aerials sprouted ungracefully from the blue slate roofs; prams and push-chairs, with sleeping babies in them, cluttered the little front gardens.

I turned the bend in the road, where we first used to catch a glimpse of the trees in the Park. ('So lucky to have a park near by; you might be miles away from London.') The Council school across the way was just the same; brick walls, forbidding high windows, asphalted playground with 'Boys', 'Girls' and 'Infants' inscribed above the three iron gateways. But I noticed a new and unfamiliar name on the white-painted board outside; and a new canteen adjoined the school yard. School dinners, of course; nobody ran home now at twelve o'clock for dinner with Mum; Mum as likely as not wouldn't be there.

On round the corner, and there it was — the fifth house from the end. Just the same, solid, brick and friendly; till you noticed that the iron railings bordering the little front garden had gone for scrap during the War, and the fancy iron gate that used to bang behind us as we rushed home from school had gone, too. It looked a trifle bare, exposed to the road like that. We used to be proud of our little iron railings that shut us away from the world.

Up the seven steps to the front door, with a glance at the bay window to see if Mother had twitched aside the lace curtain and was waving from within. But the lace curtains had gone; there were unfamiliar ones now. Bang on the knocker, the polished brass knocker that was shined up proudly each morning; but the knocker wasn't there any more. Only an unfriendly-looking electric bell, with two metal name-plates beside it. And I knew that when I pressed it, no warm welcome would meet me as the door was opened; only an inquiring stare when I told them that this was once home.

1

Beginnings

MORE than two World Wars ago, a young Welsh doctor and his wife pushed a mailcart up this same tree-lined road. The houses were newly-built, and the district was what the house-agents called 'desirable'. It was still called a mailcart then, the big high black perambulator with its two large wheels and two small, its glossy leather hood smelling of polish, its box seats, one at each end, over which you could lay a floor if you were making a bed for the new baby. The desirable district was New Cross, in South London, and the road was Waller Road. All the roads around were named after seventeenth and eighteenth century worthies — Waller, Erlanger, Pepys, Arbuthnot, Jerningham. Worthy names for worthy roads; and the young couple were proud to be living there.

He was in a curly-brimmed bowler and a black overcoat with an astrakhan collar. She was in a broad-brimmed hat, piled with fruit and flowers; feather-boa'ed, trimly corseted, voluminously skirted. Beside them ran a little boy in a blue serge sailor suit with a floppy tie and a whistle and lanyard. Of the baby in the mailcart you couldn't have seen much because of all the frills and furbelows, for a new baby must always be protected from the dangers of sun and air beneath layers of clothing and veiling. But the couple were obviously content with their family. George V had just come to the throne; the new house in the modern residential street was admired by all (had it not gas and a geyser?) and the baby in the mailcart was just what they wanted — a girl. It was 1910 and life was good.

In fact, as soon as I could know or feel anything, I was aware, through my parents, that I had been born into a goodly heritage. Nothing, it seemed then, could have given a child a better start. It was an age of satisfaction. There was horror and want in the streets — I

6

caught glimpses of barefoot children, heard angry voices shouting outside the pubs at night, listened to talk of murders and burglaries, and people still spoke of Jack the Ripper, and of notorious Charlie Peace, arch-criminal of the last century, who had lived only a few streets away. But our little home was inviolate; our station in life the most desirable that could be imagined. Nothing could touch our own safe family.

I used to count my blessings, the blessings which everybody knew came from living in a house with a bay window, in a yellow-brick road with trees all along it. It was a comfortable life. Ours was, of course, a world of classes; nobody then had discovered anything wrong with the threefold division into which we had been born — upper, middle and lower. We belonged, I was told, to the middle classes. Not the upper class, which would be altogether too superior; not the lower class, which would mean going to board-school and dropping your aitches and having a dirty face; but to the satisfactory, in-between middle class, where little boys wore sailor suits like my brother, and little girls wore white on Sundays.

My father was a professional man, I also learned. This didn't mean money; money anyway was not the criterion; but it did mean education, and that was important. Was he not a medical man? Then again, we lived in London. London, they told me, time and time again, was the best place in the world into which to be born. We didn't live in the City, which was busy and crowded, but in the suburbs, which were residential and quiet. You couldn't have chosen a more suitable place if you'd tried. And the acacia trees and the Park made it just like the country.

Then, too, I discovered, we were British. How lucky to have been born into the right nation, the top nation, the one with the Empire marked in red on the map, the Empire that children saluted every year on Empire Day when there were flags and marching and patriotic songs. The British, everybody knew, were masters of the world. And the wars of the past were all over; history-book affairs. There would be peace for ever now;

nobody would go to war any more.

In short, there was nothing else a child could desire, they told me. Tightly rolled in this warm ball of comfort, I spent my earliest years in a pleasant haze of contentment. How fortunate we were to have been born just here, just now, just like this!

Father, born in Anglesey and reared in Wales in an age when young men of ambition studied hard and 'got on' (which meant coming to London, of course), had begun to train as a doctor at Bangor University. He was the typical Welshman of the turn of the century — short, dark, limpid-eyed, with handsome whiskers, a curly forelock, a Welsh lilt to his voice, and a passionate Celtic temper, which flared up and was gone. Life to him was a constant challenge, full of wonder, full of things to do and worlds to conquer. In the middle of his training his father had died, and left the little family in sore straits, so he was forced to cut short his medical studies and go as a young, partly-qualified assistant to a local doctor, after the manner of his time.

He would tell us hair-raising stories of rough rides in pony and trap up mountain passes in Snowdonia, to visit the sick; of critical operations performed with a pen-knife on scrubbed farmhouse tables when snow outside made the roads impassable; of patients brought down steep hillsides on home-made stretchers to the waiting ambulance two or three fields below; of children dying of diphtheria, young girls sickening with the dreaded tuberculosis, old men writhing in the mental agonies of delirium tremens brought about by drink; of midnight watches by pneumonia bedsides for the 'crisis' which would restore life or take it away; of raging epidemics due to foul water or lack of sanitation, when tents had to be pitched in fields to receive the patients the local hospital could not cram in. The life of a country doctor in those times was full of the troubles of the age.

Yet it was full, too, of humour and zest, and Father was the first to appreciate them. We used to laugh at his tales of gullible patients and doting relatives, listen open-mouthed to his accounts of country spells and witcheries calculated to cure any disorder, and chuckle over his character-sketches of country people of an age long gone. Gradually, however, as times changed, Father found his semi-qualified position increasingly difficult. New medical legislation barred the door of formal medicine to him for ever, and at last he had to turn to the bypaths of medical practice, becoming medical adviser or research chemist to a variety of firms, but abandoning sadly the round of the G.P.

It was an unhappy compromise for him to make, for he had in abundance the qualities of integrity, discernment and personal kindliness which, with the requisite skill, could have made a success of doctoring. However, his life henceforth was to be one long compromise, and somehow the chance of using his remarkable abilities to the full never seemed to come his way.

Before giving up general practice, he had at last come to London, his Mecca, as assistant to a Dr Milburn in Myddelton Square, Islington, where he met and married the young governess to the doctor's two children. Gentle, quiet-voiced and as mild as he was passionate, my mother adored him, bore with him, laughed at him, coaxed and persuaded him, and saw him through a multitude of disappointments and frustrations. She and Father set up house together in Waller Road. Everything was to the liking of a young couple at the beginning of the century. The house, which had been built only a few years before, backed onto Telegraph Hill Park, where, so they said, the beacons had flashed the news of Trafalgar and Waterloo; a bit of history which Father loved. There was a long narrow uphill garden at the rear, and a smaller one in front. There was a tradesmen's entrance, a bathroom with real hot water from the geyser, bay windows with Virginia creeper trailing over them, covering the house with autumn glory. The neighbours were quiet, the shops just around the corner, and the trams at the bottom of the road. There was even a school a quarter of a mile away, not the Board school opposite but a 'good class' school as they called it then, with one building for boys and another for girls; the Haberdashers' Aske's School in Jerningham Road.

The only trouble was that the house was too large. So my mother's sister, a schoolteacher and unmarried, came to live with the young couple, taking over the top floor. Into this tight little world of respectability and contentment came, first a boy, in 1903, called Aubrey after the old family name from Wales, and nearly seven years later, in 1910, a girl.

There had been no Eileens in the family at all, and it was considered at the time rather an outlandish name, Irish or Scottish rather than Welsh, and by some, not even quite nice. Why not Gertrude, or Phyllis, or Helen, or Marjorie? But Mother obstinately clung to the name she liked, and so my second name had to be something acceptable to the neighbourhood — good solid Winifred, which would do for anybody and could not possibly cause offence.

People must have wondered somewhat, when the couple first moved in and started their family, about this strangely assorted pair; the stocky little Welsh doctor and his tall graceful young wife; so different, yet so obviously united. They didn't look as though they suited each other at all; yet this was clearly a love-match. In those days, of course, you married forever, and to love and to cherish was the height of Mother's ambition. She loved and cherished through thick and thin; through Father's storms and tempers, through money worries and family problems, through all the stresses of childbearing in the little back bedroom overlooking the garden, and child-rearing in the narrow terraced house with its thirty-three stairs. Perhaps it was the sheer hard work of it all that kept her so slim.

Mother was slender, oval-faced, with warm brown eyes full of affection, and a warm wide smile to match. She wore her hair in the fashion of the age — piled up in great swathes around her head. I loved to tiptoe into her bedroom in the mornings, and see her in her frilly white cotton nightgown with the wide collar and the full sleeves, sitting at the dressing-table and brushing her long soft hair. 'I used to be able to sit on it when

I was a girl,' she would say, a little wistfully. I would watch the smooth strokes of the brush on the shining hair, and think of a waterfall, rippling and flowing. Then she would twist it up high, and pin it with a multitude of hairpins, and standing, corseted and camisoled and petticoated before the mirror, put on the long-skirted blue serge dress with the spotted collar and cuffs, and fix the net modesty vest at her throat. You always wore a modesty vest, as it was called, to cover yourself if your neckline was low. You had a collection of them, tucked, lace-inserted, or embroidered, fastening with tiny gold safety-pins to the camisole underneath, and neatly covering the neck; a relic, no doubt, of the Edwardian high collar. (Our kindergarten teacher still wore a boned collar that reached right up round her throat, nearly to her ears, and we used to wonder how she could turn her head without being throttled.) If it was Sunday she would put on her shiny black or dark-blue silk that rustled a little when she walked. It had floating panels at each side, and in this, I was sure, she was the most beautiful mother in the world.

Nobody except Mother ever saw Father in less than full attire; except occasionally for a fleeting moment when he was emerging from the bedroom, fastening his gold cuff-links into the stiff cuffs of his white shirt before putting on the high-collared black coat that went with his pin-striped trousers. He would have been deeply shocked to be seen in any state of undress, let alone in bed. A gentleman was always perfectly attired, even at seven o'clock in the morning.

Short, lively, with brilliant brown eyes that took in everything, and a well-trimmed moustache and whiskers, he made up in dignity what he lacked in stature. His expressive face could beam approval or delight, as instantly as it could darken with anger; and while it was comfortable to sit on his knee in the old red leather armchair and play with the golden guinea he dangled on his watch-chain, it was a terrible thing to be the recipient of his rage, even if it was over a trifle and instantly forgotten. But in spite of frustrations and furies, Father enjoyed life to the full, and you could see that he did. His step was quick and light; he marched, rather than walked, down the road, as if on adventure bent; as indeed he usually was. Life to him was a perpetual adventure. He was the pioneer, the trail-blazer, the man of ideas, of enthusiasms, of optimism; even though he had by now to abandon the doctor's practice in elegant Myddelton Square for a modest little house in South London, and chemical research in the basement.

Neighbours liked him for the twinkle in his eye; churchgoers respected his regularity and decorum. Mother calmed him, upheld him, bore with him and adored him; and he, in his erratic, passionate way, was as devoted to her. You could tell that from the way his eyes rested on her dark head as he leaned against the piano-top to sing; and the way she glanced up from the keys to meet his gaze. For the whole of their married life they were only apart for two weeks, and even then they wrote to each other every day.

Father and Mother were both content with the little home in Waller Road. Now that he was no longer in doctoring,

Father didn't need a big place with a surgery; he had found himself work as medical adviser to a firm of industrial chemists, and he could do it at home, with occasional journeys to London on the lurching tram that conveniently passed the bottom of the road. He had his regrets, no doubt, and, as a married man with the inevitable family to follow, he could see no possibility of finishing his studies. There were no mature student grants in those days; no benefactors who could put him back on the road to medicine. No matter; life was full of opportunities, and with his usual optimism he set to work to conduct his many and mysterious chemical experiments, down in the dim regions of the basement. He set up a laboratory for himself, alongside the stone sink and the big copper and the mangle and the dolly-tub that were the normal basement furniture of the houses in our road.

Later, Father spread his wings and took a proper laboratory in a back street round the corner. A laboratory sounded to me very grand, though I couldn't make out what he did there. Father and my brother, who had an equally scientific turn of mind, spent all their spare time round there at what he solemnly called 'The Industrial Chemical Laboratories', though it was only a cobwebby building in a corner of Harry Roberts' coal yard. Mother and I used to take them round their tea in a Thermos flask on Saturdays, and I would talk to old Harry and be invited in for a cup of his mother's strong sweet tea in her dark little parlour overlooking the yard. At home, Father spent most of his time in the basement, a white coat over his black jacket and pin-striped trousers, doing strange things with glass retorts and bunsen burners; once started on research of any kind, he could never stop, and his brilliant butterfly mind was for ever working out new inventions and discoveries.

True, it was difficult on Mondays, when the basement was needed for the enormous family wash. Father had to be banished to his study upstairs, or to 'The Industrial Chemical Laboratories'. But by and large, though there were certain inconveniences, the yellow-brick house was a good place in which to start a family. He and Mother certainly wished for nothing better.

It was a rented house, of course; nobody we knew ever bought a house, unless they had suddenly come into a vast amount of money. To rent was perfectly satisfactory; you felt just as much of a house-owner that way. Nobody we knew ever wanted to move, either; none of our neighbours ever moved house, unless it was at the very end of their married lives when the children had left home, and even then it was looked upon as rather daring to retire to the country or the sea. Nothing, certainly, would budge Father from the home that was as near perfection as he could hope for. 'Why move?' he would ask. People in those days expected to go on living in the same place till they died; and indeed, that was precisely what my parents did. As for me, I couldn't conceive of any other home than this, the tall narrow house with the bay window and the seven steps up to the front door.

Our house was a house of stairs; thirty-three of them if you counted from the bottom to the very top. Starting from the basement, where the tradesmen's entrance was from the street, you climbed five steep linoleumed steps, past the dark little recess where we hung our hats and coats, to the brown-varnished door with its panes of coloured glass that led to the breakfast-room and kitchen. Every house had its coloured glass; and was proud of it, too.

I always thought it sounded very grand to have a breakfast-room. It was only our family who called it that; in every other house it was the living-room, for every day. Father, however, thought differently; there had always been a breakfast-room in the big houses where he had been the doctor's assistant and Mother the governess, so there must be one in his own. Most of the year, it was a gloomy room, with its bay window opening onto the yard that divided the back of our house from the back of the one next door. All you could see was wooden fence and brick wall, with never a glimpse of green. By contrast the kitchen, which opened out of it, was lighter and happier; it gave onto the garden, and Mother worked in summer-time with the door wide open, so that she could see the trees, and the lilac bush in bloom, and let the sunlight stream in to make bright patterns on the floor. But never a hint of sun reached the breakfast-room, even in the height of summer weather.

It was cosy enough in winter, though, when the fire burned brightly in the blackleaded grate, the kettle sang on its hob, and the old collie dog Gelert dozed on the hearthrug, snuffling gently in his sleep. Father had his special red leather armchair beside the fire, though it was worn a little; it had been with him since his earliest doctoring days, Mother had her carpet-chair, as we called it, on the opposite side of the fire; carpet-chairs, with sling seats of stout carpet-like material, and varnished wooden arms and back, were popular along our road.

Family meals were taken at the big table in the middle, with Mother's white starched cloth spread over the green bobble-edged table cover. When the meal was over, she would take the silver crumb-slice that had been given her as a wedding present, along with the usual toast rack and cruet set and serviette rings that every bride received, and sweep the crumbs from the cloth so that the table could revert to its usual purpose. At night, when the heavy curtains were drawn to keep out the November fogs and the February dampness, even our dull old breakfast-room seemed a comfortable place. Mother would light the gas mantle, and start the ironing, the smell of newly-ironed aprons and shirts and sheets and pillowcases giving the room a homely air; the sizzle of the flat-irons as they heated on the fire mingled with the bump-bump of her rhythmic ironing as she pressed each garment and hung it on the brass fireguard rail to air.

Good smells often came from the kitchen too, in winter-time, where Mother would be taking hot scones from the old black oven. For her, the little kitchen, with its scrubbed table, its dark stone sink in the corner, and its wobbly home-made cupboards where she kept all the groceries, must have left a lot to be desired. Nobody bothered about 'kitchen fitments' then; and nobody had heard of refinements like vacuum cleaners or

23

refrigerators; indeed, they couldn't have installed a vacuum cleaner, for no one had electricity, and even gas was an uncertain, flickering affair that certainly wouldn't have supported a refrigerator. Mother kept the meat and the perishables in what she called 'the safe', with a perforated zinc door to keep out the flies, and lived in perpetual fear in summer-time of something 'going off' — which quite often it did.

Up another five stairs, also linoleumed, and you were at street level, where the big front door, with its inevitable panes of coloured glass, opened onto the narrow hall. With the hall, our house at last began to assume a certain dignity. The hall was an important place; visitors were received there; the grandfather clock ticked there; the carved oak hall stand, Father's pride, held the family's sticks and umbrellas and parasols, and gloves in a little drawer. Life really began, I used to think, at the hall, with the sunny bay-windowed dining-room opening out of it, full of the best carved oak furniture Father had bought for his wedding.

The dining-room was bright and looked

out onto the road with its acacia trees; it was special, too, for everything good, like Christmas and parties and roast Sunday dinners, always happened in the dining-room. Father and Mother were immensely proud of all the carved oak; especially the sideboard, with its tiny mirrored shelves, full of knick-knacks and little flower-vases, and the carved lions' heads on the handles to the cupboards and drawers. It was a wicked piece of furniture to dust and polish, but it spoke of glory; Father had bought it, and Father adored it. There was a carved table and six carved chairs to match, besides the green plush couch and Father's deep-buttoned armchair, and the ebony table in the bay which held the aspidistra in its brass bowl and the huge family Bible with all our names and dates of birth and christenings written on the fly-leaf. There were draped lace curtains, and thick green baize ones to draw over them at dusk, and Venetian blinds. Venetian blinds were a sign of respectability at the windows in our road; you scrubbed them, slat by slat, out in the garden at spring-cleaning time; you drew them in summer so that the sun shouldn't make the upholstery fade; and in winter to shut out the dark, and of course, as a mark of respect, whenever there was a funeral in the street, with the black horses with their dipping black plumes drawing the hearse at a solemn pace. Funerals were frightening things, and I was always glad when we drew down the Venetian blinds.

There was a piano, too, in the dining-room; our family's pride and joy; rosewood, polished, candle-lit and glorious. Mother played it and Father sang to it; later, I practised my piano pieces at it, and my brother struggled to learn the violin to Aunt Jane's accompaniment. But only when Father wasn't working in his curtained-off study next door.

We were always a little in awe of Father's study; really, an alcove off the dining-room, but in those days a man expected a place for retirement. Here Father read, smoked and meditated, Mother always seeing that he was supplied with Player's Navy Cut tobacco at sixpence ha'penny for a two-ounce tin. Even Mother thought twice about disturbing him when he was behind the blue-and-green tapestry curtains. The study was a dim place full of books and little tables and reading-lamps with green globes, fuelled by paraffin, the floor stacked with old medical journals, newspapers, encyclopaedias and magazines which Father was always going to sort and never did.

Father was a great reader, and a great buyer and borrower of books. His taste was catholic; his study shelves held rows and rows of medical and scientific manuals, mixed up with all the classics — Milton and Shakespeare in red covers, with gold lettering on the spines, Thackeray and H. G. Wells and the other 'moderns' of his time. Certain books, however, were banned. No Shelley; and no Oscar Wilde; one was an atheist, and the other worse, though nobody would ever tell me why. There was one particular favourite of Father's called *Self-Help-Smiles* or so I thought; a curious title, I told myself and a curious subject — why write a book about smiles? It took me years to find that the book was on that very Victorian subject, self-help, of which Father vehemently approved; and its author was one Samuel Smiles. Father never allowed his books to be touched without permission, nor his papers to be disturbed by dusting; Mother was always longing to put them in some sort of order, but Father insisted that in the chaos he always knew just where everything was — though, as he frequently lost things and sent the whole house into uproar until they were found, we privately doubted his system. But the study was his domain; even with the curtains open, we were nervous of going inside.

Up from the hall, another twelve steps — the linoleum giving way to red and blue Turkey carpet — led to the best bedroom and bathroom floor. Most of Mother's and Father's bedroom was taken up with the high brass bed, with white curtains at the head and foot, a heavy white crochet coverlet, and heavy blankets. Nobody in our house could sleep unless weighed down by blankets to keep out the cold of the open windows. Father was determined about the open windows. 'Nothing like good fresh air to keep you healthy,' he would say, throwing up the sash to let a piercing draught howl through the bedroom.

On one side of the bed Father kept his green-shaded oil reading lamp; he needed very little sleep, and used to read till the small hours by its steady gentle light — Shakespeare, the Bible and Einstein every night, a little bit of each 'to store in the mind' as he put it. On the other side were Mother's bedside treasures; books of all sorts, little vases of flowers picked from the garden, letters from friends; she was a great letter-writer. A large mahogany cupboard with a mirrored door contained Father's black jackets and striped trousers, and Mother's long-skirted coats and dresses; a shining mahogany dressing-table held her lavender-scented handkerchiefs and Sunday gloves, and Father's collar-box for his starched collars. A bow-fronted chest of drawers held everything else, including the household linen, which often overflowed into two tin trunks in the little bathroom next door.

Everyone shivered in our bathroom, except on special days when an oil stove was put there to warm the air. It was a bare little room with its geyser and uninviting white bath and basin, and we didn't much care for going into it on winter mornings to take the cold baths on which Father was so keen. Cold plunges were the best possible tonic for the nerves, he would say; good for the health, like the open windows. 'Look at me,' he told us. 'Never had a day's illness, and all due to six inches of cold water every morning.' Indeed he never missed his daily plunge, to the very end of his life, and though he couldn't persuade Mother to take it up, he insisted on it for his children. When we grumbled, sponging ourselves in the six inches of cold water measured out for us on the bleakest of January days, Father would tell us we were lucky to have a bathroom at all. Plenty of houses he knew hadn't got one, let alone a separate lavatory next door.

Still more stairs followed, six from the best bedroom up to the third floor, and five more to the top. Here were my aunt's rooms and the children's bedrooms, once we had been promoted from the white-curtained cot in which babies invariably began their lives next to their parents' bed. The Turkey carpet that led up from the hall had long since given out up here, and it was linoleum again to the attic-rooms; the gas jets had given out too, and candles in white enamelled candlesticks were taken up the last flight of stairs, throwing flickering shadows along the length of the narrow passage. All the bedrooms were simple places; iron beds, with the obligatory white curtain frill at head and foot; linoleumed floors; wooden chests and cupboards. There was a special type of bedroom chair, white-painted with a cane bottom; it wouldn't have seemed right to have anything more comfortable in the bedroom, which, as people pointed out, was only a place to sleep in. My aunt had a wash-stand and towel-horse in her bedroom, for it was a long way down all those stairs to the one little bathroom below. Wash-stands were always the same; yellowish wood, with marble tops and china jugs and basins and toothbrush holders; and your towel and face flannel were always damp, because there was never any heating to dry them by. My parents bedroom, indeed, had a fireplace, but nobody ever lit the fire except when there was illness. If there was ice on the window-sill, you took the oil stove upstairs 'to warm the air'. It smoked if you put the wick up too high, and went out if you pushed it down too low; and of course it didn't warm the bed at all. A hot water bottle did that; and my parents thought they were very modern when they bought an aluminium one instead of the usual one of brown stone.

Stairs; stairs; stairs; there were just too many of them. Thirty-three stairs, climbing from floor to floor; all to be carpeted or linoleumed, with stair-rods to be polished and surfaces to be cleaned, with dustpan and brush, or a pail and scrubbing-brush and a bar of yellow Sunlight soap. Mother must have run up and down those stairs dozens of times every day; but she didn't mind. A house of their own to rent for as long as they lived — that to my parents was bliss. The house, stairs and all, was the high spot, the hallmark, of their marriage. It was home, and always would be; home, where they lived and loved and presided; the frame for their family.

If one's earliest memory is perhaps significant, then mine must have been so in this little world of contentment, for it was of groping through the bars of my cot to seek Mother's hand in the deep darkness of the night, and finding it there ready to hold and caress. There, in a nutshell, seems to be the whole mother-and-child relationship. Seeking and finding; warmth and comfort and solace; darkness, and content. A good way to start life. Two or three more years were to pass before the world my parents knew was to be shattered by war; yet in those few quiet years I had time to take sure root in a home I believed to be the best in the world, and to be loved; naturally one loved, and was loved by, one's relations. It was as simple as that.

The second glimpse of memory is riding in my pram — it was just beginning to be called a perambulator then, having been, for all the years before, a mailcart good and proper, and Mother often slipped into the old use of the word even now. We were going down the road past the Council school, and I shouted my delight as the children came running out.

'I'm going there!' I cried, longing for the day when I should be big enough to run across the road to school. But this blithe remark was met, to my astonishment, with disapproval on the part of Frances, the 'girl', who was pushing the pram; we were not grand enough to have a maid or a nurse, but just grand enough to have a daily girl.

'No, you don't, Miss,' said Frances sternly. 'It's not the thing. You'll go to a nice school where they speak proper.' Children, she went on to explain, were of two kinds, 'rough' and 'nice'. I, it appeared, was to mix only with the latter sort.

I was duly puzzled by this, my first meeting with the class-distinctions which still ruled the world in the days just before the First War, and for a good while after. I already knew about the middle classes, the comfortable position which I always thought of as the tasty middle of the sandwich. Now I knew that there were classes amongst children too; the rough ones and the nice. I was informed, quite firmly and irrevocably, to which one I belonged, and to which kind of school I was going. I accepted the distinction with surprise, but without question. In those days you knew where you were and what was expected of you, and you did it. It was a safe, well-regulated, unworried world; and it was not till I grew older and myself felt the first tremors and cracks of the crumbling class system when World War One had begun to split it apart, that I felt any need to question these accepted codes.

From time to time, however, even those of us who lived sheltered lives caught glimpses, fleeting ones, of the world of the Rough from which, by Heaven's bounty, we had been preserved. Little street boys came to the door of our basement — the tradesmen's entrance that spoke of gentility — and I caught a brief sight, as I was hanging round the skirts of Frances or my mother, of bare feet, very dirty; rough jerseys with worn elbows, and tousled hair.

The boys came round with buckets of horse manure, which they hawked from house to house around our quiet street with its gardens. 'Penny a bucket! Penny a bucket! Do yer garden good!' they would shout, thrusting the malodorous bucket underneath our noses. I was fascinated by these boys, and tried hard to get a chance of watching them at work.

Sometimes I was lucky enough to be able to slip out and see them. Whenever the milkman came, I was privileged to run outside and hold out the metal can into which the milkman would ladle his milk, and this was occasionally a chance to watch for the street boys with their buckets. Sometimes, too, Frances would hear one of those new-fangled things, aeroplanes, humming overhead, and then also I was allowed to run outside into the street to gaze wonderingly up into the sky; everybody ran out to see an aeroplane. If a horse and cart had just been up the road, clip-clopping along with the bread or the cats' meat, a throng of little boys would follow with eagle eyes, shovels at the ready to catch any droppings and transfer them to the clanking iron buckets in their hands. This they sold from house to house, making, as I thought, a princely sum in such a simple manner that anybody could do the same. What a good way of making money, I thought, and longed to be out and about with my own bucket following the horses. My heart beat fast at the prospect of having so much money to spend. The Saturday penny, later increased to twopence, went quite a long way, it is true, at Mrs Evans', the sweetshop, or at the Penny Bazaar; 'The Rainbow' cost one penny, and a bag of jelly babies could be bought with the other, or two pink and white sugar mice with black eyes and string tails. But from following the horses, what wealth could be amassed! Not only sugar mice, but oranges and chocolate bars and black boot-laces of liquorice and tiny china dolls just as big as the joint of your little finger. All from horse manure!

At last I plucked up courage to ask Frances for a bucket. 'The one under the sink would do quite well,' I told her. 'We only use that on washing day.' But again, as in the case of the Council school, I was in for a surprise.

'Going round behind the horses, Miss!'

Frances was flabbergasted. 'Whatever next? Your Mum would have a fit, really she would. Nice little girls don't do that.'

So here it was again, then; the strange division into two worlds, the rough and the nice. Rough boys might run behind the horses, but nice little girls couldn't. Again I retired, baffled but unprotesting. It seemed a pity that the rough children got all the fun.

The sounds from the 'rough' world outside, however, impinged nearly every night into the comfortable fireside world of home. Towards evening, we would become subtly aware of the life outside; the wild mysterious life of the streets; the boys with their tousled hair. Iron hoops would trundle along pavements; sticks would jerk a savage rhythm along railings; roller-skates would whirr through the gathering darkness; cat-calling and whistling would sound eerily from the distances; whistling of children at play in the blue dusk, of hiders and seekers, of lads after girls. Last of all, about nine o'clock, the age-old haunting cry would come, of the boys rounding up their fellows from the emptying streets: 'All home! All ho-o-me!' It was a sad, strange cry, bringing, in the autumn evenings, a sadness into the peaceful gas-lit world of our home, a hint of distant melancholy which used to disturb my dreams.

Outside there was the darkening blue of the pavements, the misty vapours of the Park, the pools of gaslight from the tall iron lamps at the street corners. But inside, when the curtains were pulled, the thick green ones over the draped lace, the gas-lamps lit, with careful application of the match to the fragile pyramid of the mantle, and careful turning up of the quivering flame till it glowed steadily, a throbbing, golden, singing globe of light; when the fire crackled in the grate, and the kettle purred on the hob, and the old collie dog slept on the black hearth rug, and there was the smell of newly-ironed pinafores and bread-and-milk — then the plaintive cries outside would be forgotten, and all my life would be warm and certain, ordered and lovely.

2

Monday

I HAD in my vivid imagination a mental colour for each day of the week. Monday was a dull pewter grey, drab as the dank smell of the washing and the workaday world in general. By Tuesday things were looking up; the house was nutty-sweet with the smell of freshly ironed linen, so Tuesday was a pale silvery-blue.

By Wednesday the week had really got going; pale blue was succeeded by azure like the summer sky. Thursday was green and peaceful; Friday, taking its cue from the fried fish which appeared on every dinner table down our road, was golden-brown like the tasty fillets hot from the pan. Saturday, a day on which anything might happen, was scarlet in glory. Sunday was white, pristine and untouched; after which the greyness of Monday reflected the greyness of my spirits.

On Monday the household was wakened early, as befitted the stern conception of Duty first, Pleasure afterwards, on which we were reared. No lying in bed; to work, to work. Everybody knew it was washing day, and lifted an eye to the sky outside to see whether the sheets would blow. The housewife who was the first along the road to get a line of snowy linen billowing in the back garden was entitled to a smug sense of satisfaction.

By the time I was seven, I was considered old enough to lend a hand on washing day. Frances, the daily girl, had now departed. For some months I had realised dimly that her days with us were numbered; our family fortunes, never very stable, had run lower than ever, and even a girl was now out of the question. Frances went to help her father in the fish business, which he successfully conducted in one of the back streets half a mile away; whenever I had been taken there on a walk, the family at the fish-shop had been lavish with sweets and biscuits, and I had the feeling that the fishmonger's fortunes were, curiously, in a better way than our own.

Anyway we had to get on without Frances. She gave me a parting hug and was gone. Mother was determined, however, that though the family prestige had been shaken, the running of the household should go on as smoothly as before. Nobody should ever guess that this was a servantless house. Shining white table napkins and cloths appeared, beautifully and painstakingly laundered, on our tables as before; the clothes were all immaculate; the rosewood piano top shone with polish; the brass knocker on the front door gleamed like gold, though I guessed Mother had to get up at crack of dawn to do the cleaning of it, before anybody was about to notice her. The only household task with which she had any help at all now — and everybody along the road employed help for this, for no self-respecting housewife would ever be seen on hands and knees in the street — was the cleaning of the front steps.

Twice a week, wet or fine, an army of step-ladies, as we called them, used to advance clanking up the road, metal buckets swinging at their hips, scrubbing-brushes in their hands, sacking aprons firmly pinned round ample waists, a man's cap topping their hair. Their job was to scrub the steps leading up to the front doors at sixpence a time, hearth-stone and water being provided by the housewife. Each household had its preference in step ladies; but of late years, the honours had always gone to the same person, the step-lady of all step-ladies, Lightning Lizzie.

Lightning Lizzie had earned her name by the amazing speed with which she did the steps from house to house along the road. By the time one of the old brigade of cleaners was just heaving herself up from her knees at the bottom step of one house, Lightning Lizzie had done two or three more, and was already half way up the road, taking everybody else's custom. She was small and spare, with a long angular face, pointed chilly-looking nose, and snapping grey eyes that missed nothing. Lightning Lizzie alone was not fat and cheerful like the others; never called you 'ducks', never produced a sweet for you from capacious skirt pockets. Nor did she wear a man's cap like the others; her hair was pushed lankly back from a bony forehead, from which it flapped as she worked and was pushed back again with raw red hands as she scrubbed; but oh, how she worked!

I used to watch spellbound as her thin arms moved skilfully over the steps, and the grey stone changed to dazzling white as she scrubbed and hearthstoned. Almost before you could count ten, Lightning Lizzie had done the whole flight and was off next door.

Lightning Lizzie did her steps so well that many housewives gave her more than the customary sixpence, and she had all the other step-ladies beaten. They muttered darkly after her, but even they had to concede her a grudging admiration for the skill with which she plied her trade.

Lightning Lizzie, however, was now the only bit of domestic help that was to come our way for a long time. So I had to set to and help on washing day, at least during the time I happened to be home from school. I helped reluctantly; I would much rather have been out in the garden playing, but work had to be done, and the sooner you did it, the sooner it was over.

Mother got up very early and came down in clothes that meant business. After Sunday's black silk, Monday's garb, of blue serge with a white embroidered modesty vest at the neck, seemed dull and shabby. She would put on an apron, and, while the porridge was boiling, go down the worn linoleumed steps to the big cold basement to light the copper fire. This was a tricky business: the copper was ancient and cracked, and the fire took a long time to get up; yet the whole of our working day was dependent on the copper fire burning well, and if it went out, Monday's entire routine was disrupted.

'I'll just run down and see how the copper fire's burning,' Mother would say half a dozen times during breakfast, and jumping up from the table would go below for a tour of inspection, returning with a face filled with joy or gloom according to the state of the fire. I would raise an anxious face from my bowl of porridge whenever she came back. 'Is it going?' I would ask; and if the answer was yes, then I knew the day would be a success; if not, I would have to mind my p's and q's, for the whole morning would be a tricky one.

Breakfast done and the copper fire coaxed up at last, we would descend to the basement for the work of the day. Washing was a fearsome business. Clothes had to be boiled in the copper; lifted, steamy and dripping, by means of wooden sticks to the stone sink for rinsing; blued with the blue-bag; mangled in the huge wooden rollers of the iron mangle that stood, four or five feet high, in the far corner of the basement; and carried out up the backyard over slippery flagstones in a weighty wicker basket to be hung on the line in the garden.

Some of the clothes had to be starched as well, and that too meant work: mixing the starch, waiting till it was ready, dipping the garments in one by one. When all these processes had been completed, the final triumphant moment came at last; when you had pegged out every garment, you grabbed the piece of rope hanging from the pulley on the clothes-post, and hoisted the whole heavy line up, up, up to the sky, till the sheets and shirts, pinafores and tablecloths and combinations, flapped and blew in the sharp wind, drying to a glorious whiteness.

Meanwhile my first task was to collect the laundry. 'Just run up and get the things from the bedrooms,' Mother would tell me, and up the three flights of stairs I would climb — four if you counted from the basement — to load myself up with combinations, white petticoats, camisoles with square embroidered tops, bodices of every description, underskirts, blouses, modesty vests, woollen stockings and knickers, Father's shirts and long pants, my brother's school clothing, my own white pinafores with the frills round the armholes that I was just growing out of. I had worn pinafores happily for seven years, but now a new vogue was coming in, and little girls wore brown holland smocks over their dresses. The smocks were becoming and modern, but as yet the family fortunes wouldn't run to these, and I had to wear out my old white cotton pinafores to the end. Combinations, too, were on the way out.

47

Nobody at school wore them; they wore vests instead; but although I begged for respite from the scratchy uncomfortable woollen combinations, my family were firm believers in 'wool next the skin' and would not hear of anything so scanty as vests.

Down I would stagger with my arms full of clothes, collecting odd doyleys and antimacassars, lace-edged dressing-table mats and crochet-bordered huckaback towels on the way; down to the basement, which already smelled of steam and hard yellow soap. Clouds of steam would billow up from the copper whenever Mother lifted the wooden lid, and the ceiling was wreathed in swirling veils of vapour which hung depressingly above us while we worked.

Soon the stone floor grew slippery with water, and anyone who went upstairs to the kitchen would leave wet footmarks on the linoleum. On worked Mother without pause, boiling, scrubbing on the ridged wooden scrubbing-board, washing in the stone sink, up to her elbows in soapsuds, rinsing, blueing, starching. My job was to dip the blue-bag in the cold water in the shallow sink, and swirl it round and round till the water looked like the Mediterranean, blue and translucent. In went the yellowish clothes, and out they came to my constant surprise, not blue at all but dazzling white. It was a triumph when all the clothes were ready for the final mangling, and we dragged them across in the basket to the old mangle by the back door.

'Whatever you do, child,' warned Mother a hundred times a day on Mondays, 'don't trap your fingers in the mangle.' But I scarcely needed any warning; to me the whole contraption was terrifying — the huge iron frame with its curly scrollwork, the big scrubbed wooden rollers that turned so slowly, the great black handle that squeaked as it went round. I could barely reach the handle when it was in its topmost position, but manfully I would struggle to keep it turning, and watch the garments one by one dropping into the big clothes basket on the wet floor beneath. At last the squeaking and turning were done, the last garment went into the pile, and we had to carry the heavy load up the slippery outside steps to the garden.

Pegging the clothes I always enjoyed. There were our neighbours each side — Gilbert's mother, large and gay and hearty, singing as she pegged out Gilbert's little striped tunics and trousers, and always good for a bit of local gossip or a joke. Gilbert was my friend, and I admired him tremendously in those red striped trousers. What fun it must be to be a boy and wear trousers! On the other side, Ethel's mother was, rather dolefully, pegging out the family's washing. Ethel's mother had a hard life, and even a breezy morning, when the sun shone and we knew the clothes would dry, left her dull and dispirited. I guessed Sunday hadn't been too happy a day for her.

'Nice drying morning!' Mother would call to Gilbert's mother, struggling to peg down a sheet that was flapping deliriously in the wind; and Gilbert, tagging at her heels, would signal to me that when all this business of washing was over, we would go up the garden to the gooseberry bushes and play noughts and crosses through the palings. There was a gay feeling in the air; clothes were drying, the work was done, and we were all enjoying the freshness of the morning and the sense of triumph which came when we saw Monday's washing, clean and crisp and smelling of soap and sunshine, blowing on the line that was tied to the old pear-tree's topmost bough.

The clothes swung in the breeze, and I would have to duck my head to avoid the great sheets that would flap suddenly into my face if I wasn't careful, and sting my cheeks with their dripping hems. Socks and stockings danced in the wind; cotton knickers filled out embarrassingly, and shamelessly displayed themselves on the line; pinafores and summer dresses bellied and flapped in a kind of maenad frenzy. When the last spare inch of line was filled with clothes, we would survey our work with pride, and go into the house again, conscious of a morning's work well done. The sky outside would be white with the billowing of sheets, the blowing of garments, while we watched it for signs of rain from the open kitchen door where we were scrubbing potatoes for dinner.

Cold meat on Mondays was one of the things that made me hate this particular meal. The remains of Sunday's joint looked stringy and unappetising, served up with floury yellow potatoes and dark cabbage which I detested.

'Don't you loathe cold meat on Monday?' one of my school friends had confided to me as we ran home to dinner one day. '*My* mother fries me bacon and eggs for Monday dinner — it's lovely!'

I envied her her good fortune, but was much too timid to suggest to Mother that we do the same. Cold meat on Monday followed as surely as did roast meat on Sunday in our family, and it would be an act of gross impropriety if I were to demand anything different.

On Monday Mother worked so hard that by evening she was exhausted; but on Tuesday she was at it again, ironing the clean clothes with pride, till every frill was perfect, every tuck and pleat in place. Our irons were heavy objects which had to be heated over a clear fire in the kitchen, and then lifted carefully with a kettle-holder over the handle, and tested against Mother's cheek to see if the heat was right. If the fire wasn't clear enough, the ironing had to wait, because the irons would get smoky and dirty. It was time-consuming. While one iron was being used, the other was heating on the fire, and it required no little skill to make sure that time wasn't wasted as one iron grew cold and the other hot.

'Don't you ever burn yourself when you put the iron to your cheek like that?' I asked Mother one day. It looked every moment as though she would get burned, but with the skill of years she had come to know exactly when the heat was right and exactly how near to the iron she could go. Mother laughed and told me not to worry, but I was worried all the same.

'When Frances did the ironing,' I reminded her, 'she used to spit on the iron to see if it was hot, and when the spit bounced off, it was ready. Couldn't you do that?'

'Gracious, no, child,' said Mother in horror. 'A nasty unhygienic habit. I'll not burn myself, I do assure you.' And she went holding the sizzling iron half an inch from her cheek, while I looked on fascinated and appalled.

The ironing board had to be balanced carefully between the table and the brass fireguard which always shielded the kitchen fire. You could, I had heard, buy ironing boards on folding legs, but no such luxury had ever come our way; Mother continued to iron as best she could, balancing the board precariously and keeping it out of the way of our cat and dog, who were inclined to come wandering round our legs and bumping the board awry. Hour after hour Mother ironed; white cotton nightdresses, voluminous, with frilly necks and sleeves, still faintly reminiscent of the leg-of-muttons Mother and Aunt Jane had worn not so very long ago; blouses with puff sleeves, modesty vests with little crystal buttons between which you had to manoeuvre the iron with delicacy; enormous tablecloths, traycloths, towels, handkerchiefs; nothing was missed. What Mother had done in the days of our babyhood, when the long clothes and pelisses, the frilly bibs and bonnets and numerous petticoats and binders all had to be meticulously ironed every day, I just couldn't imagine.

Ironing was hot work, especially in summer, and Mother would frequently pause to push back the hair from her wet forehead and pass a hand over her brow before bending again to her task. No wonder a small friend of mine had been heard to add to his evening prayers one particularly torrid night: 'And please don't let Mother get so hot with the ironing!'

But it was a clean job; and as the newly-pressed and folded clothes piled up on the table beside her, Mother's face would relax and she would survey the mounting load with justifiable pride. A well-turned-out set of garments and household linen was one of the things that built up a family's prestige, servant or no servant. And Mother, however tired she was, would never let so much as a handkerchief get by without being ironed.

Tuesday, silvery-blue with the freshly ironed clothes and the easing of tension, passed into Wednesday; azure Wednesday, as I imagined it, when skies were clear and the heaviest tasks of the household done. Wednesday was altogether a lighter and merrier day. Mother worked about the house, but now she was polishing furniture and rubbing silver and brass till it shone. My duties, if I were at home, would be to dust the enormous tiered oak sideboard in the dining-room, a job I hated because of all the surfaces, the little shelves and mirrors, the curved nooks and crannies in the cupboards that were a nightmare to get clean. But this was soon over, and Wednesday was melting into Thursday — quiet green Thursday, when Mother sometimes had time to sit down in the afternoons and do embroidery — traycloths, or initialled handkerchiefs, or the yoke of a best frock for me. In summer she took her sewing out into the garden and sat beneath the lilac bush, where later we would have tea; in winter she sat by the fire, and did all her sewing jobs by its gentle glow, with old Gelert looking up now and again from the hearthrug and pushing his nose against her skirt. Teatime then would be a comfortable time, with toast made with the old iron toasting-fork, and dripping, brown and tasty, on top.

Friday, golden-brown, and the end of school for the week; fish frying for our supper, and the weekend before me. My spirits always lightened on Friday night. Two whole days before me. On Saturday, the day when anything might happen — cheerful red Saturday, that I loved — I got up in the morning ready for whatever might come. Play in the Park at the top of the hill; shopping expeditions; visitors. Saturday was a bright day, full of excitement; excitement that mounted towards evening, because tomorrow would be Sunday — the day that crowned the week, the day when little girls wore white. I fell asleep in the attic bedroom on Saturday nights, full of the blissful knowledge that Heaven was just around the corner; Sunday, the day of days, would soon be here. Sunday, the family day when we could all be together.

And then all too soon, white Sunday had passed, and it was grey Monday again. Grey because there was work to do; grey because the labour of wash-day was on us once more; grey because of the copper fire's uncertainty, the effort of hauling all those heavy clothes down to the basement, washing and mangling and hanging out; and bringing the great basket in with all the garments to be ironed.

However much we enjoyed the week, I used to think, we never seemed to get away from Monday. Wouldn't it be wonderful if the week could start on Tuesday, with the worst of it behind us? But there it was; inevitable Monday. Ah well, it was just one of those things you had to put up with. Like all the other housewives along the road, Mother never thought her lot was hard. It was just life; just Monday.

3

Green Places

I COULDN'T live, as a child, without my two green places the garden and the Park. The long, sloping, uphill garden was to me a private world; the Park was the public world, the wide open spaces where we played. Both were necessary, for every child needs to escape. My escape to the garden began when I stepped out of the kitchen door, and into the little paved arbour Father had made, with the green and white striped tent to give shade in the summer-time.

The arbour was a family place, but it was the threshold to adventure. Big lilac trees screened it on one side, and the ivied trellis on the other, so that you couldn't see the neighbouring houses at all. And the tent made it even more private.

It was a simple enough affair, Father's tent; just an awning of green and white canvas fixed up on four metal poles. To him it was a place to gather and sit in, to have tea in the shade; but to a child it had a quality of its own, an atmosphere of romance I couldn't even start to explain. How could you explain, for instance, that the tent wasn't a tent at all, but an Eastern palace — one of those canvas palaces where the wind from the Sahara — was it the Sahara? my geography was never much good — billowed out the richly embroidered sides while princesses and sultans disported themselves within. When there wasn't a wind, little black boys in bright tunics swung palm-leaf fans above your head; you were the princess, of course; and strange Oriental music came from pipes and unknown instruments in the background. You only had to look up at the tent-poles, with those onion-shaped wooden domes on top, to know that this was truly Eastern. Ali Baba sat under onion-shaped domes like those; it was in my picture-book.

There weren't really any little black boys, of course, and the only fans we used were the fly-swatters for the wretched mosquitoes that in summer made those afternoons in the arbour intolerable. All the same, it was fun to dream.

When you sat there on a summer's day, soft sounds would drift in to the green and white tent; Gilbert's father mowing the lawn — whirr, whirr to the left, whirr, whirr to the right, with the mower heaving a kind of indrawn breath as it turned the corners. The long back gardens were all so close that you could hear the summer sounds right the way up the street; Walter's mother leaning from her bedroom window and calling her unfortunate son — 'Wall-eee! Wall-eee!' — how we used to tease him about that name! Bertie's father busy with some do-it-yourself job in the garden shed; hammer, hammer, 'Bertie — hold it steady now,' hammer, hammer. Gilbert and Walter and Bertie were all my friends, and the sounds that came from their houses were cheerful and companionable. By contrast, poor Ethel next door had a stormy home, and we put our hands over our ears when her father, whom everybody called Jos, was in one of his rages. No wonder Ethel's mother looked so sad when she hung out the clothes on Monday mornings.

No wireless set blared out to break the peace of those little gardens. Nobody had got one yet. Occasionally we would hear the churning of a gramophone; Jos next door had one, the kind with a horn, which he played in his more sociable moments; but the old records only came faintly from the cool depths of the house; no one would have thought of playing music in the garden.

Instead, we sat and talked; Father in his summer Panama hat — his only concession to the weather, for he always wore the same immaculate shirt and tie, the same dark coat with the striped trousers. Open-necked shirts were not for him; a lazy fashion, he called them, and stuck uncomfortably to his wing collars and starched cuffs. Mother would be in one of her pretty Liberty cottons; every year we would take a trip up to the 'West End' to buy summer fabrics at Liberty's — tiny flower patterns in soft colours, which made the softness of Mother's dark hair and the gentleness of her face even more appealing. I loved to sit and watch her sewing, her needle plying in and out with regularity, her face bent above her work.

Aunt Jane, when she joined us after school, would sit with a book. She was a great reader. I would watch her too, with a trace of awe, for was she not a schoolteacher and didn't she know everything? I used to wonder why she bothered to read books. She must know everything in them already. Aunt Jane, being something of a career woman for those days, favoured a crisp blouse and a serge skirt. Privately I thought it must be very uncomfortable; but since the female world seemed to be divided into home people like Mother in Liberty dresses and career people like Aunt Jane in serge skirts, perhaps one had to accept one's uniform as one accepted one's status in life. What would mine be in the far-off future when I would put up my hair and wear long dresses and either marry or go to work. You could not do both!

A little more freedom was allowed us children in the summer; my brother wore a cricket shirt, and I had short sleeves to my cotton dresses. There were still a good many years to go before the sleeveless dress arrived on the scene, and when it did, Father never looked on it with favour. It showed too much, he said.

Tired of sitting under the canvas — even if it was an Eastern palace — I would get up and venture beyond the arbour onto the lawn that sloped upwards into the hot sunshine. It must have been a tiny lawn, but it seemed like vast acres when you were small. Here, bordered by flowerbeds, the grass would be green and cool — cool enough to lie down on, with Gelert, our faithful old collie, beside me, and smell the fresh, earthy smell of the grass that you could only appreciate when you were low down near it.

There was a lot going on down there, I thought, propping my chin on my hands and watching the miniature life among the stalks of the grasses. Tiny winged creatures fluttered for a moment; insects made their painful way through forests of grass; occasionally a worm reared up from its hole, and usually there were ants. I loved the ants. It gave me the sense of being Gulliver among the pygmies to watch the laborious processions of ants crossing and recrossing their innumerable unseen paths in the jungle of grasses. What a difficult life they must have, I would think; all that trouble and effort, all that stumbling and climbing and swarming round stones and pebbles, hauling themselves and the mysterious burdens up the mountainous slopes of the earth, scurrying back again to do the same thing all over again.

Once I became so entranced with the ant life in our garden that I collected some ants into a jam jar and took them to school to show the teacher. I broke the jam jar in the cloakroom when somebody knocked into me, and ants ran everywhere over the stone floor. Little girls climbed on the locker seats to avoid them, teachers lifted up their skirts and fled. Nobody was pleased, and I felt sadly disappointed; what a lot they'd missed!

Our flower-beds were full of homely flowers; London Pride, its pink stems proudly upright, its faint scent borne on the air; flaming poppies with scarlet outsides, and insides stained a blue-black;

pansies with their inquiring, innocent faces; and on the damp shady patch beneath the pear tree, Solomon's Seal, with the white pearly blossoms gracefully held aloft on juicy stems. The rambler roses hid the wooden palings on Ethel's side of the garden. They dripped down in summer like a pink flood, and around them the bees buzzed with an incessant hum.

My favourite was the little moss rose, which Mother had carefully planted. Even its name, I thought, was lovely. The moss rose was romantic, with its tiny buds and delicate petals; so romantic, indeed, that someone in our neighbourhood had even been named after it. She was called Miss Rose Moss, and she taught piano in a little neat house behind a privet hedge.

I would have loved to go and learn the piano from someone with such a beautiful name. Did she, I wondered, match her name, with pink cheeks and a delicate little head? But though we often passed her house with its shining brass plate on the gate, 'Miss Rose Moss, LRAM, Piano Lessons', we never got further in our inquiries than spelling out her name. I was too young to have piano lessons, anyway; and by the time I was old enough, little Miss Rose Moss was — unaccountably — dead.

Up the slope, where the lawn ended, was the most interesting part of the garden; the pond and the pear tree. This was where romance began; for you were out of view of the grown-ups under the shade of the pear tree and nobody could see you and inquire what you were doing, or tell you not to. The pond was quite small but big enough for me; Father had made it, cementing round the edges and constructing a tiny island in the middle where the occasional jewel-eyed toad would sit, sunning itself, its wrinkled face like a little wizened old man. When you took it onto your hand, its skin felt cold and clammy against yours, and you would wait for it to jump, with a shiver of delight when those skinny, splayed brown legs leapt into the pond again.

No fish swam in there, but there were myriads of tiny creatures; water spiders and water boatmen, skating over the surface, and strange weeds that waved underwater, and made me think of 'The

Forsaken Merman', the haunting poem which the bigger ones at kindergarten recited. The greeny-blue depths of the pond were a world of their own. My brother sailed his boats here, but I preferred to dream above the watery, weed-swayed surface. It was a fascinating other-realm.

Into the depths of the pond fell, in spring-time, the white petals of the pear tree which leaned above it. It was old and gnarled and had been there long before the houses were built; it too belonged to another world, the world of the almost-country. Its bark was rough and textured to the touch, and if you shinned up it with your knees, reaching for the lowest bough with your right hand and swinging yourself up onto it, your bare skin got scratched and your fingers torn. But it was worth it.

Once up on that bough, it was again a different world. How many different worlds there were out here in the garden! Here, you were half a creature of the air. You looked down on the lawn, the green and white tent where the family sat resting, the little narrow gardens

with their wooden palings running up
the hill, their hen-coops and sheds; and
then you looked up through the green
leaves and saw patches of sky above
you, and the flying clouds. It was much
nearer, the sky. Climb just one branch
higher, and your head began to swim; a
dizzy lightness filled you, and you hung
on tight with hands and knees. Climb
a third bough, if you dared, and there
you were almost at the top, the wind in
your hair, your body trembling with the
excitement of it all, and with the feel of
the tree swaying slightly, ever so slightly,
in the breeze. Now you could see, if you
plucked up courage to look, right over
the houses and the chimney-pots into the
next road; into the world; into infinity.
Perhaps if you were to climb the very
highest tree in the neighbourhood, you
would even see the sea, and that would
be your crowning moment. I had no idea
how far the sea was, but I was sure you
could see it somewhere.

This must be how God feels, I would
think, looking down from the sky over
the whole of his creation. Seeing all
the little gardens, all the little houses,

all the little people going about their business. How he must long to stop them sometimes when he saw them doing anything silly! And did he feel pain when one of them got hurt — like falling down in the road and cutting a knee — and joy when one of them was happy — like being bought a whole bag of sweets at Mrs Evans' shop? He must be very pleased with himself I thought, clinging to my topmost bough, when he saw the orderliness of our little suburb; all those tiny gardens, all the wooden palings running parallel up the hill, all the little people planting their lettuces and digging with spades and pushing their wheelbarrows so busily. And all his doing! I knew now what the Bible meant when it said that God looked on his creation and saw it was good.

Down again, sliding from branch to branch, grazing knees and elbows, and reaching the ground again in one great rush, hoping you hadn't torn anything. Never mind, the grown-ups sitting there in the tent couldn't see. Past the pond and up the sloping path to where the fruit bushes were; a private place this, the only place in the whole house or garden where you could hide by the hour from grown-ups and not be found. I loved this wilder part, where raspberry canes grew thick and high, the soft red globes hanging deliciously on summer afternoons, and the gooseberries growing plump and green, covered in tiny hairs like the back of Mr Smith's hand when I used to watch him slicing bacon in his grocery shop. You could crawl between the rows of bushes on hands and knees, near to the smell of the earth, and be completely invisible to the grown-ups. You would hear them coming up the garden calling you, but there was no need to answer; in here you could stay safe and unseen.

The smell of the fruit bushes was a heady smell, quite unlike anything else in the garden. It must be rather like the jungle, I would imagine, safely curled beneath the jungle-green of the canes. I would reach up and put one of the rich red raspberries in my mouth — one was allowed me, but never more — or a great globular gooseberry that felt rough against the tongue, breaking into glorious juiciness as my teeth broke the skin of it. The strong smell of fruit made me feel almost drunk; I would crouch unseen, hearing vague sounds from the other end of the garden, but unwilling to go back and join the family under the tent. Just a little while longer.

Scrambling from solitude, I would explore now the further reaches of the garden, where there was a tangle of vegetables on either side. A plump marrow would hide beneath fleshy leaves; great clumps of rhubarb, like giant fans, spread out around me; runner beans tower above, their fresh green clusters tickling my head. This was a strange part of the garden, filled with a sense of sadness. Nobody ever came up here except to tend the vegetables or light a bonfire; the ashes of dead fires were everywhere, and with them, broken flowerpots and compost heaps that you could stir with your foot to make armies of beetles scurry away. Overhead, at the very end, was a grassy bank above which poplars swayed; they were the trees that marked the boundary between our road and the next. Who lived in those houses the other side of the fence I neither knew nor cared; they were unknown territory, and beyond them lay the even wider stretches of the Park. A shiver would come over me, kicking my heels here among the old flower-pots and the rubbish, and suddenly I would long to run down the garden to the safety of the little green-tented arbour and the family.

Across the sunny lawn, past the pond and the pear tree, to the shade of the tent, and Father smoking his pipe in the deck-chair while Mother sat sewing. It was comfortable to be back amongst them. The only trouble was that they would keep asking me what I'd been doing.

I never did know how to answer. What *had* I been doing? Dreaming over a pond, watching an underwater world? Climbing a tree and being God? Hiding away in a nowhere-land of red raspberries and green gooseberries? Feeling a touch of the sadness of the world among the broken flower-pots and ashes of dead fires? How could you tell all this to the grown-ups? There simply were not words enough; and if there were, they wouldn't understand.

My other green place was the Park — Telegraph Hill Park, so short a distance away that I could be out of the house, down the seven steps, round the corner and inside the Park gates in less time than it took to say the multiplication tables up to ten. It was the place where I escaped on Saturday mornings, and in the holidays when I had done my chores of dusting and errand-running at home. It was also the nearest I could get to the country — the real country, which, as far back as I could remember had been in my bones. It took marriage and the years following it for me ever to fulfil my secret, desperate need and really live in the country; but from earliest days I would do my best to pretend that our London suburb, if not quite the country, was at least something like it.

Our road had trees in it, acacia trees delicate in summer against the sky, and green verges to the pavement, for both of which I was deeply thankful. We also had a garden back and front, and if you hid deep enough in the currant bushes or climbed high enough in the pear tree you could pretend that the houses next door were not there, and that instead of looking out onto a sea of slate roofs and yellow brick, you were scanning a horizon of cornfields against a blue distance, or meadows shivering in the sunlight and knee-deep in cow-parsley. But it took a lot of pretending.

If I craned my head from my attic window, I could just catch a glimpse, sideways between the chimney pots and through a gap in the brick walls of the houses, of waving tree-tops in our little park. I clung to that beatific vision of trees which might almost, so very nearly, be the country; and when life was particularly worrying — which it was at times — there was comfort in climbing on the shaky table under the window, and balancing precariously on the sill, to gaze out at the little triangle of green that meant the peace, the beauty, the steadfastness of the country — almost the country.

'Can't think why you're so crazy about the country,' Father grumbled. 'Isn't London good enough for you? Why,

London's the metropolis of the whole world; you're a lucky child to be born here.'

I was not quite sure what metropolis meant, but I was quite sure that however long you lived in London, you needed — desperately needed — the country. There was something about London parks and gardens which was spurious, self-conscious: you could enjoy them, but you couldn't get any comfort from them; they didn't belong to you, nor did you belong to them.

But get amongst the fields and the open skies, and you would belong; of that I was convinced. They would take you to themselves, till you were part of a whole, your worries lessened, your mind at ease. I didn't know how I was so sure about this, but on the few occasions when we had at last got rid of London houses and streets and London parks, and gone to the real country, however briefly, the knowledge had come to me. It might be unreasonable to Father; but I knew it was true.

Meanwhile we had to make do with the Park. On Saturday mornings, as soon as I had helped clear away the breakfast things and dusted the hateful sideboard, I would flee away round the corner to the Park. Wonderful Park, green in summer, gold and bronze in autumn, frosty and silent in winter, and most glorious of all in spring! What matter if the bushes were the park variety with little labels underneath, that the park-keeper in his brown uniform walked over the grass picking up paper bags with the end of his spike, that a bell was rung at closing-time to coax out the last courting couples before the iron gates were shut? It only needed a little imagination to turn the flower-beds into cottage gardens where the plants grew unlabelled, the grass playing-field into a meadow where buttercups blossomed, the formal little pond into a real pond where cows came down to drink, and the concrete paths into moorland tracks leading into infinity.

When we were in romantic mood, my friends and I, we would linger by the pond, where fat white ducks waddled comically along the bank, and moorhens, gleaming green and tawny, dipped and floated in the shadowy water. An enormous weeping willow overhung this pond, and how I longed to disregard the nasty little metal notices that said 'Keep off the Grass' and climb over the low wire to run down to the very water's edge, beneath the benison of the weeping willow's green trailing branches, and discover who knows what mysteries by the bank, where the shadows were deep and glassy, and the rushes waved high. You never knew what you might see if only you were allowed down there; minnows perhaps, silently darting, or toads, water-rats, frogs. But alas, I never got as far as the water's edge; being a law abiding child, I never dared flaunt the park-keeper's little notices, but had to be content with leaning over the wire fence and gazing from afar.

Here were the seats where the lovers used to sit on summer evenings. 'What do they do all the time?' young Gilbert used to ask me wonderingly. 'Just sitting there! They never seem to talk, or play games or anything.'

'Perhaps they just like holding hands,' I told him. 'Or looking into each other's eyes. That's what they always seem to do.'

Gilbert sat down on the grass opposite me in his little red striped tunic and trousers, and peered with fierce concentration into my eyes. 'I think that's silly,' he said. 'There's nothing there to see.'

Certainly it did not seem much fun spending all your time looking into somebody's eyes when you might be playing Catch or Last Man Home. But then grown-ups, we knew, were unpredictable. With all that time to spare, they spent it on such silly things.

The lovers kept to themselves, anyway, and didn't trouble us as we played; in fact they seemed to try to get away from us. Once you ran through the big iron gates with the familiar notice outside — 'A Bell will be rung at Closing Time; Dogs must be Led' (which the wits amongst us translated as 'A Dog will be Wrung at Closing Time; Bells must be Lead') — the whole park, except for the lovers, was your playground.

There was plenty to do. We played Hide and Seek all over the Park, with

the bandstand as Home; took pieces
of chalk with us in our pockets for
Hare and Hounds — the park-keeper
didn't approve of the chalk marks
everywhere, but never interfered. Or
we played wild games, the boys chasing
the girls, round the hillocks and through
the shrubberies. The best game of all
was an invention of our own, involving
maidens taken prisoner and barons pacing
their battlements, the battlements being
the concrete platform with its iron railings
which stood out on a lofty jutting crag
at one end of the Park. No matter
that the lofty jutting crag overhung the
Public Conveniences; you could forget
about them, and pace your airy terrace
watching for the first sign of the invading
army over the horizon, or awaiting the
messenger who would tell you the fate
of your beautiful only daughter, captured
by bandits. 'Sire, she pines in a lonely
tower; wilt thou not send forth a knight
in shining armour to rescue her on his
milk-white steed?' We used to get a bit
muddled with all the thee's and thou's,
but it added to the romance.

There were places to run down, and

places to jump from. The steep hill, down which we ran to fall over painfully and inevitably at the bottom, grazing our knees, was a test of courage. We dreaded it, yet we never failed the test.

'Go on, run down! Dare you!'

And we dared, the wind in our ears, the gradient beneath looking terrifying as we ran; we knew there was a tumble at the end, but still we ran. The girls ran wildly, screaming, hair flying, big bows flopping and bobbing at the end of pigtails, skirts billowing in the wind, whilst the boys followed them whooping. One of the boys used to wear a straw hat that faced us with a problem; nobody quite knew what to do with it, as it invariably flew off when he ran. He turned up to play, with the straw hat firmly anchored to the lapel of his jacket by a thick black cord with a clip at the end, as was the way with such headgear. But it never stayed clipped on for long. The Park didn't seem quite the place for such sartorial glory.

'Hang it on a tree,' suggested someone.

'Shove it under a seat,' said somebody else.

'Hide it in the bandstand,' offered another.

So the poor straw hat was disposed of somehow, whilst its owner galloped off to seek adventure on his fiery charger. Whoever could hope to find adventure, wearing a straw hat?

There was a refreshment booth in the Park, where you could buy large penny glasses of fizzy lemonade, and buns full of currants. I used to think it very unfair that I was never allowed to make any purchases there. Mother had the firm conviction that nothing bought at a booth or a stall was edible — in fact it might be little short of poison; and she was probably right in those days. But the prohibition rankled; what would I have given, on a scorching summer morning when my throat was dry with thirst, after running in flight from a band of brigands, for a cool drink of lemonade out of a tall thick glass? Strangely, none of the other children were ever forbidden to spend their Saturday pennies on these luxuries; but perhaps the other parents were not so food-conscious. Mother definitely was. Everything, down to the lemonade, in our house was home-made.

The boys scorned lemonade, and went for ginger-beer in stone jars with captive marbles in the top. In winter they used to ask for huge thick mugs of Bovril, steaming hot from the hands of the fat lady who served the drinks; grand when there was ice two inches thick on the pond, and the trees were white with rime. I used to be given a sip sometimes, wondering all the while whether it would be poisoned; but somehow all my friends survived. But it always seemed an anticlimax, after a morning's play in the Park, to go tamely home and fill a tumbler with water at the kitchen sink, or beg a mug of cocoa from Mother.

It so often did seem an anticlimax to leave the green places and exchange them for slates and mortar and yellow brick. The garden and the Park — they were so necessary; a breath of the country, for which I pined.

It took a lot of pretending to turn the narrow uphill garden into some country paradise; or the Park, within its iron railings, into the wide open spaces for which I longed. Yet sometimes it happened. Without my knowing it, I was transported from bricks and mortar to the green places where romance dwelled. Magic things can happen when you are a child.

4

In the Kitchen

OUR kitchen was the heart of the house, and Mother's life centred round it. In it she got the meals, washed the dishes, baked for the family; the kitchen was her domain. I used to love the smell of baking when I came in from play on a Saturday morning; a warm nutty-sweet smell that meant pleasures to come — and pleasures to share, too, when she let me help.

I always thought how beautiful she looked there at the scrubbed kitchen table, presiding over it in her big white apron with the frills round the armholes and the strings tied behind her waist. If I was helping, it would mean a rush round the house to find the little green velvet hassock to stand upon, to reach the table-top. Sleeves up and pinafore on and I was ready for cooking.

There always seemed to be puddings

to stir on Saturday mornings. Puddings were one of the great stand-by's of mealtimes. Every family had them. Plump currant puddings, steamed or boiled in a cloth; roly-poly, round and fat; suet puddings that were 'good for you'. There was Queen of Puddings, too, the one with the lovely name, and the equally lovely contents: all creamy with milk and jam and meringue, whipped up by Mother with the little old metal whisk that her own mother had used. You couldn't have a meal without a pudding, or at least a tart. Treacle tart, golden and sticky; jam tart, red and criss-crossed with an ingenious lattice of pastry; apple tart, made with apples from the old tree in a corner of the garden, that only bore fruit every second year.

I loved to help mix the puddings in the big earthenware basin, yellow outside and blue within. There were no short cuts then; no mixers or beaters or blenders; you used what Mother called 'elbow grease' — that quick turn of the hand and arm that sent the contents whizzing round the bowl. No packet mixes, either; Mother certainly wouldn't have used them, even if our grocer, kind Mr Smith round the corner, had stocked them. Mother had been brought up on Mrs Beeton, and nothing less would do. Though we didn't use her lavish recipes as they were — we couldn't have afforded them — Mother did wonders with the simple ingredients from the family grocer's shop. Flour kept in the big white and blue enamelled bin; bread in a crock; currants and spices in little glass jars ranged along cupboard shelves. Making a pudding with all these ingredients took a long time, for flour had to be sieved through a fine sieve; lard carefully softened and crumbled; currants to be washed and picked over by hand. But there seemed to be all the time in the world on Saturday mornings, for Mother liked cooking, and I loved to help.

Our kitchen table was a stout old wooden one, which I often had to scrub, using good old soap and water and a great scrubbing-brush. For pastry, at which Mother was a dab hand, she used a marble slab; it was lovely on a hot summer morning to run in and put your hand on its smooth coolness.

Washing-up was done in a bowl on the table, for our old brown stone sink was awkwardly placed in the darkest corner of the kitchen, and nobody liked using it. Much better to wash up at the table, with the kitchen door open to the sunlight, and the birds singing in the ivy outside.

We had no hot water; nobody had in our road; and all the washing-up water had to be heated on the stove, or in wintertime, in one of the two big black kettles with curving handles and elegant spouts which were always kept by the fireside; one on top of the fire, the other singing on the hob. Our cooking stove was set back in a tiled alcove. I wasn't allowed to use this, in case I burned my fingers; but occasionally Mother let me put in, with great care, a tray of buns I had made or a batch of little fat pastry-men with currants for eyes and currant buttons down their waistcoats.

Mother's kitchen utensils were fun to take out of the drawer beneath the table. Wooden spoons in many sizes; pastry cutters, big and small; lots of sieves (you sieved everything in those days); and a big flat masher which was used to mash the greens. Our greens, after long boiling with a dash of bicarbonate of soda 'to keep the colour', used to be strained and mashed flat with this implement; no wonder I didn't like the resultant pulp, but that was how every family prepared its greens then.

My jobs in the kitchen on Saturdays were the picking over of currants and the stirring of puddings or cakes, with the promise of a spoon to be licked at the end of the proceedings. On Saturdays before Christmas I would never fail to stand there on my hassock, picking the pounds of currants for the Christmas puddings and cakes, or chopping peel till my fingers ached. But the Christmas smell in the kitchen, of good things boiling on the stove and biscuits baking in the oven, made up for the trouble.

Every Saturday morning Mother baked a large fruit cake for Sunday tea. Our tea-table wouldn't have been complete without this cake, set on a crocheted doyley on the best blue plate. It was plump and curranty, mixed with brown sugar and treacle till it looked dark and inviting. I was too young to make proper cakes, but I could manage little fancy ones for tea-time; coconut ones with cherries on top (and one for my mouth at the end), and butterfly cakes with the tops sliced off and cut into two little wings to be set daintily side by side. I was proud of my butterfly cakes.

In holiday-time Mother and I did sweet-making. We made rich Everton toffee, that melted deliciously in the mouth, and was cooled in square tins on the kitchen window-sill; and coconut ice, sweet and sickly, pink and white with cochineal. We made doughnuts, too, mixing the sweet dough and watching it sizzle away temptingly in the frying-pan on top of the stove; the one occasion when I was allowed to cook at the stove, under Mother's watchful eye. Then we put jam in the hole in the middle, and set the doughnuts on a top shelf so that my brother couldn't filch one on his way through the kitchen. Nothing smelled as good as doughnuts fresh from the pan.

Making out the grocery order for Mr Smith, the family grocer, was an event I enjoyed. As soon as I could write clearly enough, this became my job. I would take a pencil and, leaning heavily on the kitchen table, write to Mother's dictation. The first few words did not even have to be dictated, because they were always the same, and I soon knew them by heart. I recited them like a chant:

Two pounds of Gran,
Two pounds of Dem,
Two pounds of Lump,
And three half-pounds of Best Fresh
    Butter.

Mr Smith's grocery order seldom varied. The Gran was granulated sugar, which arrived in thick blue bags; the Dem was demerara, brown and gritty, also in thick blue bags. The Lump was a special box of cube sugar, kept exclusively for friends and relations who came to tea; you couldn't offer them Gran or Dem; instead, you filled the blue and white sugar bowl with cubes, and rummaged round in the sideboard drawer for the silver sugar tongs that had been one of Mother's wedding presents. For every day, the table was set with a bowl of Gran, whilst the Dem was kept to sprinkle over the breakfast porridge.

The Best Fresh Butter, in separate half-pound packets, had to be Best Fresh and nothing else. Mr Smith knew better than to send us around the New Zealand stuff, which Mother did not trust. British, said Mother, was always Best. You never knew how long that New Zealand butter had been travelling round the world. When the butter arrived in the grocery box, it had to be taken out immediately and put into the 'safe' to keep cool. Mr Smith the grocer had slapped it up into rectangles, from the great mound of butter on the marble slab in his shop, and wrapped it in greaseproof paper; but it was still often beginning to melt when it reached our house in the grocery box on a Friday afternoon.

After the Gran and the Dem and the Best Fresh Butter I would wait, with my pencil poised, for what would come next. It might be currants for the Sunday cake, packed in cones of blue paper; or rice, or tapioca, or semolina, all similarly wrapped in paper cones, great stand-by's for weekday puddings. Rice was an essential on any grocery order, for Father had to have a rice pudding every day of his life. If the rest of us were not having it, Father's rice pudding would be set before him in an oval dish on the dinner-table, for him alone; and woe betide the family if it wasn't there. Nothing else would do.

Biscuits figured every week on the grocery order; in paper bags, personally filled by Mr Smith from the row of glass-topped biscuit boxes in front of the counter. Nobody bought biscuits in packets then; you selected your own, ordered your choice, and the bags were made up. You could order broken biscuits at half price, but Mother had to be very hard up with the week's housekeeping money to do this; there was something not quite respectable in ordering broken biscuits from Mr Smith, though we children used to buy them with our pocket money; you could get a lot for a halfpenny. When we were expecting visitors, Mother would sometimes order my favourite — chocolate bourbons, with the rich brown chocolate sandwiched between layers of biscuit, and the outsides crunchy with sugar. But usually it was shortcake biscuits, or Oval Maries — which I didn't like at all — when money was running low.

Soap went onto the order regularly; yellow kitchen soap in good thick bars, which you had to cut up for household use; red Lifebuoy soap with its disinfectant smell, for grubby hands and knees; and special lavender toilet soap for the bathroom. For washing-day there would be packets of Hudson's Soap, the only soap powder anyone used, and even then something of a novelty. Plenty of people still did the washing with hard yellow soap, or boiled up soap-scraps into a greeny-yellow liquid to save money. There would be whitening, too, for the step-girl to scour the front steps with; knife powder for cleaning the knives; and Silvo for shining up the spoons, a job which I enjoyed because you could make funny faces while you did it and see them reflected in the bowl of the spoon. Brasso was an essential, of course, for polishing the door knocker. It was a sign of respectability to have a nicely burnished door knocker, and nobody would ever allow a knocker to get tarnished and risk the ignominy of being called a bad housewife.

Cocoa appeared on the list, a puzzling word I could never spell; those a's and o's were always tricky. There was Lipton's tea, too, and once every few months coffee, which nobody used in our house except for visitors. Coffee, when it arrived with the grocery order in its dark blue paper bag, always smelled delicious, and I loved ladling it out into the coffee tin while the kitchen was filled with its rich odour. We sometimes bought jam and marmalade, when Mother wasn't making her own; cereals never. They were American novelties, Mother said, and we wouldn't touch them. Porridge, now, was different; that was good for you, as everyone knew, and you could cook it overnight in a haybox and save fuel.

Mother was very skilled in making the money go round, though sometimes it was short enough. A housekeeping entry in her 'Boots the Chemist's Home Diary' for 1917, a book which Mother religiously bought at the beginning of each year, lists provisions and their prices for the third week in January — Mother never got very far with her entries in 'Accounts' though she unfailingly entered the simple events of every day:

Grocery and provisions 14s. 8½d. [for the four of us and Aunt Jane]

Butcher 6s. 9½d. [plus 2d. in the margin — whatever did she buy from him for twopence?]

Baker and Confectioner 5s. 0d.

Fish and Poultry 2½d. [Herrings, probably, to be grilled for a tasty supper.]

Greengrocery 6s. 10d. [plus a penny in the margin, for a parsnip].

Milk, butter, eggs 7s. 9d.

Newspapers 8d. [though Mother often bought my penny *Rainbow* for me, and my brother's *Junior Mechanic*, an expensive journal at sixpence].

Chemist and Doctor 3d. [no National Health in those days, of course, and you paid for all your medicines]

And the week ends gloriously with Mother lashing out on a 'Hambone' for Saturday dinner — at 1s. 3d.

Mr Smith's groceries came round every Friday afternoon by way of Henry and his barrow. Henry was Mr Smith's 'man', a poor scrawny creature in ill-fitting clothes, thin wrists protruding from too-short sleeves, a muffler at his neck instead of a collar, and boots with broken laces. I accepted Henry for what he was — a simple soul, unable to take any better job because nobody could understand what he said. Henry had a cleft palate, mouthing his words in a throaty voice with accompanying nods, grimaces and shakings of his cadaverous head; and he brought his goods in an old soap-box on wheels which he had made in the manner of a porter's trolley. But he was never alarming; he would knock at our basement door and unload the grocery box from his trolley with a wide gap-toothed smile, and I would give him the halfpenny Mother had kept for him — Henry never left without his halfpenny — before he shambled off into the street again to deliver his groceries to the next house along the road. We took poor Henry for granted in our neighbourhood, and never questioned whether anything could be done for him; he was one of the unfortunates, like the vacant-faced babies we saw sometimes, lolling in prams, or the idiots who went muttering to themselves along the streets. The world was full of people like Henry.

But apart from the weekly order, nearly every day one or other of us children would have to 'run round to Mr Smith's' for something or other; another box of matches for Father's pipe, a pound of candles for the bedrooms when we'd run short, or a half-pound bag of biscuits when Mother had not had time to bake a cake for the unexpected visitor. 'Running round to Mr Smith's' was something we took for granted as a job for children. It took five minutes there and five minutes back, but it often took longer because Mr Smith's shop was such an enticing place.

In summer, especially, Mr Smith's shop was a haven of dimness from the scorching streets outside. It had a green and white awning outside, rather like the green and white canvas Father put up in the garden, and it was cool and pleasant to reach it after running — I always ran — through the dusty roads beneath the dusty plane trees. Inside, all would be shadowy, and it would take me some time to get used to the twilight. Then I would see Mr Smith himself standing, arms akimbo, behind the counter; serene and smiling. Mr Smith was always smiling. His round pink face reminded me of the slices of pink ham that he cut from the machine for the customers' orders. It was like the face of a baby, so smooth and pink and scrubbed and innocent. When I arrived Mr Smith would stick his thumbs into his waistcoat above the starched white apron he wore round his middle, and invite me to sit on the high wooden stool beside his counter before I got down to the serious business of shopping.

It was nice to sit up there, dangling my feet and exchanging pleasantries; gossip about school and home; comments on the weather. It made me feel very grown-up to be talking about the weather. 'Nice morning,' Mr Smith would say, glancing out of his shop door towards the sky, which was anyhow veiled by the green shade outside. 'Don't think we need worry about rain today.'

Usually grown-ups' conversation about the weather bored me. They were always talking about whether it was going to rain, as though this would be a disaster, whereas to me rain was often quite fun — you could splash through the puddles when no one was looking, and watch the little rivulets rushing down the gutter. But the grown-ups did keep on rather a long time talking about the weather, before getting down to interesting conversation.

Still, when you were sitting here on Mr Smith's high stool, it seemed very important to be talking about the weather. It made me feel that I was really somebody; not just a little girl taking a message or running an errand, but a young lady who had to be entertained with exchanges about the weather.

When we had agreed that no, it didn't look like rain, Mr Smith would dive into one of the glass-topped tins that bordered the counter and produce a biscuit for me to nibble. On good days it was a Bourbon — chocolate-flavoured and crisp with sugar. On less lucky occasions it was a ginger snap, sometimes even an Oval Marie — but always a biscuit. Biscuits between meals were frowned on at home, and I used to wonder if he ever told Mother that he gave me biscuits. From his wink, I guessed he didn't.

If nobody was in a hurry for me to bring back the shopping, Mr Smith would offer to take me on a conducted tour of the dim realms at the back of the shop. He knew I liked this, because it gave me the chance of weighing myself — free — on the weighing machine. Inside I would go, blinking the sunshine out of my eyes to get used to the musty darkness of those back rooms. All around stood cardboard cartons, bins and barrels, sacks of meal, parcels of groceries waiting to be delivered by poor Henry. Over in the far corner stood the scales.

Mr Smith would invite me to get up on them, putting a friendly foot on the wobbling plate at the bottom to make me appear heavier than I was. I would watch, fascinated, the great black hand swinging round, and join in the pretence that I was as heavy as the traditional 'fat lady'. Then I would go through to the shop again, smelling the fragrance of biscuits and flour and vinegar, seeing the tiny motes of dust dancing in sunbeams across the dim wooden floor; and wonder what other treat Mr Smith would have in store for me this morning.

If I was lucky, it would be the bacon slicer. 'They'll never let you touch that!' my brother used to warn me, with a kind of half-envious horror. 'Why, it's so sharp, you'll slice your finger off in no time! Right off, like this — ' and he would make the gesture of a fierce steel blade cutting through flesh with a tearing sound. But I was not alarmed. I knew no harm could come to me in Mr Smith's friendly little shop.

I would go behind the counter, with trepidation mixed with delight, mount a sugar-box turned on its side, and, stretching on tiptoe, grasp the handle, and with rhythmical regularity push the blade back and forth, back and forth, while thin wafers of 'streaky' or 'back' sliced themselves off the end and plopped onto the marble slab beneath. What other child had the joy of doing this? Dear benevolent Mr Smith, who knew what little girls liked, and how they enjoyed scoring over elder brothers!

Mr Smith had two assistants, Mr Davies and Miss Hobbs, who served on opposite sides of the shop and kept up a constant barrage of banter across the floor. I never quite knew whether these two were deadly enemies or very good friends. Mr Davies would start on me as soon as I came into the shop, with Mother's shopping list in my hand.

'Here, give it to me, Miss — I'll serve you. No good showing it to *her* — she can't read, y'know.' With a scornful toss of the head at poor plump Miss Hobbs on the other side, weighing out coffee into blue paper bags, Mr Davies took the shopping list from me.

I would turn, fascinated and horrified, to view this grown-up who had never even mastered her A B C. Could there really be people of her age who couldn't read? It was hard to believe; yet Mr Davies appeared totally serious. I turned from studying Miss Hobbs to studying him. There wasn't a smile on his face, so he couldn't be joking.

After all the years and years Miss Hobbs must have spent at school, I would think; and she would meet my worried stare with a flounce of her navy-blue skirts and a flash of her dark handsome eye at her enemy, who was slicing cheese now, with a bit of wire, in apparent unconcern.

'That's all *he* knows!' she would mutter darkly. 'Come over here, lovey, and let me do your Mum's order for you. He'll give you all the wrong things, like as not — never had a grain of sense, he didn't.' And bewildered, I would take the shopping list from Mr Davies and put it into Miss Hobbs' hand, noting her outraged expression, and hoping that Mr Davies, tossing his yellow slabs of cheese onto greaseproof paper and muttering into his whiskers, wouldn't be offended. There was certainly a lot of winking and grimacing going on from counter to counter, that I couldn't understand at all. Did grown-ups really bicker like this?

My brother and I, of course, constantly argued, as befitted brother and sister, and thought nothing of it. But to hear grownups like Mr Davies and Miss Hobbs slanging each other like that was incomprehensible. It wasn't even like Jos's rages next door. They seemed to be quite enjoying it. And good-natured Mr Smith's pink face was still smiling, so clearly he didn't mind. He never once told them to 'agree' as our parents were always telling us. Many were the wordy battles I heard waged from side to side of the little grocery shop, and they always left me bewildered.

Miss Hobbs's name was Mary, and Mr Davies would tease her continually in my hearing by getting her into a furious mood, and then singing softly with one eye on me,

Kind, kind and gentle is she,
Kind is my Mary.

Whereupon the flashing eyes would snap and the full lips pout, and I would be torn between loyalty to Mr Davies, who would slip the odd cheese cracker into my hand as he made up half a pound for Mother, or invite me to try one of his dried apricots as he weighed them out, and loyalty to poor Miss Hobbs, whom I always considered was very badly treated. For Miss Hobbs it was who invariably came to my rescue on the humiliating occasions when nobody gave me a shopping-list and I had to carry the message in my head.

I used to dread these moments; the shame of running blithely into the shop, to pull up short with that pang at the heart which foretold a complete lapse of memory. What was it now? Sugar? But surely we had plenty of that; there had been the usual two pounds of Gran and two pounds of Dem on the grocery order. Could it be something else we'd run out of like tapioca or rice? Or biscuits? No, for Mother had been baking. How *could* anybody remember?

Miss Hobbs would tell me to sit on the stool and wait till I thought of it; I would swing my legs with apparent unconcern; it looked better than to dangle them, as though you really didn't care whether your feet reached the floor or not — and my feet came nowhere near the floor. I would wait there, crestfallen, but trying desperately not to show it; trying to look as if it was the most natural thing in the world to sit on a stool cooling off in the shade of the shop on a hot summer's day.

Humiliation was even harder to bear when other customers came in. 'Don't you feel well, dearie?' kind old ladies would ask me, as they came in for a pound of Best Fresh Butter, not that Empire sort, please.

'Sitting there to get over the heat, are you?' old gentlemen would inquire as they bought dog biscuits for their pets, or blacking for their boots.

How could I tell them that I had just forgotten what I came for? As though I were an idiot, like those poor children I saw with lolling heads and open mouths and dribbling chins, being pushed about in babies' go-carts when they should have been walking. I, who went to school and could do lessons, and yet forgot messages like any half-wit? I, who was considered intelligent, and who now couldn't remember whether it was a pound of candles or a pound of lard . . .

Mr Smith's shop was full of sweet-smelling goods, to fill the modest cupboards of the neighbourhood; goods which now seem peculiarly of their age. Who ever hears now of Epps's Cocoa, or Mazawattee Tea, with the poster of the little girl dressed up in Granny's mob cap and spectacles, drinking tea from a china cup? Who ever hears now of the old-fashioned family grocer who would cut bacon to the taste of each individual customer — Number Six, or Number Seven, or Number Eight on the bacon slicer? Or mix a pound of biscuits, taking half a dozen from this tin and half a dozen from that, to please the family? Mr Smith would do all these things and more besides; and, I am pretty sure, would never have let any customer from his 'neighbourhood' go short, however difficult they might find it to pay. In the war years, when food was hard to come by, he would press a packet of butter into my hand, or half a dozen eggs in a box, with nods and smiles and whispers, under cover of the back of the shop — 'For your Mum, but keep it dark'. I could never understand this secrecy, knowing nothing at all about rationing; however worried my parents might have been in the days of the First World War, they never let their own private problems cloud the happiness of us children. All I knew was that Mr Smith was not only our family grocer but our family friend, and that he was always kind.

Indeed, food was taken for granted; plain food, perhaps, but always plenty of it. Plenty of Mother's home-baked cakes and puddings; plenty of fresh bread and butter; plenty of apples and oranges on the table in the dining-room, and home-made jams and jellies, and marmalade when the Seville oranges came in and the whole house smelled of Mother's marmalade-making. Good food to eat was one of the basics of family life. And we were taught to be grateful. 'For what we are about to receive,' we recited before every meal, 'may the Lord make us truly thankful.' And we were; Mother saw to that.

5

Jonesandhiggins

THE great shopping day of the week was always on Saturday, when Mother and Aunt Jane would get ready, after dinner, to go to Jonesandhiggins. This was really two words, Jones and Higgins, but we said them so often and so quickly in our house that for years I thought it was all one word — Jonesandhiggins. Jonesandhiggins was a large department store in Rye Lane, Peckham, and it sold everything from boots to wallpaper, from ladies' blouses to lampshades, bedroom suites to kitchen sinks. Whenever we wanted to buy anything we could not get at Mr Smith's or the local shops, we saved the purchase up for Saturday, when all the world went to Jonesandhiggins.

My parents remembered it from long before, when they used to buy their leg-of-mutton blouses there, their braided skirts and button boots, and gentlemen's long underwear. It boasted half a dozen plate glass windows, with arcades through which you could walk admiring the dummies of elegant papas in City clothes, mammas with parasols, and simpering children in school tunics. All the shop-walkers and assistants knew Mother and Aunt Jane, and took a personal interest in seeing they always got what they wanted, and that we children were fitted out to the best advantage with whatever the store could provide.

Jonesandhiggins was nearly two miles away, and we had to set out early after Saturday dinner to walk there and back. We nearly always walked to save money; a penny each way on the tram was a considerable item — as my parents used to say, it 'mounted up'. My family had been brought up to count every copper and never to ride where their legs would carry them.

'Be thankful for good health to walk at all,' was Mother's reply whenever I grumbled at having to trudge so far in the heat of a summer's day.

Occasionally we would take the tram

111

home, laden with parcels and baskets, when it was manifestly impossible to walk; but this was a rare luxury. As for taking a tram both ways, that was unheard-of. Wastefulness was a sin; and to waste twopence when you could walk was not only foolish but morally reprehensible.

The walk was a depressing one, through little back streets where children played in the gutters and women stared from open doors, their hair scraped back in topknots, leaning on their brooms with vacant eyes. I was always mightily glad when we came out of the dingy streets into the gay bright bustle of the 'Lane' as our main thoroughfare was called.

The Lane on a Saturday afternoon was crammed with flower stalls; large women in men's caps and with black shawls draped round them chanted their wares: 'Here y'are, ducky, only tuppence for this loverly bunch.' 'Two a penny, varlets, two a penny, get yer Mum to buy yer some.' I never dared ask Mother to buy any flowers; they were luxuries; besides, hadn't we got plenty in the garden at home? Nevertheless the smell of the 'varlets' was sweet, and reminded me of wet woods where they poked through the long grass. The smell of the daffodils was lovely, too; it followed you through the busy street, and the memory of their dazzling yellow swam before your eyes.

Sometimes there was a balloon stall, too, and occasionally I would spend my Saturday penny on a bright balloon. It was a trifle awkward trailing it behind all the way to Jonesandhiggins, and usually it burst with an exasperating pop before the afternoon was out. But the man with the balloons looked so kindly and wrinkled, his back bent under his great burden of coloured balloons, and his voice was so wheedling. It was worth it, for a penny; choosing the colour — should it be the sky-blue or the Guardsman red? — and letting it float upward on the end of its fragile string.

We passed quite close to the Penny Bazaar, which was a wonderful place to spend your pocket-money; but on the days we were bound for Jonesandhiggins nothing was allowed to distract Mother and Aunt Jane from their destination. We would cross by the busy island in the main road, where cars and horses and carts and bicycles and the occasional red bus came sweeping round, and I would hold hard onto a grown-up's hand to prevent myself from being engulfed in the traffic. There would be the smell of motor oil, and the smell of fresh horse droppings, too, which the birds would peck; and of course, people, people, all bustling around intent on shopping or business, and taking little notice of a small child trailing along with a balloon.

At last we had reached the other side, and were entering the cool glass arcades where the dummies stood, and the draped lengths of fabric for curtains and dresses, and the piles of kitchen pots and pans. We generally went in by the Boot and Shoe department, which led the way into most of the others, and it was here that my heart invariably sank, if anybody during the previous week had mentioned the subject of button boots.

The first two years of my school life were made miserable by those button boots. They were the fashion at the time, and Mother and Aunt Jane thought them suitable wear for wet days at school; but Mother and Aunt Jane didn't have to do them up. I longed in silence for any other kind of footwear but button boots. The buttonholes, when the boots were new, were so hard and slit-like that they hurt your fingers, and you didn't always have a button-hook. Even if you had, it invariably hooked the wrong button into the hole. I would sit on the wooden locker in the cloakroom at school long after all the other children had gone home, wrestling with my button boots and choking back the tears.

Getting them off was easy. You just ripped gloriously and they were undone. But getting them on! As often as not, I would be forced to walk out into the road with the buttons half undone, and pretend not to notice the grins and glances of my schoolmates outside. Some of the older girls wore fashionable button boots that came right up to the knee; but then they knew how to manage them. Mine were the unfashionable sort, coming half way up the calf; but that was bad enough. I prayed and prayed for the fashion of button boots to go out, and for some easier form of shoe to come in. Who could understand the vagaries of fashion? certainly not a little girl. And every time we went to Jonesandhiggins to buy a new pair, I would throw out desperate hints, only half hoping they would be taken up.

'Strap shoes are pretty,' I would suggest, gazing at a pair in the showcase. But nobody would even hear my remark. 'Or what about those?' as some luckier child proudly walked out of the Boot and Shoe department in a pair of laced brown shoes. At any rate you could learn how to do up laces; but buttonholes seemed to have a life of their own that defied anyone's expertise. Mother and Aunt Jane firmly stuck to the button boots, and it wasn't till years later that the fashion changed and 'went out' as mysteriously as it had come in. I was profoundly thankful.

Nearly every week we went up Jonesandhiggins' thickly carpeted stairs to the Drapery and the Ladies' Wear. How luxurious that carpet felt as you

116

walked slowly, savouring every step! Upstairs we would replenish the family wardrobe. It might be a new shirt-blouse for Aunt Jane to wear to her school; highnecked, severely buttoned down the front, and fastened with a large cameo brooch. Or a flannel nightgown with a huge frilly collar and frilly cuffs. Or — in spite of my wishful glances towards the new modern vests in the showcases — another pair of woollen combinations for me.

'*Can't* I have vests this time?' I would plead; but the answer was always the same. 'Our family have always worn wool next the skin, and we don't want you to catch your death of cold!' So it was more tickly combinations, with sleeves that showed under your party dresses, and legs that scratched when you sat down. I used to feel helpless and hopeless, standing there while the grown-ups bought all these clothes against which I didn't dare protest. Somewhere there must be somebody who would understand how a child just wanted to be comfortable, free of all that clothing.

In the ladies' department I usually got a sweet or two. As a very small child, I could dimly remember being lifted up to sit on the counter and recite the poem I had learnt by heart:

King Bruce of Scotland flung himself
    down
  In a lonely mood to think . . .

I didn't like it much; it was about spiders, and I abominated those. But people made me learn it, and seemed unduly pleased when I repeated it. Parents in those days were very proud of their children's accomplishments, and lost no time in showing them off even if it was only to an admiring audience of shopgirls. Since that day they had all got to know me well, patted my head and asked me that idiotic question 'How are you getting on at school?' Why did ladies always ask you that, I wondered? If you said 'Very well' they thought you conceited, and if you said 'Badly' they scolded you.

Leading out of the Drapery was the Millinery, and this never failed to entrance me. We seldom bought anything there, but it was fun to walk across those thick carpets and view the fashions. Hats were in all their glory, and held a peculiar fascination for me, for to wear a really large conspicuous hat, feathers, fruit and all, was the sign of actually being grown-up. First you put up your hair; then you went out and bought yourself a magnificent hat and were a girl no longer.

Here were displayed, on little gilt stands in luxurious abundance, such hats as I dreamed of wearing when my turn came to put my hair up. It was past — but only just past — the era of the glorious cornucopias and Harvest Festivals of hats, when one walked bowed down beneath a weight of fruit and flowers that Covent Garden itself could scarcely equal. But hats were still broad and belligerent, adorned with a bird of paradise, or a bunch of such gleaming artificial cherries that you could almost eat them. Veils, too, were in fashion; the heavy motoring veil was only just past its day, but something of the kind was still needed for those few — very few — rich people who travelled in a motor-car, or in an omnibus and were exposed to all the airs of heaven; for many cars were still open affairs, and on the tops of all the buses you travelled in the glorious outdoors.

I would never leave the Millinery without a glance at the grandmothers' bonnets, which had a showcase all to themselves. They were comic, bunched-up little affairs in black satin and velvet, decked with jet beads called mysteriously 'bugles', though they didn't look like bugles to me, and why anyway would a dear little old grandmother want a bugle on her hat? They often had crystallised violets as well — or that's how I thought of them, recalling the crystallised violets that you bought at the sweetshop for decorating birthday cakes — and were tied under the chin with long black satin streamers. These bonnets were correct headgear for the granny of the day. All my friends' grandmothers had bonnets like them, and I used to look forward to the time when my mother would be wearing one, and I could help her choose the prettiest from the stands in

Jonesandhiggins.

School hats were not in the Millinery, but in School Outfitting next door. I would see them amongst the navy serge tunics with the heavy box-pleats in front, and the thick navy bloomers. Some of the schoolgirls round us had already adopted the fashion of the soft straw or Panama hat for summer, and the felt for winter. Our headmistress, however, belonged to a past age, and was a stickler for the old ways. She still saw her girls in the uniform of thirty years ago. So we wore stiff straw boaters to school all the year round — uncomfortable and unpractical and universally hated.

You slung them up on a peg in the cloakroom, and the peg went through the crown. Or you wore them in the street when you passed the boys' school, and the boys nipped up behind you and smartly tipped the brim over your eyes, which hurt abominably. Altogether the straw boaters were distasteful objects, but still we wore them and still they were sold in the School Outfitting department. I longed to be big enough to choose my own hats.

Our purchases made upstairs and duly paid for — the change used to be sent across the ceiling in one of those wonderful aerial runway affairs that you never see in shops nowadays — we would make our way down to the Soft Furnishings and Household Goods. Mother would look longingly at the lace curtains draped so lavishly in folds and festoons, as at the best drawing-room windows.

'Ours really are getting very shabby,' she would sigh, 'but I suppose they'll have to do another season.' And she would look regretfully at the delicate lace patterns of birds and flowers and ornamental urns. 'A pity we get all the sun at the front of the house; they turn yellow so quickly.'

The tablecloths would next catch Mother's eye. Tables in polite society as we knew it were invariably covered with a dark green or brown chenille cover, with bobbles at the edge. Our cover on the dining-room table hung down in just this fashion, making a wonderful hiding-place for secret games on wet days. You could sit in there unseen and overhear bits of the grown-ups conversation, always in the hope of hearing something to your advantage like advance news of a party or an outing; though in fact all you ever did hear was dull conversation about Aunt May or Uncle Ernest or whether the grocer had charged too much for that pound of streaky.

The lampshades would always arouse my admiration. Lampshades were made in pale-coloured china or glass, fluted or scalloped, patterned or flowered, to go over the gas mantles that were used universally in our suburb. Nobody in our road had electricity yet. Most parlours and drawing-rooms also had large standard lamps, for which you could buy enormous red silk shades. We had such a lamp at home, fuelled by oil in a shining brass container beneath the light; its shade was a huge bulbous affair of silk; but it was never used. Indeed I doubt if it could be lit at all; oil was a messy, smelly affair. In the hall, many of our friends hung shades of jangling glass beads that caught the light and jingled slightly when the draught from the opening front door set them a-quiver. I thought these very grand, and was always begging Mother to buy one for our front hall; but she considered them distasteful.

'Vulgar things I call them,' she would say about the wonderful glass beads. 'I'd never have one of those in *my* house.' I would pass them regretfully in Jonesandhiggins, wondering why the grownups thought so many things 'vulgar' that were beautiful to me.

The object I coveted most of all in the furniture section was a huge brass bowl for our aspidistra. No home, of course, was complete without its aspidistra, that huge shiny spiky-leaved creature that almost had a will of its own, I used to believe. Once you had an aspidistra in the house, it grew larger and larger, more and more shiny and spiky every day, till it seemed to take up more room and attract more attention than anything else. The whole household tended it reverently, watering it with care, and making most complicated arrangements for its welfare whenever the family went away on holiday, just as if it were a pet.

Whenever it rained, in the heat of summer, it was my task to see that the aspidistra got its share. I would rush out with the plant in my arms and place it strategically on the top of the front steps, where it would get a nice healthy share of rain and also the drips from the doorway. All up and down the road, people were doing the same. The leaves were polished regularly with a rag to make them shine, and of course dusted daily. Mother was very proud of the aspidistra Father had bought her when they set up home, and I longed to have enough money to buy her one of the fashionable Benares-ware brass pots to put it in, instead of the cracked china bowl it had at present. But Benares-ware cost a lot, and could not be bought with Saturday pennies.

At the Carpeting, Mother would pause wistfully, contemplating the riches spread out before her. Carpeting was a costly business, only undertaken when you got married, or when, many years later, your original carpet had worn threadbare. Ours had not yet reached this stage, though the pattern on the carpet in the dining-room was wearing out in many places, especially where our old collie used to sleep on it.

Turkey carpet was considered the most desirable; rich shades of crimson and blue, lending a solid, important air to the best room in the suburban home. Ours had been Turkey once, but the red and blue had faded to a kind of uniform mauve. One day, I thought, I shall be rich enough to buy Mother carpeting for every room in the house, even the attic bedrooms, which only had a bare linoleum floor. Carpeting, too, for every one of the flights of stairs, with thick pile like that on the stairs at Jonesandhiggins. Wouldn't that be the height of extravagance?

'When our ship comes in,' Mother would say a little sadly; and I would think that whatever she meant, the mysterious vessel was a long time making harbour, for she said it so often.

It was in the Kitchen Department that Mother would really let herself go. She would walk entranced between the rows of kitchen pots and pans, the carpet-sweepers and the scrubbing-boards, calling attention to this new device or that.

'Well, that's something novel!' she

would exclaim. 'I'd like to have a trial with that.' And the salesman would step forward briskly, hoping for a chance to 'send a man along' to demonstrate the virtues of this new labour-saving device or the other. Mother was very proud of her housewifely skill, and was always on the look-out for something to save time or trouble and give her leisure to do the other things that always called for attention — polishing silver, or turning sheets sides-to-middle. Not that she grumbled; everybody took it for granted then that housework was a heavy job; but still it would be nice to try out new inventions now and again.

One day we bought a Bissels carpet-sweeper. It was quite the latest thing in household gadgetry for homes that were not, of course, electric; and it did away for ever, so the salesman told us, with the drudgery of sweeping carpets by hand, scattering tea-leaves over them to take up the dust, and going over them with the broom, or using dustpan and brush beneath the furniture. The Bissels was new and shining, with a polished handle, two brushes which swept up the dust, and a box underneath to trap the sweepings. Unfortunately it all too often trapped the fingers as well when you emptied it, as I was soon painfully to discover.

Aids for washing day were few and far between until the advent of electricity; and that was a long way off in our suburb. Yet Mother always had an ear and eye open for new devices to make a better job of it. Once she had heard from Aunt Jane's Scottish friend Nickie — Mrs Nicholson, who was a fellow-teacher and dropped in most afternoons for a cup of tea on her way home — that Scottish peasants used to tread the sheets round and round with their feet in the clear running water of the burns. We hadn't any clear running water, but next washing day Mother filled a big tub with suds and got me to take off my shoes and socks and paddle round in my bare feet in the tub, supposedly treading the sheets clean.

This seemed a grand idea, and I trod and trod to my heart's delight, drenching myself in the process and deluging the basement floor inches deep in soapy water. The sheets, however, appeared none the cleaner; in fact some of them were distinctly dirtier where I had let them fall over the edge of the tub; so Nickie's bright idea was carried no further. It might be all right for Scottish peasants, but it didn't do for us.

Nickie, however, was a great one for gadgetry, and she soon persuaded Mother and Aunt Jane to buy a 'dolly'. The dolly consisted of a round metal plunger with perforations all round it, attached to a long pole. You plunged the pole up and down in a specially designed wooden tub, thus washing the clothes clean by a suction method. We bought the dolly and its bucket, and bore them home in triumph, getting the pole stuck into all the other passengers on the tram and calling forth rude comments from little boys as we walked up the road with it.

But alas, the dolly didn't do the work any better than the Scottish peasant idea. We begrudged the hard-earned money wasted on this useless gadget, and soon the poor dolly was relegated to a far corner of the basement, where it languished propped up against the heavy old mangle, until my brother and I discovered the uses of the stick as a hobby-horse or a ship's mast for games in the garden. The bucket was used for various purposes, and Mother henceforth abandoned all thought of easing the washing-day burden, and, since we could not afford the expense of sending anything away to the laundry, continued her Monday toil in the good old way.

Nickie, however, was not to be defeated in her passion for labour-saving. She recommended to Mother a wonderful new pressure cooker, one of the earliest of its kind. It was a large metal container, so big that I could scarcely carry it, into which you fitted little metal baskets containing meat, vegetables and pudding, sealing the whole up tightly and putting it on the top of the stove to cook. It was a clumsy affair, and cost a good deal more than Mother could really afford, but Nickie swore to its efficiency, so home we came from Jonesandhiggins on the penny tram with our new machine.

We had already tried various dodges for reducing the amount of fuel needed to cook for a family. During the War Mother had made up a hay box, into which we used to put such things as rice pudding or porridge to cook overnight. The results tasted to me soggy and unappetising, but it did save fuel. Unfortunately the hay box came to a sudden end when the cat had kittens in it, and we abandoned it for ever. The new pressure cooker, however, so Nickie assured us, would save money and fuel and time galore; so we tried it out in great excitement.

But again the results tasted to us insipid. Father complained that the meat tasted of currant pudding, the carrots of cabbage and the cabbage of swede; and gradually the poor pressure cooker went the way of the washing dolly. It wasn't even as useful as the dolly, for you couldn't play any games with a pressure cooker, and it was too heavy to bath the dolls in. Mother should have been warned by these disastrous ventures into the world of gadgetry, but she still, though washing by hand and cooking with the usual big iron pots and pans, insisted on leaving Jonesandhiggins by the Kitchen Department so that she could 'just see if there was anything new'.

But eventually even Mother dared not dawdle any longer. There was still the long walk home; and tea to get ready for any visitors who might drop in. Saturday tea-time was a great time for visiting amongst our friends and relations.

We would reach home tired and hungry, and while Aunt Jane put the kettle on the fire for tea, Mother would take a pencil and jot down her purchases in the 'Boots the Chemist's Home Diary and Ladies' Notebook' that was her great stand-by for keeping the family finances steady. The 1917 Diary records some of her expenses at Jonesandhiggins: my brother's navy serge school suit (he was fourteen), £2. 3s.; his flannel shirts, 7s. 11d. each; school boots were 12s. 6d.; Mother's new shoes were 17s. 9d.; and my own shoes 7s. 3d. and 1s. 11½d. for a pair of patent leather party shoes and a pair of plimsolls for school. Jonesandhiggins was a reasonable store, everybody said; you didn't get overcharged, and you always got value for money.

You got a lot more than value for money, too, when you shopped at

Jonesandhiggins, I used to think. You got novelty and excitement; you got friendliness from the shop assistants; you got a glimpse into a dream-world where a suburban house could be furnished from top to bottom with Turkey carpets and aspidistra-pots and kitchen labour-saving devices; you got a picture of yourself as you would be when you were really grown-up and a lady with dresses like Mother's and Aunt Jane's, and any hat you liked to choose.

When I'm grown up, I thought, I'll always shop at Jonesandhiggins. I'll take the tram — yes, a whole penny — from the Fire Station to Rye Lane; push through the glass swing doors and buy and buy and buy. And then I'll ride all the way home again with everything I've bought. Even if it does cost another penny. I'll be rich, perhaps, one day.

6

Relations

LIKE every other family down our road, we had relations by the score. Though we didn't ourselves have any grandparents, we had aunts and uncles, cousins, first and second and even third, and cousins many times 'removed'; I often wondered who removed them, and where to. Not to speak of the multitudes of elderly friends of our parents, who styled themselves 'aunt' or 'uncle' and certainly considered themselves permanent members of the family. It was these people whom I remembered nightly in my prayers; were they not 'aunts-and-uncles-and-all-kind-friends'?

Families reached far in those days, and no self-respecting child would feel complete without them. They visited frequently, coming long distances by tram or bus or train, or even on foot; visiting, indeed, was one of the major pleasures of life for the grown-ups; and we in turn visited those who visited us. Though I noticed they seldom did anything except sip tea and talk.

To me these visits were unspeakably boring, though I couldn't admit it. We were supposed to look pleased to see our relations, however much we hated having to stand on tiptoe and plant a kiss on those parchment-like faces with whiskery chins. Most of the relations I was taken to see were elderly, and female, and either spinsters or widows, with little recollection of small children. I suppose these were the ones whom my parents considered needed visiting the most; but I didn't think much of their choice. I wished they would visit without us in tow; but it was no use wishing that, children tagged along as a matter of course, never expecting any preferential treatment either; it was a grown-ups' world and we had to put up with it.

Occasionally a more than usually imaginative aunt would provide a book for a child to leaf through, or even more occasionally a toy to play with.

The books and toys were never very interesting, usually weary-looking objects left over from a past generation, joyless in the extreme. I would sit on a hard chair, trying to reach the floor with my toes; it gave me much more confidence when I succeeded, for there is nothing like having to dangle your legs in the air to undermine any self-respect you started off with.

The chair was not often a comfortable one. It usually had arms which were designed for grown-ups, sticking into bits of a child's anatomy with a perverse kind of spitefulness. As a special concession, I would sometimes be offered a stool, which was even worse, since these had no backs to lean against. You had to sit up very straight, and were painfully conscious of your inferior status at floor-level. Seldom did any of the conversation hold any interest to a small child. It was usually of the familiar Saturday evening type — 'How's Charlie?' 'What became of poor Agnes?' Long sighs, during which I felt myself keyed up with anticipation: how *was* Charlie, and what *did* become of poor Agnes? But usually poor Agnes and her kind were sighed over and nodded over with sideways glances at me. A pity, I thought; it would have been nice to have something to spin a story about, those endless stories I would invent every night in bed so as to get myself to sleep. Poor Agnes sounded as likely a candidate as any for the role of heroine, if only I knew her fate.

When conversation was temporarily exhausted, or when my fidgets seemed to be getting the better of me, our relations would suggest, in a voice which gave promise of a real treat, that we should all 'go round the garden'. I knew better than to look forward to this. Indeed my spirits would sink even lower; going round the garden, I knew from experience, could be even more tedious than sitting on a stool looking at faded picture-books in olive-green covers; grown-ups missed so many wonderful chances when they decided to 'go round the garden', and a child's disappointment would be made even worse. All that space — those lovely lawns, those trees waiting to be climbed — and nobody took any notice of them, just walked sedately round the flower-beds inspecting every plant. When they might have gone bursting through those glass verandah doors (all gardens seemed to open off verandahs) with whoops of joy, and skipping onto the lawns to turn cartwheels! Even when they walked round the kitchen garden, they would never stop and grab a plump gooseberry and feel the juice running from their mouths; never reach up and pick a ripe apple from the bough. Instead they would simply say 'The gooseberries are doing nicely this year' or 'Quite a good crop of apples, don't you think?' It was all such waste.

No; they walked demurely round the garden, stopping at every plant and bush, to bend and inspect it, and tell or listen to its history. I never knew flowers could have such histories. 'Now this,' the hostess would say, with fearful deliberation as she stopped dead in her tracks for the third time in two minutes, 'I got as a cutting from Cousin So-and-So.' Then she would pause, her hand clapped to her brow. 'No, I'm telling you wrong; it was dear Cousin Somebody Else — or was it? Let me

138

think, now.' She paused. 'Wrong again; it was dear old Mrs Thingummy down the road. I brought it home when it was the tiniest plant, and just look at it now.' I looked, and saw nothing but a few green leaves sprouting dustily from the ground. What conceivable interest could dear Mrs Thingummy's cutting have for Mother or me? But the grown-ups would stop and linger and chat, and go on from there to discuss Mrs Thingummy's latest illness and how all the little Thingummies were doing, while I kicked at the gravel with the toe of my shoe and looked longingly at all that grass that nobody seemed to want to play on, all those trees waiting to be climbed. The whole golden afternoon was crumbling in a long recital about cuttings and illnesses, when the garden was ready, waiting to be explored.

When at last it became quite obvious that they were going to do nothing but perambulate from flower-bed to flower-bed, I would concentrate my thoughts on tea. At least this was something to look forward to. There would be cake — if you had eaten your bread-and-butter — and sometimes even two kinds of cake, an unheard-of luxury. There was only one snag: they would rarely give me a table to eat from. Grown-ups seemed to prefer to eat in their laps, a precarious business at which I was unutterably clumsy. At home, tea was always taken at the big square table; you sat sensibly in comfort and safety, and knew what to do. But here, you were given a cup and saucer, and a plate as well, sometimes even a knife. What did you do with them? Uncomfortably islanded on chair or stool, there would be nothing to do except balance it all on the knee; and conveying all that tempting food to your mouth without dropping a spoon or worse — upsetting a plate — was almost impossible. The shame when you heard something clattering to the floor, or worst of all, felt a tide of warm tea enveloping your lap as the cup tilted, took a long time to live down. Just one more waste, like all that time in the garden; all this lovely food, and agony to eat it. How inscrutable were the grown-ups, who had power to do anything they liked, and then made things so difficult. When I was grown up, I would think, toying with a piece of cake and hoping I wasn't dropping any crumbs, I would organise this whole business of visiting very differently.

There was one exception to the agonies of visiting relations. This was when we went to see our one really grand relative. She lived in a large house, double-fronted, the ultimate, to us, in architectural luxury; and with an enormous garden, in a very select part of the south-eastern suburbs — Gipsy Hill. The house didn't even have a number. It had just a name, a fact which set it apart from all the other houses we knew, and indicated a romantic life-style. I was suitably impressed. Fancy a letter arriving, bearing no number but simply a name; it must confer an honour, almost, on the postman who brought it.

In addition to a name and not a number, and an exciting address like Gipsy Hill, the house actually had a maid. No other family I ever knew kept a maid, a real one in black dress and white apron, with a bonnet with strings down the back. This was grandeur indeed. When you rang the bell, the maid answered the door, and you didn't have to kiss her, you only had to kiss the black-dressed, well-corseted lady in the drawing-room at the end of the hall. (It was a proper hall, too, not a passage.)

Visiting here was totally different from visiting at any other relation's. In the first place, you had to wait to be asked. When the summons came, as it did with kindly regularity every four months or so, we dressed in our Sunday clothes, not our Saturday ones, and set off by tram for the long, swaying ride into the wealthier suburbs. As the tram climbed the steep hill at the end, creaking and groaning as it passed larger and still larger houses, with greener and still greener gardens, my spirits would rise. Great things were in store.

In the second place, we were asked in the morning; not the afternoon. To lunch — which we called dinner. Or rather, luncheon. I would roll the unfamiliar word round my mouth; it held such luxury. In the third place, this particular aunt seemed to know by instinct what children liked and didn't like to do

— which could not be said of many of our relations.

She didn't for instance, expect you to eat up all your food if there were dishes you didn't like. Neither did she call you faddy. This saved a lot of distress, as one of the things I was not good at was eating other people's dinners; they mostly tasted horrible.

Here, however, the midday meal held no terrors. Nobody even expected you to eat up your greens. In fact, you weren't given any greens; you could just wave them airily away when the maid brought them round, the dish carefully poised above your left shoulder. It was wonderful to be able to take only what you wanted, and not what the grown-ups thought you ought to eat.

Sometimes, when there wasn't a maid in attendance, there was something even more interesting — a food lift. It was a strange contrivance which I had never seen in anyone else's house, nor was I to see again except in public restaurants. Instead of the dishes being on the table, or handed by the maid, they were brought up from the kitchens below, with strange grindings and groanings of ropes and pulleys, on a lift. Our hostess would press a button, and the lift would majestically ascend, for her to open a pair of little doors and produce food from within like the conjuror's rabbit out of a hat. This food lift used to rivet our attention; we could hardly eat for thinking of it, listening to its grumbles and groans, watching it open. It quite made up for the unaccustomed worry of having to balance a crackling starched table napkin on the knee without having to stoop to retrieve it from the polished floor.

We would have plates of roast beef with lots of deliciously browned potatoes to which we children helped ourselves rather too lavishly for Mother or Aunt Jane's approval; but what was the point of having your food offered you by a maid, or handed you by a smiling hostess, if you didn't take as much as you wanted? For pudding, to which we always looked forward, there was usually sherry trifle. About this sherry trifle there was a lot of talk in our family. Strong liquor was never allowed under any circumstances whatsoever, on the principle that one sip would drive you straight into the arms of the Demon Drink. Didn't the Band of Hope tell you so? and Father emphatically agreed. But sherry in the trifle — well, that was another matter. A delicate matter, that made Mother wrestle with her conscience.

'It's only cooking sherry,' she would say, as though that gave it more affinity with Mrs Beeton than with the Demon Drink. But it *was* sherry all the same, argued Father. You could taste it, as we children knew, through the layers of cream and custard and jam and sponge cake; and of course, because it was forbidden, it tasted all the nicer. I used to know just how Eve felt in the Garden of Eden when she partook of the forbidden fruit, and imagine myself doing the same — only, of course, with clothes on.

Then, too, conscience could be circumvented. You were *told* to eat what your hostess offered you, so if you were offered sherry trifle you were doing Right, not Wrong, by eating it. At any rate it tasted wonderful, and since Father didn't accompany us on these occasions, we all ate it up with gusto. And when biscuits and cheese arrived on the groaning food lift, it completed my private bliss at being considered grown-up. We never had biscuits and cheese at home.

Sometimes I even wished there had been wine on the table. This would have been tempting Providence indeed, but wouldn't it be wonderful if just once I could try a sip — nothing more — of the strong drink everyone was perpetually warning me against? I had no idea how strong drink tasted; and I certainly shared my parents' horror of the local gin-palaces, as they called them, those shoddy, down-at-heel public houses, situated on the corners of the meanest streets, where the smell of sawdust on the floors mingled with the whiff of alcohol and the odour of not-very-well-washed humanity, to give me a proper repugnance of 'drinking'. There was one of these places not far from Mr Smith's the grocer's, where I went on errands, and I used to cross to the other side when I passed it, so as not to be 'enticed in'. It was a beery looking establishment, and when we went by it sometimes, late on a Saturday night after the Church Social, there would be a crowd of dispirited-looking women and tired children outside, waiting for the drink-sodden inmates to roll out and fight in the gutter.

But that was drink at one end of the social scale; I vaguely felt that drink at the other end was altogether different. Wine at table — now that would be the ultimate in sophistication. But all we got, even at this grand house, was what we got at home for a treat on Sundays — a tall greenish bottle of Lime Juice standing at the corner of the table.

Even so, I would remind myself a table which held a bottle of Lime Juice every day of the week, when it wasn't even Sunday, was luxury indeed. I really couldn't expect wine as well, and anyway there was always the trifle with its cooking sherry, after which I always used to imagine I felt rakishly dizzy.

After luncheon, and a suitable rest for the ladies while I leafed through the pages of a children's book, our hostess would suggest that we 'go round the garden'. This wasn't the signal for boredom, as it was in everybody else's house; it was the moment I looked forward to, second only to the luncheon table. True, proceedings would start in the usual way, with the accustomed trail round the flower-beds, stopping at each clump and seedling, but this particular aunt of ours seemed to have sympathy with childhood fidgets, and as soon as she noticed my dragging feet, she would suggest I should 'run along now and explore the Wood'.

The Wood! This was the moment I had been waiting for. There was nothing I could have enjoyed more. The Wood, for all its grand sound, was only a moderate-sized coppice, but it was what I always yearned for, a bit of the country. The tall trees were clustered together at the far end of the garden, intersected by mossy paths which rambled in all directions, so that you could get pleasurably lost with the certain knowledge that someone would be sure, later, to come and find you. Here I would wander at will, listening to the delicious soughing of the wind in the topmost branches, watching the swaying of the tall trunks, stopping to note the call of a bird, sometimes — on lucky days — even spotting the whisk of a tail, a squirrel! There were nuts on the ground to pick up as souvenirs or to nibble; pine cones to collect in your pinafore, if you were wearing one; leaves to scuffle through in your best shoes, at the risk of scratching the new brown leather. There were so many things you could do in the Wood, while the grownups pottered on their dull little ceremonial round of the formal flower-beds.

I would stand at the foot of the tallest tree I could find, looking dizzily up into the branches, at the patches of blue sky and scudding cloud that seemed such a long way away; or stroke the rough bark and hold my breath in case — just in case — there might be a dryad in the tree. Dryads did live in trees, I knew; we'd read about them in school, and my great ambition was to see one. But they never lived in suburban gardens, I was sure, only in a Wood like this one. It was worth taking a chance, keeping perfectly still while the bees hummed and the birds chattered, listening. Sometimes there was a rustle; could that be the dryad stirring? I hesitated to ask the grown-ups, for fear of being laughed at, for they did laugh at the strangest things. But I never did actually see one. Perhaps they were shy, or perhaps they were hard to catch a glimpse of, like the Guardian Angel that everybody had, though nobody ever saw it.

Nevertheless, within that wood, something — dryad or not — had cast a spell on me. I walked carefully, quietly, so as not to disturb the pool of stillness which rippled all around me as I stole through the gaps between the tall trees, sniffing the smell of the pines. If only I could stay here for ever in this wood, doing nothing, being nothing, just living; far away from the world of school and sums, the dusting of the sideboard at home, the unaccountable ways of grown-ups. I could be happy here.

And then I would hear someone calling, and drag myself away, back to the garden. The trees thinned out; the mossy paths broadened into gravelled walks, the ferns and bushes gave way to geraniums and pelargoniums and all those other flowers with names ending uglily in — um. We would walk up to the terrace outside the drawing-room and there, I knew, tea would be set out; tea with plenty of plum cake, and lots of home-made jam in little glass dishes. True, there would be the usual trouble about balancing cup and saucer on your lap, for even this kindly aunt never seemed to have tea in a sensible way, round the table. But there would be things we never got at anybody else's houses: cucumber sandwiches cut very thin with the edges neatly nipped off so that there were no crusts, and handed by a maid in a cap and apron; and salmon sandwiches with juicy slices of tomato inside, that slipped about deliciously as you ate. All this and plum cake too; what more could a child ask?

Staying with relations was something you had to do sometimes, when the grown-ups told you to; and this I didn't like at all. In fact, the relations with whom I was usually sent to stay, under the mistaken impression that I was enjoying it, were horrifying indeed. Of course they meant well; all our relations did that, for they were kindly folk. But they just didn't understand children; not even if they had children of their own.

I knew when I was going to be sent to stay with someone by all the whispering that went on as a school holiday approached. First it would be whispering, and then it would be something called 'catching the postman', which meant someone running out to the hall in the mornings to pick up the post so that I shouldn't notice where the letter came from. They wouldn't tell me very long before the date, because I might make objections, or start to feel homesick before I got there. When at last the plan could be concealed no longer, I was told, with many assurances that I would 'enjoy it when I got there'; a sure sign, to me, that I was in for something bad.

The suburb where I was sent to stay was considered one of the trendy ones in those days. It was the newly-built Hampstead Garden Suburb, a desirable estate in North-West London where every house had its own garden and there was a careful plan for beauty coupled with utility, and things like Community

Centres and Educational Institutes to provide the necessary culture. It would be even more desirable than our own suburb, I was assured by Mother and Aunt Jane — though Father doubted it; he was a fervent Londoner. Mother would tell me that it was even nearer the country than our own neighbourhood, knowing this would be an attraction; but I already knew it was only 'pretend' country where the green bits still had rails round them and the trees had been planted by the Corporation instead of just growing.

The cousin with whom I stayed was about the same age as me — a little older, in fact, just old enough for me to wear her conveniently passed-on dresses, which didn't suit me, for they were slightly trendy like the Garden Suburb itself. Her family did everything in their power to make me welcome, and I knew I was expected to enjoy myself; but it was purgatory of the worst kind, the kind you had to pretend to enjoy. I dreaded it.

First of all, you arrived in time for midday dinner; and here there was no possibility of avoiding the things you didn't like, for your plate was piled high in the mistaken idea that the guest was being given a good meal. I would watch my little weekend bag being carried upstairs, and feel that my last chance had passed by; now I couldn't get away. I would have to stay here alone until someone came and fetched me. A wave of misery would wash over me, making it more than ever impossible to sit down at the family dinner table and enjoy a good meal. If I could get away without everybody remarking on all that uneaten food, it was the most I could hope for.

There was just so much of it. Even to look at it was overwhelming. 'Leaving a clean plate' was expected behaviour, especially when you went away on a visit, and of course you had to try to please your hostess. But why did they pile the plate so high, with mountains of mashed potatoes, rivers of gravy, hillocks of hated greens? The greens seemed to come in every available form, for Garden City folk prided themselves on their kitchen gardens and home-produced vegetables. There were hideous tight-looking brussels sprouts, sickly pale cauliflowers, mushy cabbage, and even mushier carrots and swedes and turnips. It was as if every vegetable in the Garden Suburb had heaped itself in horrid glee upon my plate.

At home I hated the stuff but Father, who of course as a doctor knew all about Vitamin C, would lecture us on the benefit of green vegetables and the horrors of scurvy. I would be prevailed on to eat a little, but this was altogether different. This was purgatory. I would sit and eye the stuff with loathing; toy with it at the end of a fork; push it to the corner of my plate, and look round to see if I had been observed. I always was. 'Eat them up,' I was told. 'They're straight from the garden — lovely. They'll do you good.'

In the end, having struggled my way through as much as I could, leaving the mountain of potato barely dented, the hills of vegetables untouched, I would lay down knife and fork and hope for the best. My cousin, who liked such things, would shoot me a superior look, knowing that it would not be long before the defection was noticed.

'Is that really all she can eat?' Why did they address remarks to me in the third person, I wondered? 'Try her with a little more swede. Or another spoonful of carrot — that lot's gone cold by now.' And yet more of the stuff would be loaded onto my plate. It was no good, either, trying to eat it up and be done with it. If I did manage that feat, it would be the signal for even more of the horror to be piled onto my plate; 'you see, she wants some more; come along, pass the cabbage, now, pass the sprouts.' You just couldn't win.

They told me I had a sparrow's appetite, which did nothing to relieve my embarrassment. Eventually my loaded plate would be carried off while I sat pink-cheeked with misery, shame struggling with relief as I saw the last of the hated greens. Pudding could never be as bad as that dreaded first course.

Shortly after lunch, my cousin and I would be bundled off for a walk together. Our walk would always lead us through the green and pleasant roads of the Garden Suburb towards the house of a friend of hers, who could be relied upon, my cousin knew, to join us so that two could be company while three was none. The two girls walked ahead, giggling happily, exchanging notes about school, whilst I dawdled along behind them, miserably conscious that I wasn't wanted. Under other circumstances I would have enjoyed the tree-lined roads, the little grassy commons, the white fences and the flowering hedges of the Garden Suburb, even if it wasn't the country. But to tag along behind two chattering girls, alone and unwanted, was depressing. It was even more depressing when we finally reached home and I was eagerly questioned about the walk.

'Did you enjoy it, dear?' they would ask, taking my hat and coat and bundling me in again beside the fire. 'All that fresh air — you had a lovely time, didn't you?'

I couldn't tell the truth, so I wriggled and blushed and assured them that of course I had enjoyed it tremendously, while behind our backs my cousin dared me, with warning grimaces, to let on that there had been a third party on our walk and that I'd been left out in the cold.

I could get through tea-time well enough. Bread and butter tastes much the same, wherever you eat it; and there were often fancy scones and seed cake, which I adored. But as the shadows fell and the lamps were lighted, the dreaded time approached when I would have to go upstairs to share a bedroom with my cousin. It had all been so well prepared; it was all so kindly meant. But to me it was a fearful ordeal, for I knew what to expect. It happened every time.

I would undress as slowly as I could, and lie shivering in the darkness in the bed next to my cousin, watching the lamplight shining in from the road outside. It all looked so peaceful. Yet I lay awake, just waiting for it to happen. My dreadful little cousin would begin the torture. She knew my particular susceptibilities; we had both read *Uncle Tom's Cabin*, where Little Eva, the innocent child who had contracted some dire disease, lay dying in her white bed — just like the white bed in which I now lay, stiff with fright.

My cousin would rise in her white nightgown, fearful in the shadows from the gas-lamp outside, and fling out her arms in a sort of ecstasy of suffering. Her long hair would fall about her face, her eyes stare with horror, her breath come in great convulsive gasps, till I really believed she herself was dying — dying there with only me to see. All the death-throes of the poor child were faithfully enacted; the gulps, the sighs, the struggles for breath, the final death-rattle which left her, with agonizing slowness, lifeless against the pillow. In the half-light I could see her white face, her staring eyes glassy in their sockets. It was too horrible to be borne. I would scream and scream, till horrified grown-ups came pounding up the stairs and into the little bedroom, where my cousin lay innocently asleep, and only I was screaming.

'Poor child, she's homesick. She wants her mother,' they would say soothingly. I knew perfectly well that it wasn't a case of homesickness, though at that moment I would have given anything to be home in my own bed. I didn't even particularly want my mother, except to calm my terrors. But how could I

159

tell them the truth? If only, I thought wildly, if only it meant that I need not come here any more; need never again struggle through those awful meals, go on those hated walks, or witness, helpless in the darkness, the death-throes of Little Eva! But I knew, even as the grown-ups calmed me down and left me, that as soon as the next holidays came round, off I would go again to stay in the Garden Suburb.

Only another term, I would think, lying in bed, and they will be whispering together again; saying brightly 'You'll enjoy it when you get there.'

How I wished I could have told them the truth! But you never did in those days. It was one of the penalties of having relations; you had to visit them, and worse, you had to go and stay with them.

7

Fear and Trembling

I WONDER how many grown-ups understand the enormous cloud of fear which can at any moment loom up to darken a small child's sunniest day? Children are happy enough on the surface; but they have unplumbed depths of dread and anxiety that nobody knows about except themselves.

Fear leaps back at me from the past in the most chance encounter, the most passing scent or sound or movement recalling an earlier terror. Perhaps fear never really dies, but is only buried. Though I lived the most sheltered life, fear was always there, just behind me; sometimes of material things, sometimes of things intangible. I only knew that both types of fear could fill the day with foreboding, and most of all the night.

Amongst the material objects that terrified me were the spiders — those

161

great black hairy things with uncountable legs, that planted themselves, the very personification of evil, in the bath just as you were about to get in; or crawled disgustingly from under the kitchen sink when you went to put down the cat's plate for her dinner.

It was no use my elders telling me that spiders were clean and wouldn't hurt you; the fear was far more primitive than that. Spiders were and still are — unclean to me in an allegorical way, seeming to embody all the powers of Satan, the Devil, Beelzebub or whatever you called him. They were sin itself crawling across the floor. I had a horrible recurrent nightmare of being buried alive under a vast, heaving mass of spiders, unable to breathe, unable to free myself or call for help. I would wake sweating with terror, clutching the bedclothes, my heart hammering with fear, and scream and scream until somebody came.

Often they scolded me for being naughty and bringing them upstairs from supper or the warm fireside — was it really only the beginning of the night, and not the deep middle it had seemed? — but

I was totally unable to communicate to them the terror that had filled my dreams. I would scarcely dare to go to sleep again, and would lie cowering, trying to keep awake till morning, cold with misery and sick with remembering.

Then there was the dreadful moment when you had to pass under a certain railway arch just as a steam train was thundering overhead. This was horror pure and simple; paralysing, blotting out reason entirely. People laughed and told you that the arch was strong enough and that the train couldn't possibly fall through and annihilate you; but all your world was tearing and roaring and thundering in your ears, shaking your whole body, quenching your spirit.

Trains were terrible things. They could be — and still are — devils indeed. When you were on a station platform and the express came roaring in, straight for you with all its power and might, to wipe you out — then you flew for protection to hide your head in Mother's skirts. They laughed again at this, but laughter did not even touch the fear.

Strangely enough — or sensibly enough, if you consider it aright — the Great War, which broke out soon after my fourth birthday, hardly entered my consciousness at all as something to be afraid of. I was safe in my little world, with Mother, Father, my brother and Aunt Jane. Having them, everything was all right. People talked over my head about bombs and air-raids, and we had our share of them; often I was awakened by the wailing of the siren in the middle of the night, and would stand at the foot of my bed, clutching a blanket round my nightgown, waiting for someone to come and take me to the shelter which Father had made for us in the basement downstairs.

The shelter was a snug little place. It was barricaded with sandbags, and we children enjoyed the novel experience of sitting cosily inside, being read to from story-books, and drinking warm cocoa, with nobody telling us to go to sleep, although it was the middle of the night. Once the house rocked when a bomb fell near, but I felt only the excitement and none of the fear.

I did notice, however, that the grown-ups' faces often paled when they opened the newspaper. I used to watch Mother scanning the casualty lists, as I later discovered they were, on the back page; and one morning in the kitchen I found her in tears.

To me, the war so far had been just one gigantic game in which everybody tried to score one better than the others — like Ludo or cards. Now I came to understand, suddenly, that it was something more; they were killing each other. It had got beyond a game.

But one thing stood out clear. 'Do the Germans cry as well?' I asked Mother; and when she nodded through her tears, I saw the answer definite and simple. 'Then why don't they stop?' I demanded. 'Why doesn't everybody stop?'

My mother, not trusting herself to speak, shook her head; and, alarmed by her unaccustomed tears, I said no more. But for years afterwards I still saw the issue in black and white, just like that; and strangely, that is how I still see it in the last resort. In a dawning way, it was the beginning of the personal pacifism which has remained with me to the present day, through the Second World War and beyond, and in the spiritual sense has led me to become a Quaker.

Only twice did the War strike a momentary fear into me, as I played happily in house and garden, and busied myself with the cares of my little world. One night I was snatched up from the comfort of our homely little shelter and carried through the street door, wrapped in a blanket, to watch a huge sausage of flame suspended unbelievably in the dark sky. It was the first of the Zeppelins to be brought down, and fell, as we learned later, in the grounds of a friend of ours at Northaw, near Potters Bar. For years we kept a piece of the blackened and scarred metalwork, which fell from the burning zeppelin, on the mantelpiece, as a memento.

For a moment I was desperately afraid; I did not know why. I was too young to realise that there were men up there, dying in the flames; but the tragedy of it somehow stabbed at my heart. The cold night, the crowds in the streets, the burning shape in the sky, filled me with terror, and I knew there was something momentous happening.

The other moment was more of sadness than fear, yet it brought a sense of foreboding which shadowed me for a long time. Aunt Jane's friend Nickie — the one with the passion for gadgets — worked hard as a widowed teacher to keep her little family of two girls and a boy, a boy whom she adored. Nickie was a tiny birdlike little person with a shrewd Scots face, twinkling eyes, and a sharp yet kindly tongue. She always had a joke with us children when she dropped in every day for a chat, on her way home from a long teaching day somewhere in the back streets of south London.

We had all stood outside early one morning to watch Nickie's handsome young son, resplendent in his kilt, marching off with a contingent of other young fellows to fight for his country. I had felt a lifting of the heart as I watched the six-footer with his kilt swinging and his bare knees glinting in the morning sunshine. 'There he goes!' someone had said; and I followed the tall young figure in the Scots uniform till the little band had marched out of sight.

A few months later Nickie came in as usual on her way up the hill home; but the twinkle had gone from her eyes; her sharp tongue was silent; she made no jokes with me, and I saw she was dressed in black. Nickie never got over the death of her fine young son. I felt, without being told, the first chill breath of war piercing the warmth of our little world. Something could happen, something from outside, that could turn laughter into silence and change people from the kindly folk you knew into blocks of stone. That had happened to Nickie. I felt curiously unsafe.

The war left only these few fears behind; but other fears were ever present, the fears that haunt a child whatever his surroundings and however sheltered his life. There was, for instance, the constant dread of burglars.

Living in a city, almost every week we heard tales of burglaries and house breakings; bits read out of the paper and hastily suppressed because the children were listening; dark hints dropped by Frances, the daily girl; chance words spoken when Mother met an acquaintance in the street or visitors came to tea.

'Night before last; no, they didn't take anything; got in round the back; that's enough, the children are coming . . . '

I knew all about burglars, whatever my elders thought, and I dreaded their coming with more than a physical fear. Once a burglar had broken into the safe stronghold of your home, it would never be the same again. Its security, its very integrity somehow, would be shattered for ever; the powers of evil would have entered your life.

'From all perils and dangers of this night,' the Vicar prayed in church. I knew just why he prayed with such intensity to be protected; he must feel the same as me. As night drew on, the dread of burglars would creep upon me. Perhaps at this very moment, when I was lighting my candle for bed, they were secretly plotting in the privet bushes by the back door, waiting to seize their moment. I would go up to bed, wait until the goodnights were said, the candle blown out and the door shut and then, shivering, climb out of bed and crouching in my nightgown on the cold linoleum, gingerly lift the bottom of the bedspread, straining in the darkness to discern a darker figure in the dusty shadows under the bed, who-knows-what monster of iniquity concealed beneath the sagging springs of the mattress.

Or I would slide up the sash of the window, and leaning out into the cold night, chant a protective ritual into the back yard below, intended to scare any waiting burglar who might be hiding behind the dustbins.

'My Father's at home, and he's got a gun, and I've a brother too, and he's got an air-gun.' No burglar, I devoutly hoped, would dare to proceed against so heavily protected a stronghold after that; yet I only half-believed that I was safe.

Once there was a real burglar in our neighbourhood, and then it was as though my most awful fears, for a few terrifying moments, had come true. I was dead asleep, when into my consciousness came noise and shouting, the sound of people running, bushes being rent apart, fences creaking as fugitives and pursuers clambered over the garden palings outside.

For one instant I lay paralysed with terror; then in a flash, I had torn off the bedclothes and was dashing, in bare feet, into Aunt Jane's room next door, seeking any shelter, any reassurance. Aunt Jane had the window open, and was leaning out in her nightgown, calling to my parents, who were likewise shouting up to her from their open window below. Some burglar had been surprised at work in a nearby house, and all the neighbourhood was giving chase.

Over the little back gardens they sped, a shouting, tumultuous crowd, men in night attire, screaming women. They climbed on hen-houses, vaulted over garden sheds, tore through bushes, and finally, like a maenad throng, the valiant few who were left in the chase swarmed over the brick wall at the end of the row of gardens and were lost to sight. Police whistles sounded; babies wailed; I was cold with fright.

We never heard what happened to the burglar; indeed, in the morning, the family put on a united front of bland surprise. Had there been a disturbance in the night? Oh yes, it must have been somebody's dog that got out. Nothing to worry about. Burglars? Of course not. But the glances over our heads, the forced brightness, gave the lie to such words of comfort. You cannot deceive a child.

For weeks I went to bed in a sweat of terror lest that frightful midnight scene should repeat itself. Perhaps the burglars would come back, all the more terrible because they had been foiled the first time? The trouble was that I could not now even confide in the family; they themselves were ranged on the other side, the side of the sensible people, the disbelievers, the disclaimers. My searchings under the bed, my chants from the window were intensified to the point of obsession.

Then there were all the childhood magics and rituals, which you disregarded at your peril. The grown-ups knew nothing about these, for they belonged to the children — at school, in the park, around the streets. They were closely guarded secrets from the family, but in the tightly-knit fellowship of childhood, everyone knew the rules and kept them, or paid the penalty. At seven or eight you are still so new to life that you are never quite sure where you are likely to overstep the mark and call down the wrath of the unknown powers that rule your world. So you play safe, however difficult it may be.

The rituals were passed down by word of mouth, in some private place like the school cloakroom. 'Don't you *ever* step on a patterned tile on the way home from school,' one little girl whispered to me darkly. 'Or when you get home — know what? Your mother'll be dead!'

This ghastly possibility had never so much as occurred to me before. Home and family were always there, permanent and stable and enduring. This was a truly dreadful thought. I knew those patterned tiles; we all did in our road. They filled in the gap between a long garden wall and the edge of the pavement, just where you turned the corner; and they lined other neighbouring roads as well. I had never given much thought to them before. I noticed, now, other children avoiding them if their steps ever took them too near the wall; but what if someone pushed you and you couldn't avoid stepping where you shouldn't? The walk home, that so long had formed a quiet bridge between school and home, was now a daily agony.

I turned into the last road before home, and saw, at the bottom of the hill, the dreaded corner where the patterned tiles were. Everything now assumed sinister proportions. I seemed to feel an evil power propelling me, in spite of myself, towards the forbidden tiles. I only had to put one foot on them — just one foot — for the awful threat to be realised.

I would reach home, bang the iron gate behind me, and rush up the seven steps — and there would be no one to answer my knock and open the door. I felt sure of it. My foot hadn't touched the tiles, but the spell was so evil, I must have done something. Terrified, I waited on the step, my breath coming in long sobbing gasps, till it was opened and I fell into Mother's arms.

'Whatever's the matter, dear?' Mother's warm voice said. I couldn't tell her; it was too terrible. Disaster had been so near. I buried my face in her skirts and cried my relief away. Next day I tried a different route to school, where there weren't any patterned tiles, so life was safe again. No evil power could propel you towards them and wreck your happiness. There were so many pitfalls for the unwary.

'Do you know,' some young theologian informed me in the cloakroom one morning — the cloakroom being the place where all these mysteries were discussed, she was the minister's daughter and ought to know. 'If you ever forget to say your prayers, even once even, something dreadful will happen the same day?'

Well, of course I didn't forget my prayers — or did I? They were as much part of my morning and evening routine as washing my face or cleaning my teeth. But — well, one evening I had gone to bed without cleaning my teeth. It had been very late, I had been at a party, and it wasn't till the next morning that I'd found the dry unused toothbrush and the pink Euthymol tooth powder in the bathroom, quite untouched from the night before. There might come another time when I forgot to say my prayers, and then what would happen? I imagined all sorts of dire calamities, from losing my pencil again to getting run over by a tram in the main road.

The thought that one day I might forget my prayers altogether by some fearful oversight was a disturbing one. And then one morning when we were in the middle of mental arithmetic, I suddenly remembered that I hadn't said my prayers.

I looked across at the minister's little girl, sitting on the other side of the aisle of desks, legs tucked demurely under her chair, head well up to catch the next mental arithmetic question. I was sure she never forgot her prayers. I wished she would, one day, so that I could witness the dreadful disaster that would befall her. Do her good, the horrid child.

I hastily muttered my usual morning prayer between two bouts of mental arithmetic questions, on the principle of better late than never. It might put off, if not avert, disaster. But I was still uneasy. 'Five nines!' somebody shouted, and then 'Wake up! You're not paying attention.!'

They were talking to me, and I couldn't explain that I was just catching up on my prayers.

The morning wore on, and so did the afternoon, and still nothing had happened to me. Nothing happened on the way home from school, either. The house was still standing when I got there, and there were no signs of fire or death. Nobody was walking about wringing their hands. And I didn't die in the night, either. My informant was clearly wrong. In my prayers the next morning I added a rider to the effect that I really hadn't meant to forget them the day before, and I was glad God was sensible enough to understand.

It wasn't too difficult, at that time, to get onto really personal terms with God. In fact quite often, I would hear him speaking, or even engage him in conversation. He had become much more human than the Vicar holding forth about God's dreadful Eye that saw everything. Now, I often thought he was quite nice. It must have been the familiarity of praying to him for so many days and nights on end.

Only the week before the prayer episode, I had discovered I could enliven a dull day without any playmates by playing nought and crosses with God. I provided paper and a pencil, and God did the rest. It was quite comforting when there was nobody else to play with.

I assigned the nought to myself, and gave God the benefit of the cross. It seemed rather more respectful, somehow, towards the Deity; didn't he keep that for his special symbol? First I let him think of a square on the paper, and I marked it off for him; and then I thought of one, and marked it off for myself. Quite frequently I won. It really was something, being able to score off the Almighty.

Altogether, I knew he wouldn't do anything dreadful to me if I forgot a prayer or two. So when I next encountered the minister's daughter in the cloakroom, changing into boots at break for playing in the garden, I tackled her confidently.

'I forgot to say my prayers yesterday. And nothing happened. Nothing. So there!'

The minister's daughter looked up,

appalled. 'It will, just you wait.'

'I've waited a day,' I said, 'and I'm quite safe now. I just told God it was an accident, and he told me not to worry.'

He had, too; of that I was convinced. I was on quite good terms with him at that time.

Dreams could be terrible things. They held you prisoner, helpless. In the feverish illnesses of childhood, they could assume vast proportions, blotting out all hope, filling the night with endless horror.

Tossing and turning on hot pillows, my forehead wet, my hands clutching the bedclothes, I was completely at the mercy of these feverish dreams. There was the sinking one, where you sank down, down into nameless depths; the running one, where you ran and ran, down endless corridors, with something or someone at your heels. There was the floating one, where you drifted high among rooftops and treetops and couldn't get down to earth again. Worst of all was the sleeping-waking one, when you were conscious that the dream was finished but you couldn't release yourself from it. You were seconds from safety, but the scream wouldn't come out, the clutching hand couldn't grasp at relief. These were the delirious moments of illness, when I felt half within my body, half without; limbs heavy, like the trunks of trees; eyes filled with whirling colours and patterns; mind floating somewhere up in the sky. They were at their worst the summer I contracted scarlet fever.

Usually Father, with his doctoring knowledge, kept us all healthy, dosing us with calomel, yellow powder shaken onto the tongue from a piece of paper, ordering us Parrish's food when we looked peaky, buying Dr Collis Browne's Chlorodyne — an infallible cure for all upsets of the stomach; Dr Collis Browne himself gazed mournfully at us from the medicine cupboard, his bewhiskered features frozen onto the label of the bottle. But neither calomel, nor Parrish's food, nor even Dr Collis Browne could save me from the scarlet fever which everyone dreaded, in my seventh year. Scarlet fever in those days was a deadly disease, for which you went away to the Fever Hospital. Because the war was on, and there were air-raids nearly every night at that time, my parents would not let me go away to the Fever Hospital, but managed — goodness knows how — to get me a nurse at home. I was put to bed in my parents' bedroom, while they slept in another room; a sheet, soaked in disinfectant, was hung over the doorway, and Nurse Cameron — brisk, starched and Scottish — came to minister to me while the rest of the family were kept sternly away.

I was haunted by the dreams. First they came and went; then they came and stayed all the time, so that there was no difference between waking and sleeping; it was all one blur of horror. Gradually, as the fever lessened, I drifted back to the world again, and the sights and sounds and feelings of the bedroom began to drive out the memories of those haunting dreams. Nurse Cameron gave me blanket baths entailing the most vigorous scrubbing I had ever had. She seemed determined to get me well again by sheer force of scrubbing. She scrubbed the room as well, and everything in it, and cleaned and polished and disinfected till every trace of a germ must have been scrubbed and chased out of sight. When it was all over, she took the books I had been reading in my convalescence, made a bonfire in the garden, and burnt the lot. I was heart-broken. All those lovely pink-covered paperbacks, Stead's *Books for the Bairns*, that my brother and my parents and my Aunt Jane had brought me to read in bed — all crumbled to ashes at the top of the garden. The shock of losing all my books was worse even than that of losing all my toys. But in those days germs were enemies indeed, and nothing in the sickroom was ever allowed to go out again.

'You don't want to give everyone else your germs, do you?' Nurse Cameron asked briskly.

I was too weak to argue, but the pain was great.

Coming downstairs after such feverish illnesses was strange and dreamlike. Legs felt wobbly, the stairs seemed endless, and everyone appeared strangely foreign, as though I was entering another world. Gradually I would be absorbed back into normality; sit in the garden, shell peas for Mother in the high-backed kitchen chair, and eventually put on my school tunic again and join the rest of the children in the humdrum round of the week. But for a long while after illness, I would dread the nights; those long black stretches when the dreams would come back to haunt me; dreams I could never communicate, because they were so vague that nobody would understand.

Fear of the dark must surely be one of the primeval fears of our race; no child I have ever known has been without it. In our house of twisting stairs and long corridors, lit by trembling gas mantles or guttering candleflames, the dark was almost a tangible enemy. I used to dread being sent up to the top of the house to fetch Aunt Jane's spectacles on a winter night.

'Just run up and get them, there's a good girl. On my dressing-table shelf you know the one. You'll be able to find them; the light's on on the landing; you don't need a candle.'

My heart would sink. 'Perhaps they're in your work box in the next room?'

'No, no, of course they're not there. I know they're upstairs. Run along now;

your legs are younger than mine; don't you *want* to be a help to other people?'

This was the unkindest cut of all. I couldn't meet it with explanations, so I just had to go into action. I would start off up the three flights of stairs, thinking how little the grown-ups knew of the shapeless creatures that lay in wait round the corner by the bathroom, along the top passage, behind Aunt Jane's bedroom door.

The first flight wasn't too bad; I could still see the light from the hallway below, hear the friendly click of knitting needles, the hum of talk from the livingroom. The second flight was worse; a glimmer from the gas mantle, and the friendly sounds far off now. The third flight was the worst of all; total darkness; doorways terrifyingly shut, or more terrifyingly open, holding who knows what horrors in the gloom inside? As I gingerly pushed open the door of my aunt's bedroom and felt my way in, the wardrobe door would swing open without warning, and a great white shape would come rushing towards me — a reflection of a face, my own! It was only the full-length mirror on the front of the door, but the moment was awful as the Day of Judgment. I would stifle a scream, grab the spectacles and then, with all hell at my heels, scuttle headlong down the stairs, flight after flight, lest Something should get me from behind as I ran. Oh blessed light as I saw the open door below!

'Whenever I'm scared,' Frances the 'girl' told me once in a moment of confidence, 'I sing "Onward Christian Soldiers". Nothing can get you if you sings 'ymns.'

I tried it, but it didn't work. The headlong flight down the stairs was always the same, 'Onward Christian Soldiers' or not.

Night was the time when thoughts spread their widening circles round me, and I would lie wondering about the great mysteries of life and death, and the 'ever and ever' about which they chanted and prayed in church on Sundays. I was puzzled and frightened, in the night hours, by that 'ever and ever'. I would see myself, in the dark, a tiny speck becoming smaller and smaller, vanishing down the distances of time and beyond it; the thought of going on for ever and ever didn't comfort me; it filled me with dismay, till my mind boggled. I pondered, too, on Heaven and Hell. Church on Sundays was full of Heaven and Hell; did little devils really poke at you with toasting forks if you went to Hell, and did Heaven really mean playing on harps all day?

Religion weighed heavily on my mind as I lay wakeful in bed. Kind Mr Crabbe, who christened me, made it a gentle thing; he was a gentle person, and associating the sounds of his name, I always pictured him as a rosy little crab-apple hanging on an orchard bough, sweet and sound and wholesome. Raven-haired, lantern-jawed Mr Batterby, though, his successor, presented a very different picture of religion to worry over at nights. His God was a hard taskmaster, who exacted suffering and retribution to the full. Poor Mr Batterby, haggard in his black suit against which his white dog-collar showed so baldly, seemed engaged in a constant battle with the powers of darkness, and made sure that his congregation, down to the smallest child, should battle as well.

Mr Batterby's choice of hymns was as severe as his personal code. Not for him dear Mr Crabbe's 'All things Bright and Beautiful'; not for him 'There's a Home for Little Children, Above the Bright Blue Sky'. The hymns we sang for Mr Batterby were of sterner stuff The one that worried me most, especially at nights, was the hymn about the troops of Midian, who, it appeared, were constantly hanging around ready to pounce:

> Christian, dost thou see them
> On the holy ground?
> How the troops of Midian
> Prowl and prowl around?

And the lugubrious tune matched the words.

Prowl and prowl around, I used to think, in bed in the darkened room. That was what the Things did — the Things that lived on the landing and behind the cupboards and lurked in Aunt Jane's bedroom when I went to fetch her spectacles. The troops of Midian surrounded my bed at nights, I knew.

Suddenly, however, out of the blue, an immense comfort was vouchsafed to me. Vouchsafed, surprisingly enough, through the medium of a small girl at school, who confided it to me in a moment of earnest talk.

'Didn't you know,' she asked me, 'about the Guardian Angel?'

No, at that time I didn't know about any Guardian Angel. No such being had ever entered my theology.

'We've all got one,' she explained. 'One apiece. It stands just behind you and keeps you from harm.'

Stands just behind you — what a wonderful thought! Could this really be true? Why, then, all my midnight fears would be miraculously dispersed. How wonderful to go to bed at nights and never to fear; to walk the dark house alone, and never to fear; to meet the troops of Midian and never to fear. A Guardian Angel; why had no one ever told me?

I pictured my own Guardian Angel, shining, golden, serene, with beautiful furled wings and a white gown rather like my summer nightgowns, only purer and less earthly. It stood permanently at my back, and however quickly I turned, I knew I couldn't catch sight of it. I never caught even the flash of a wing. But never mind; there it was, the Guardian Angel who would keep a child from harm.

Life took on an entirely different hue from this time. Worries dispersed; night fears became less powerful. True, I discovered the Angel's powers were limited. They didn't for instance, extend to dolls; the very day after I heard about the Guardian Angel, my second best doll tipped out of the dolls' pram onto her china head and broke into a thousand pieces. Dolls, obviously, weren't included in this circle of safety. Perhaps, I thought, they had Guardian Angels of their own who weren't so efficient.

However, you couldn't expect miracles, even from an Angel. At any rate, it dispelled most of the terrors that haunted me by day and closed in on me at nights. I went to sleep now, with the Guardian Angel installed permanently at the back of the bed, watching serenely behind the white frilly curtain. Not even the troops of Midian could get me now.

8

Street Scene

DOWN the seven white-stone steps, newly washed by Lightning Lizzie, across the little tiled path to the twirly iron gate — push it open, listen to the clang of metal on metal, and there you were in the street. Street life — albeit a quiet tree-lined street in the leafier suburbs — was a real pleasure; there was always something to see, someone to watch. Out here in the street, anything could happen.

There were different scenes in the street for different days and seasons. Blue days, when the sky above was brilliant, the clouds scudding over the grey slate roofs and the black chimney-pots, the wind bending the fragile acacia trees that stood outside every fifth house. Grey days, when the rain came steadily down, the pavements shone like silver, and the grass that bordered them was sodden; but rain too had its excitement when it streaked down diagonally, causing passers-by to crouch beneath their wet umbrellas. I liked the shine of the rain on the rooftops, the gleam of puddles in the gutter. In my own black shiny raincoat with its matching sou'wester hat, I felt I could cope with any weather. True, Wellington boots had not yet come into fashion; you wore button boots, in which you splashed through the puddles at your peril, knowing you would get a scolding on reaching home. But the rain in the street was a challenge; it made everything — houses, rooftops, front gardens — shine and gleam with wetness, and I liked the sound of the running gutters and the sight of autumn leaves being swirled down them to block the drains along the kerb.

White days were best, of course, when snow covered the ground. They didn't happen very often, but when they did, our hilly street was covered with toboggans, racing crazily down from top to bottom, steered by small boys in navy reefer coats and little girls in tam-o'-shanters, and long woollen scarves. Tobogganing was enormous fun.

Gilbert next door had a toboggan, and when he was in the mood, and when Wally and Bertie from along the road had tired of using it, he would lend it to me. I would sit squeezed tightly behind him, holding onto his back, and squeal with fearful delight as the wooden toboggan careered wildly down the steepest part of the hill and straightened out, sliding and skidding, on the flat. Usually we were both tumbled out into the snow, and feet and fingers were frozen; but we soon tingled with warmth again as we dragged the toboggan all the way up to the top by its rope, and set off on another delirious excursion downhill.

It was quiet enough in our street, for motor traffic was still moderate, and we children had few fears about crossing the road. There were still plenty of horses about, and the sound of their clopping hooves, and the sight of the sparrows pecking at the corn on the ground where a horse had been given his nosebag for dinner, was a familiar one to us. Street corners, too, had their horse-troughs, where the horses were watered, and we would stand fascinated as the great fleshy dribbling lips, with their fringe of hairs, came up from the trough as the beast raised its head, water trickling down the great broad chest and onto the huge shaggy carthorse feet.

I used to love to look into the eyes of one of these carthorses; great liquid brown eyes which gazed sorrowfully at passers-by. What I didn't like and it was a fearsome sight — was to come across a horse that had fallen down. This happened often in slippery, snowy weather. A small crowd would gather to watch the poor creature lying there in the roadway, its great haunches shivering, the veins on them standing out, its breath coming in long gasps as it tried vainly to struggle to its legs again. The driver would shout for help, and men would come running from nowhere with ropes, and slowly, painfully, the great animal would be levered to its feet, and scrabble the ground with ironshod hooves that sent the sparks flying. Then, as it panted, its huge eyes straining with fright, someone would bring a bucket of water and give it a long comforting drink. Finally it would lumber on its way, pulling the heavy load upwards to the very top of our steep hill. I would feel sympathy with the poor beast, so mighty and yet so helpless; I would wish I could do something to ease its load, though for the most part the drivers were kindly enough, and seldom used the whip or tested a horse beyond its strength.

The milkman had a horse to draw his cart, which was shaped rather like a Roman chariot with curly sides curving triumphantly to a rounded top, behind which sat the milkman in glory, shouting his cheerful cry of 'Milk-o!' as he urged his horse along the street. Housewives would come out with their jugs, and hold them up to be filled from the big brass churn with the dippers hung from its sides; there would be the gleam of metal — every milkman took a pride in his highly polished brass — and the cheerful clink of cans and china, and the fascination of the horse which seemed to know by instinct when to stop and when to go.

There were other horse-drawn vehicles,

too, along the street, which we would watch with the round eyes of childhood. There was the cats' meat man, a horrid sight, but one from which you could not avert your eyes; the pull was too strong. The cats' meat man drove a rickety cart pulled by a bony horse; the horse, I was sure, never got any of the delicacies which hung from the sides of the cart, if delicacies they could be called — great red slabs of meat, ragged entrails, dubious-looking rabbit carcasses; we looked, and shielded our eyes, and looked again. There was a horrible fascination about the cats' meat man.

The rag and bone man was scarcely a more pleasant sight. His cart would be pulled by an even bonier animal, and the back of it was piled with old rags, tattered dresses, coats with the buttons carefully removed (buttons were precious, you never threw them away but cut them from a garment and kept them in the buttonbox), smelly blankets and even smellier mattresses from children's cots, and all the rest of the flotsam and jetsam of the houses down our road.

There was nothing the rag and bone man wouldn't collect. Old tins, bones, sofas with the horsehair hanging out, chairs with broken springs, buckets with holes in, pieces of worn linoleum from somebody's back stairs. His price was a penny a bundle — if the bundle was big enough — or a marble or a sweet or two if it was one of us children who ran out with the rubbish. His cry 'Rag and bo-o-o-one!' echoed mournfully in the dusk of an autumn evening as we watched him from the window or passed him on the way home from school. Veiled in the mists of dusk, he seemed something of a legendary figure, the rag and bone man in his tattered coat, with his unshaven face and rough black hair. Other people ran out cheerfully enough, down the steps of the tall houses, with their arms full of scrap for him, but I would shiver when I even passed him and his bony horse coming up the street.

Not all tradesmen rose to the glory of a horse and cart. The knife-grinder's little foot-propelled vehicle would toil up the hill every month or so, with the grinding-wheel at the ready, and the knife-grinder himself shouting his melancholy cry — 'Any knives? Any knives?' Most of the street cries sounded melancholy to me, as though the traders themselves were half-hearted and scarcely expected anyone to come out and do business with them. The knife-grinder, though, belied the sadness of his cry; his was a thriving business, with housewives running out with meat-knives to be sharpened for Sunday, or garden shears to be ground to a suitable fineness for cutting the privet hedges in the front gardens.

I was sometimes sent out with the family scissors, with strict injunctions to hold them always point downwards; there were grisly tales of children who didn't do this and ran, the scissors in their hands, to meet with some ghastly fate. Scissors were dangerous things, anyway; they were invariably hidden away in our house, should a thunderstorm occur; didn't they attract lightning and burn down the house? But now I would run out with the big dressmaking scissors which Mother used for cutting out my school dresses, and the little embroidery pair which Aunt Jane couldn't do without when she worked the flowery patterns on the yokes of my party frocks or the scalloped edges on the huckaback towels we kept for visitors. I would stand on tiptoe to hand them up to the knife-grinder as he sat on his high seat behind the wheel, and watch while the wheel whirred round and the sparks flew, and wonder at the dexterity of a man who could earn a tidy living, just by doing that.

Street music was often heard. The organ grinder came round regularly every Tuesday at five o'clock, with his little old barrel organ, starting at the bottom of the hill and working his way up, with suitable pauses for people to run out and give him a penny, or even twopence if they liked his music. I didn't; it was mournful and mechanical, and sounded somehow even more mournful when he tried to cheer it up a bit with a more lively tune. I didn't like him either; he was dark and swarthy, with a red and white striped muffler, and I was disappointed that he never had a monkey sitting on his organ top, like the proper Italian organ grinders about whom my mother used to tell me. I would have liked to see a little brown monkey with a wizened face, all dressed up in red with a pillbox hat, sitting up there and doing tricks. But all our organ grinder seemed to do was to grind his mechanical music soullessly up the road, looking straight ahead with vacant eyes which suddenly sharpened when a window opened or a door, and there was the prospect of a penny. His music came hauntingly on a Tuesday evening, and I would try not to listen as he stopped outside our house.

The street singers were haunting, too, and I didn't care for them either. For one thing, I always felt desperately sorry for them. Though our house was often a house of singing, nobody ever had to sing for a living. We sang for joy. There was no joy about these emaciated street singers, draggletail women in men's caps, or men in long baggy shapeless coats and battered shoes. They sang tunelessly, with heads thrown back and Adam's apples vibrating in their bony throats, their eyes fixed with painful intensity on the windows from which, they hoped, coppers would come down like manna from heaven. For some reason we never threw coppers; we would go out personally and put our pennies into their outstretched caps. I used to hate doing it, but do it I had to; even the least affluent of our neighbours always gave to the street singers. It was at least better to see them taking their money from your hand, rather than grovelling in the gutter for their meagre livelihood.

One street musician who occasionally came our way, and was quite a different person, was the Irish whistling man. We loved it when the whistling man came along the road, particularly since we never knew when he was coming. The Irish whistling man always seemed a cut above the street singer; at the first notes of his whistle, coming from between pursed lips in a merry brown face, heads would pop out of windows, children would run out and follow him, and soon his pocket was full of money. He would strut along, hands in pockets, cheerfully whistling, as though money was the last thought in his mind; indeed I think he thoroughly enjoyed his job. With his Irishman's broad grin and his twinkly blue eyes, he seemed to be bringing real music to us, out of the skies. His was a pure, a piercing but melodious whistle, a whistle to prise the pennies out of anybody's purse. Strolling along with his head in the air he seemed, as no doubt he felt, master of his art.

Once or twice street music of a livelier kind came jauntily up our street. We would run out crying 'The one man band!' And in truth it was a one man band; the musician himself you could scarcely see for his load of instruments — for pounding, drumming, clashing, clanging, twanging or twitching; and he did it with a will. You could see he was having a wonderful time. It must have taken considerable skill to manoeuvre all those instruments — there were at least half a dozen of them — with only two hands and two feet, and a knee jerking up and down. His progress was slow, but accompanied by a gaggle of children all demanding to 'have a go', which they never did. Pennies came his way readily enough, even sixpences; and I was surprised he didn't come more often. But perhaps he had a larger audience to play to than the houses up our street. Whoever this solitary musician was — and he was never seen anywhere else, and never appeared to live anywhere — he was certainly good at his job, and his clashing and clanging made merry music.

Towards evening, if you were out so late on a winter afternoon, you would see the muffin man marching up the road balancing his great wooden tray on the top of his head. He marched with purposeful tread, ringing a brass bell with a cheerful note and steadying his tray with his other hand, and occasionally he would pause in his march to look around and survey the street, as though he were bestowing a favour on us all by offering us such a luscious treat for a winter tea. When we could afford muffins — which wasn't every week — I would be sent to buy them, and bring them back wrapped in my mother's white teacloth, to be toasted on the old wire toasting-fork before the reddening fire. Fat with butter and deliciously browned on top, they turned our modest Saturday tea-time into a feast. With the green baize curtains drawn across the white lace ones, and the gaslamp softly purring, home seemed a very cosy place when you sat and ate muffins for tea.

Later, on dark evenings, the lamplighter would come round, always at a regular time, pausing at each street lamp-post and reaching up his long pole with the little hook on the end to turn on the gas. A small globe of light would leap from the dusk, and one by one every post up the street would flower into beauty. I loved the lamplighting time. On a winter's evening, when the dusk lay blue around, the long line of yellow lamps was a joy to see. By that time, of course, the streets would be deserted; a few random footfalls would denote somebody quietly making their homeward way, from pub or club or Church social; an occasional cyclist would whirr softly past, his tyres making a hissing sound on the road surface, his bell sounding when he reached the corner by our house. Even more occasionally a motor-cycle would break the evening peace, putt-putting up the hill or down; a lad on his way home from his girl-friend's, or a couple in their 'combination', the husband valiant in front, the wife and baby huddled beneath a waterproof cape in the side-car, cowering and protesting when he took the corner too fast. Sometimes a motorcar came our way; but cars were rarities in our street, and it was still something of a thrill to be invited to ride in one. 'They've got a car' would mean the ultimate in luxury, and certainly we never even dreamed of possessing one. The most we ever did was to go for a ride in the car belonging to an aunt and uncle, and that was only once a year.

Precisely at twenty past nine each night the postman would call with the late mail. If we were up at such an hour, which wasn't often, we would hear his sharp rat-tat at each door-knocker as he made his way up the street; for it was not enough just to push the letters through the shining brass letter-boxes; he had to announce his arrival at each house with that peculiar staccato knock of his, and we would have been indignant if he hadn't done so.

I would hear him far down the road, and go to the window, if it wasn't bedtime, to watch his progress; zigzag from side to side, knowing exactly when and where he would cross the street — five houses one side and then five the other. I always hoped there might be, just possibly, something for us, and often there was, for our family were all great letter-writers. With the penny post and no telephone, letter-writing came naturally. The hope of 'something in the post' would be my excuse for sitting up so late, and when the rat-tat did sound, I would dash out into the dim little hall with its single gas-globe burning, to pick up the letter from the mat and run triumphant with it into the warm kitchen at the back of the house.

Street games in summertime were common enough in our suburb, though we were never allowed to join the street children having fun outside. 'The garden's the proper place for games,' we were told, and we would be shepherded out onto the grassy patch beyond the kitchen door. I was always rather sorry about this; Gilbert and Ethel were nice enough neighbours to play with through the wooden palings, but you could have much more fun, I thought, with the groups of knickerbockered little boys and full skirted little girls who played around the lamp-post at the corner of the road, or dragged their hoop-sticks along the railings of the houses, or leaped about the chalked pavement playing mysterious hopping games, the rules of which I could never understand.

The iron railings were a source of great delight to the street children, and of extreme annoyance to the householders. Each house had its own little front garden, with steps leading down to the tradesmen's entrance in the basement; and to protect the dusty privet hedges each householder was proud to possess a set of curly iron railings bordering the road. We would hear the clash of metal on metal as the boys ran with their hoops along the pavement, invariably steering them against the railings; and the rhythmic beat of the hoop-sticks, iron bars with a crook at the end, as they played a tattoo alongside each house on the way home; the traditional end of the game. Indeed, the hoop-sticks were often more popular than the hoops themselves, and many an angry householder would appear at the top of the steps threatening 'the law' on the rough-jerseyed crowd of boys in the road outside. Then there would be a scuffle of iron-shod boots up the hill, or round the corner, away from danger, and a defiant cat-call or two which the householder would have to pretend not to hear. It was no joke to encounter a gang of derisive little boys, even if they were a safe distance away. More than one window in our street had had its pane smashed by a stone late on a Saturday night, when the street boys were around.

In spring and summer, little girls skipped in the street, or sometimes on the coloured tiling in front of the houses, between the bottom step and the front gate. We thought they were lucky to be allowed to skip there; nobody was allowed even to play in the front garden in our family. The girls counted as they skipped, or chanted familiar rhymes — 'Salt, mustard, vinegar, pepper', two of them turning the rope while the third skipped in the middle. Pigtails would go flying, skirts billow up showing quantities of navy knicker, and small boys passing would shout and jeer as the girls skipped with increasing abandon.

The boys would play marbles, choosing a quiet part of the pavement under the dusty acacia trees, and squatting on their heels. A favourite game was 'glarneys', played with the big shining marbles with swirls of colour inside them. You borrowed a farthing from somebody richer than yourself, supported it just clear of the pavement on a matchstick, and bowled your marbles at it from between your legs, hoping to score a hit; more difficult than it seemed.

Then there was fivestones, played alike by girls and boys, when you threw the tiny stones up in the air and caught them in your hand; and hopscotch, at which the little girls were always defter than the boys, jumping from chalked square to chalked square with sparrow-like lightness. All these games we never played ourselves, but watched from afar; as we watched the occasional soap-box derby, the race in wooden carts to which old pram-wheels had been fitted, and at certain seasons of the year the moss grottoes, studded with miniature flower-heads, beside which children begged for pennies, and, come November, the absurd stuffed guys with their grotesque hats and painted masks, which brought in a few coppers the barefoot street-urchins could not obtain in any other way.

I used to pass these poor children of the streets with mingled fear, distaste and pity when our walks to Jonesandhiggins or journeys to some distant tram-stop took us past the seedier quarters of the suburb. They had close-cropped, prickly heads, to ward off the nits, rough jerseys and tattered cut-down trousers, beneath which grubby knees showed above torn stockings — if they wore stockings at all. It was the lucky ones who wore boots, albeit often with flapping soles, and a size or two too large or small. Boots were one of the charities supplied to deserving schoolchildren by the powers-that-be in the board-school across the road. But boots, the better ones at least, were frequently 'popped' at the pawnbrokers' with the three golden balls above it in the main road, and their owners would have to go barefoot half the week until they were 'redeemed' on pay-night. Street-arabs they were called, these thin, bony children with the harsh voices and the dirty feet. They would stand and stare at us better-clad ones, wiping tattered sleeves across runny noses in the biting wind of a winter's day, and I would wonder uncomfortably what sort of homes they came from. We caught glimpses, sometimes, of the various Buildings and Dwellings where they lived. Grimy children would be playing on the stone steps that led from tenement to tenement, and greyish washing flapped from dreary clothes-lines on windy days. Some children queued for bread and soup at the local soup-kitchen, and even scavenged the dustbins at the end of our street, especially on a Thursday when money was tight and Dad's Friday pay hadn't yet come in. They would scowl at us, and hoot at us after we had passed. Singly they were frightening enough, but in a horde they could be really alarming, and if we saw a crowd of them making their way in our direction, we would take to our heels. Lying in bed at night, I would be haunted by the memory of those snotty-nosed faces, those dirty feet scuffing in the gutter, those hungry fingers lifting the dustbin-lids and clattering them down again. And with the heartlessness of luckier children, I was glad that none of them came to my school. I would have been too scared to go to school.

The main road, Queen's Road, that led from New Cross Gate to Peckham, was totally different from the familiar side-street where we lived. It was lined with Victorian shops and houses. Hadn't it been called after Queen Victoria? And along it roared a ceaseless stream of traffic — or so it seemed to me then, though it was light enough in those days. Motor-cars, horses and carts, bicycles weaving in and out, and the big London buses with their open tops that were slowly but surely ousting the lurching trams — though Father would never travel in a bus, or 'omnibus' as he insisted on calling it, when there was a tram available. 'Newfangled!' he would comment with a snort of disapproval. Trams it had been in his youth, and trams it would remain if he could have his way.

Privately I thought the trams were

dreary things. I didn't like the droning sound they made as they lunged along the rails; and I didn't like their hard yellow-boarded seats. Buses were altogether more comfortable. They came close up to the kerb so that you didn't have to risk your safety in boarding them, as you did the trams; they were warm and cosy inside, with their upholstered seats of red and grey, at least in the bottom deck, onto which you sank luxuriously as though you were at the cinema. They didn't groan or sway, either; instead, they jigged cheerfully along, shaking you a little on your upholstered seat, but giving you a closer view of the bustling pavements, the housewives with their baskets of shopping, the old women with black shawls over their heads, the children trotting at their parents' sides.

The buses were still, as yet, open-topped ones. You climbed your way to the top, holding firmly onto the rail as the bus jerked and bounced, and fumbled along to your seat, which was made of hard wood like the tram seats. In wet weather you drew a black waterproof cover across your knees and hooked little loops of elastic onto tiny pegs at each side. It was distinctly damp up there on top of an open-decker, and cold in winter-time; but when the rain was really coming down, and shiny umbrellas hemmed you in on each side, the sight of other unfortunates shrouded and cowering beneath their wet waterproof covers gave the upper deck a matey feeling; you felt you were all in it together.

Dogs could travel on the top of the buses, and occasionally we took our own old dog along for a ride. Once he nearly met with disaster. Excited by the unaccustomed jaunt, and barking madly, he suddenly took it into his head to make a great leap over the side, and hung suspended there, choking and squealing at the end of his lead, while Father tugged helplessly, trying to save him from a plunge to death. Father tugged harder and harder, getting up from his seat and leaning over the side, red in the face with effort, and we children sat clutching his coat-tails, begging him to be careful. Visions of both dog and father going over the side together made me hold my breath in terror. Other passengers came to our aid, and soon half the upper deck was trying to haul the poor dog back to safety. We got off at the next stop, and it was a long walk home with a furious Father and a stiff-necked dog; we were all footsore and exhausted when we finally reached home. But the dog appeared quite perky, once his muscles had relaxed again; so long as we never took him near those dreadful buses again, he was perfectly content on his own four feet.

'There you are!' Father said that night. 'What did I tell you? It would never have happened on a tram. They haven't got open decks.'

Nobody dared to tell him that on a tram you wouldn't have been allowed to take a dog at all.

I could never make out where all the people came from who bustled along the main road, swarmed into the trams and buses, and crowded the shops. There were such multitudes of them, all hurrying purposefully somewhere or other, this way and that. People seemed to be going everywhere; if you were small like me, the top of your head coming only up to their knees, you seemed to be walking in a forest of moving feet and legs, flapped at by voluminous skirts, jabbed by baskets, poked by sharp elbows. Someone was for ever grabbing your hand to protect you from danger, drag you out of the way of a passing perambulator, or steer you clear of the gutter.

Once, for no particular reason, I stopped dead in my tracks, struck by a thought that in its enormous significance blinded me with wonder. All these people scurrying past me, prodding me with baskets and umbrellas, talking and chatting — they were all individuals, just like me. Each one, I thought, is an 'I' like myself, with a home to come from, a destination to go to, hopes, fears, joys and troubles — hundreds and thousands of 'I's'. It was the first time I had come face to face with the essence of 'I-ness' — the importance of everyone to himself.

It was an overpowering experience, so much so that I stood rooted to the spot, blinded like St Paul by a revelation of truth. Unlike St Paul, however, I couldn't share my experience with anybody; I had no words. A grown-up grabbed me by the hand, scolded me for dawdling, and hurried me along in the wake of the jostling crowds. I was bursting to tell them what I'd discovered; the exquisite truth was big within me; but all I could do was to submit to being towed along with the rest.

I didn't really like the main road with its swarms of people, but I couldn't deny it was full of interest. In the gutter walked sandwichmen, parading along with dignified gait, at odds with their tattered coats and bulging boots, proclaiming the virtues of things like Eno's Fruit Salts, Epps's Cocoa, Lifebuoy Soap, or exhorting you to get yourself saved because 'The End of the World is Nigh'. On the other side of the pavement there was all the glitter of the shops, though usually you didn't get much time to stop and look at their contents unless you were actually going inside.

The shops along the main road were colourful and varied. There were little sweet-shops selling every kind of sweet from large glass jars displayed temptingly in the window. There were what we called 'everything shops', where you could

216

buy almost anything you needed, from bootlaces to groceries and toilet articles. I liked these, for they had great clusters of feather dusters and giant shopping baskets flapping from their door-posts, and mysterious smells coming from inside, of flour and dry goods kept in the sacks along the narrow entrance-way, of biscuits and spice and chicken-food and toilet soap and methylated spirits.

The chemist never failed to intrigue me. He always had great glass globes in the middle of the window, glowing like Oriental jewels, with peacock blues, poppy reds and golden yellows. Nobody ever told me quite why they stood there, but certainly, if you needed a chemist's shop, you would only have to look for those glowing colours in rows along the top shelf of the window or just inside the doorway next to the shining mahogany fitments painted with their Latin names in black or gold.

Inside, there would be a faint smell of disinfectant — Jeyes' Fluid — and baby-powder and cough mixture; and if you were lucky, and your mother had a penny to spare, you could mount the wobbly step of the scales and watch the big hand move round and record your weight. But it wasn't often we had a penny to spend on such frivolous things as getting ourselves weighed.

The shop I liked best was the dairy. It stood opposite St Mary's Road, where our church was, and along a stretch of the busy main road where the houses stood back a little more graciously, hugging the remnants of their Victorian pride, their greyness relieved by a tree or two, and a border of grass. I used to love the dairy. It was patterned outside and in with green and cream tiles, the ones inside depicting scenes from the real country — a cow, in rich brown, grazing on luscious green grass, greener than any grass I had ever seen in the Park; and fat white ducks paddling in the bluest of streams. If you shut out the noise of the passing traffic from your ears, you could almost believe you were in the country.

Step inside, and you were within a cool, clean-smelling world of marble counters and tiled floors. I always went straight to the middle counter, where sat, in solitary state, an enormous white china swan, almost as big as a real one, with crisp white feathers and a beautiful curving neck, and inside, within the safety of its wings, a pile of brown eggs for sale. I always used to beg Mother to buy her eggs from the swan. If the swan had been for sale as well as the eggs inside it, I would have clamoured for Mother to buy that too, for I had never seen anything so beautiful, I thought, in all my life. How lovely it would look, standing in our hall at home, instead of the ugly carved hall-table and umbrella-stand which I had to dust on Saturday mornings. If it was the swan, why, I would keep her white and gleaming, polish the yellow beak and the bead-black eyes, and never let her lose her pristine glory. But no, the swan was not for sale.

Beside it stood homely brown baskets filled with still more eggs, bowls of cream and huge jugs of milk. We never bought cream except on birthdays, and as my Aunt Jane's fell in June and my own in July, we looked forward tremendously to the days when we could go down to the dairy and have the rich yellow cream scooped into a smaller bowl for us to eat with Aunt Jane's traditional cherries or my own traditional strawberries. But that was a once-a-year thing. Milk was a different matter.

On a hot summer morning it was our great delight to race down St Mary's Road, pulling Mother behind us, and cross to the dairy to sink gratefully into the little white iron chairs the dairy lady used to put out for customers on the tiled floor. There, from glasses set on a white marble-topped table with curly legs, we would drink our milk, brought by a girl who looked straight from the country herself, with her apple cheeks, smooth brown hair tied back in a bow, and clean white apron. The glass of milk was cold to the touch after the heat of the morning, and, out of breath from skipping beside Mother down the road, we would drink it in great refreshing gulps, watching the little beads of moisture that formed round the edges of the glass. The sun poured in, the glimpses of the green trees in St Mary's Road were almost like the country, and I was happy. I gazed at the tiled pictures of the cows in the grass and the ducks in the stream, and imagined myself far away from the streets and the people, in a peaceful place where nobody hurried you and you sat and drank cool white milk all day, and listened to the sound of the cows grazing.

Beyond the dairy, Queen's Road narrowed again, and became once more a jumble of small shops — the pawnbroker's, frequented on Fridays by black-shawled women desperate to give their children a dinner; the secondhand furniture shop, where ancient dusty desks and book-cases jostled with plump armchairs sprouting their horsehair stuffing and dark oil paintings in tatty gilt frames stacked against the walls. Sometimes, in passing, you would see a faded sepia photograph, blown up to several times its original size, framed in black, and showing some severe paterfamilias seated on a chair with a potted plant behind him, surrounded by women in high-necked blouses and cameo brooches, and a child or two in starched pinafore or knickerbocker suit. I used to feel a pang of sorrow for these unregarded families of former years, who had themselves once walked along these same streets and lived out lives so like our own. They would have had names like our own great-aunts and uncles: Theodore, Augustus, Adelaide and Maisie. They would have done all the things we did: gathered in great families, sang at the piano on Saturday nights, borne children, and finally died. Now they were forgotten — just spotted old sepia photographs in a second-hand shop, propped helplessly against the wall, valuable only for their frames. I would look at them curiously, and pass on with a feeling of mortality, a glimpse into the past, a fear about the future. It was at times like these that life suddenly took on another dimension, a mystery into which it didn't do to look too closely.

And then, round the corner, we would come on the Rye Lane street market and the Penny Bazaar. The Penny Bazaar was where we children really came into our own. We adored the market, where the covered stalls squeezed together, and there was always bustle, chatter and haggling; but we couldn't spend our pocket money there; we had to wait for the Penny Bazaar. We would push through the crowds round the market stalls, intrigued by what we saw on the way: the fish, gleaming in wet piles, the mounds of pale pink shrimps, the vegetables stacked in all their freshness and glory, pearly cabbages and cauliflowers, glassy-green brussels sprouts and juicy carrots, the babylinen stalls with long dresses in muslin and flannel swinging from the top rails and little boys' sailor suits and little girls' pinafores piled on the counter. There was, too, the second-hand book stall — 'All on this counter, two a penny' — which we could never pass without peeping inside. Usually they were only somebody's sermons, but just now and again there would be a big old-fashioned picture book or an alphabet book, or one of the paperback *Book for the Bairns* series in which we delighted, and on which we would sometimes spend the pennies we were supposed to be keeping for the Penny Bazaar.

But if the money hadn't gone on books, we would pass on to the Penny Bazaar itself, a long glittering arcade, on

223

the corner opposite Jonesandhiggins, its gaslit aisles waiting with all the treasure a child could dream of, at a penny a time. Our chins would just about come up to the level of the counter, and we would have to stand on tiptoe to get a really good view. But we knew exactly which way to go. The Penny Bazaar had everything. While our elders shopped for household necessities, we would make for the toy counters. Down the left-hand aisle, right to the far end, and there they were, all the treasures we'd been dreaming of for the past week.

There were tiny penny dolls with stiff wooden bodies and black painted hair flat on their china heads; or little china babies made all in one piece, with staring blue eyes; these were wonderful for putting to sleep in matchboxes and covering with scraps of cloth. My brother went straight for the tin soldiers in which he delighted; they stood straight in their boxes, in gaudy red and gold and blue uniforms, on little metal bases, and the best of them had muskets over their shoulders. Of course he couldn't buy a whole box unless he had come in for a windfall

— as he did sometimes from our Uncle Robert, who tipped us half-crowns — but even a penny or two bought quite a lot of soldiers, especially if you chose the ones without muskets. If you were very rich, you could buy cavalry officers, their horses leaping up on brown tin forelegs or trotting demurely along with streaming black-painted tails. They didn't stand up very well when played with on the floor at home; the foot soldiers were wobbly on their bases, and the horses usually fell over and got trodden on, and their broken legs had to be mended laboriously with matchsticks. But how proudly they showed themselves to us on the counter of the Penny Bazaar!

There was a whole counter of sweets, which Mother would never let us buy; 'you don't know what they're made of,' she would say warningly, as we gazed longingly at the gaudy-looking aniseed balls in various colours, the pink and white coconut ice and the long black shoe-laces of liquorice. But beyond the sweet counter was another one with still more tempting wares: wax crayons in their neat cardboard cartons, their ends

225

symmetrically sharpened; gay painting-books with bright covers; pencils and india-rubbers shaped like animals — now would it be the hippopotamus or the elephant? the choice took time — and shiny exercise books in blue or red with clean ruled pages inside, inviting the first scribble.

The joy of choosing something at the Penny Bazaar was so keen that it was almost pain. There was so much for a child to want, and so little money to buy it with. But usually it was the dolls' furniture that won. I would stand for minutes in contemplation of it all; away in a wonderland of my own, where I could create real people, real families, doing real things in my orange-box dolls' house that Father had made for my birthday. If you spent one penny on a china doll, you could spend the other — if you had it — on a tiny toffee-coloured chair at which the doll could sit, to eat meals at a tiny toffee-coloured table. The paint on the miniature wooden furniture was always shiny and toffee-coloured with varnish, and smelt of glue — delicious. There was even miniature food to put on the tables; minute iced cakes, perfectly-shaped fish, pink and white blancmanges, miniature trifles and sponges just like the ones we had at home for Saturday tea. If you had sixpence to spend, you could buy, one by one, a whole set of cutlery to go with the dolls' food; tiny knives and forks and spoons, in glistening silver metal, and a matching cutlery tray in silver metal as well. A penny was a lot to pay, but I paid it gladly for the tray, and then saved up over several Saturdays to buy the cutlery to go into it. If I had any birthday money I would spend it liberally on more dolls' house furniture; more toffee-coloured tables and chairs and wardrobes, a toffee-coloured dolls' bed, and best of all, a tiny grandfather clock with painted hands that you could pretend to yourself actually told the hour. Once I found, in the Penny Bazaar, a minute dolls' cot, swinging, like the cot I had had as a baby, on a metal frame. I already had a china baby, as long as my little finger, to put to bed in it, and spent a happy week visualising the pleasure I'd get, buying my little metal cot on the Saturday and installing it in the dolls' house nursery. Alas, when I went on the way to Jonesandhiggins, dragging Mother and Aunt Jane out of their way to help me make my purchase, the doll's cot was gone. The penny was warm in my hand; I'd even brought the baby along in my pocket, ready to go in the cot; disappointment was great. They never had any more penny dolls' cots at the Bazaar, and I had to make do with a matchbox instead. 'Just as good,' the grown-ups assured me with a too-brisk note of cheerfulness. But of course it wasn't; any self-respecting dolls' house owner knew that; and the little shining penny cot haunted my dreams for days afterwards. It would have been much easier to accept disappointment, had Mother and Aunt Jane not been so brisk and cheerful. Children prefer to be mourned with.

Meanwhile the grown-ups would be purposefully walking down the other aisles at the Penny Bazaar, making purchases for the house; boring things like check dusters and tea-strainers and bootlaces. Soon I would be pulled away from the enticing toy counters and hurried out into the gloom of a darkening evening. There was still a long walk home after we had left Jonesandhiggins, and my legs were already aching. But we seldom took a tram. Instead, Mother would sing all the way home, keeping our feet in marching order as we trudged through the mean streets, the market, the busy Queen's Road.

Outside the shops, the air struck cold after the heat of the Penny Bazaar. Naptha flares blazed above the stalls that were selling off the last of Saturday's wares at bargain prices, and the voices of the burly tradesmen in their white aprons or brown overalls were hoarse with a day's shouting: 'Step up, madam, step up — tea-towels down to two a penny.' 'Nice fresh fish, last of the box, do for yer tea.' We would hurry along with our string bags lumpy with purchases, back past the second-hand shop where the trader was sadly putting up his shutters — nobody ever seemed to buy any of his furniture, let alone his faded sepia photographs — past the pawnbroker's and the dairy, and the

229

chemist's and the 'everything shop' and the sweetshop, back to the end of our road. I always knew when we were nearly there, because of the big red Fire Station at the corner. Glowing out of the dark it came, resplendent with scarlet paint and brass, the waiting fire-engines at the ready within. It was a stirring sight, putting fresh strength into a child's lagging feet for the last lap home. I felt that a dozen brave men were there inside it, all ready to rush to our rescue should any guttering candle-flame or spark from the stove bring sudden disaster to our little home. It was a comfortable feeling. We would turn the corner by the Fire Station, and leave the main road with its gas-lit shop windows and clanging trams, for the leafy quietness of the side street and the last long toil up the hill. Street life was a wonderful experience, but it was good to be home.

9

Neighbours

OUR neighbours, in most of the yellow-brick houses round about, were people much like ourselves; people with families, who pottered round their long narrow gardens, cut their dusty front hedges, pushed out the babies in perambulators, and went away most summers for a week or two at Ramsgate or Margate or Brighton or Bognor, whence they sent picture postcards of the Promenade saying 'Wish you were here', and brought us home sticks of pink seaside rock. The seaside rock typified the kind concern of our neighbourhood for the families next door. Nobody ever went away without bringing home rock for the next-door children, proudly announcing it was 'lettered all the way through'. Nobody ever ate it, either; it was hard as marble and was broken into pieces with the kitchen rolling-pin, and kept stickily in pockets till finally it had to be consigned to the dustbin.

Yet if you hadn't given, or received, seaside rock from the neighbours, life wouldn't have been the same. We all knew each other, we all liked each other, or at least felt sorry for each other; and the neighbourly concern was expressed every summer by that stick of pink-and-white rock lettered all the way through.

We were, indeed, a little community in our part of Waller Road. People in the houses round about thought kindly of each other; exchanged news and gossip when we met; and felt themselves part of the suburb we all lived in, insignificant though it was to city eyes. We, in fact, belonged.

My favourite playmate and yearly bringer of Ramsgate rock was Gilbert, the little boy next door. Gilbert was round and fat, and his garments never varied; his mother made him striped tunics of red or blue and white, belted round his fat little middle, and worn above short trousers, also striped in red or blue. This was the latest fashion for small boys below school age. Sailor suits were on the way out, and being replaced by a more informal kind of dress. I thought the trousers a most convenient garment, and would have liked to wear something of the sort myself; but no little girl had ever been seen in anything but skirts, so it was no use dreaming about trousers, however convenient they would have been for my favourite occupation in the garden — climbing trees.

Gilbert also never wore a pinafore. This, too, was kept for little girls, which seemed to me grossly unfair. After all, if Gilbert's mother was prepared to wash his striped tunics every day, why could not the mothers of little girls do the same, instead of putting them into white pinafores, or, later, the holland overalls which went over our dresses? Pinafores and overalls were both inconvenient for tree-climbing, and I could not see any useful purpose being achieved by the wearing of them. But we did not argue. Boys and girls were different — in clothes, toys and tastes — and we accepted our roles as meekly as we accepted the hymn in church about 'the rich man in his castle, the poor man at his gate'. The

Lord certainly ordered our estate.

Gilbert's hair was cut in a becoming fringe, and his cheeks shone red as cherries. Altogether he was a pleasing little boy, and I longed to look like him. Since I couldn't copy his clothes, I harboured an enormous desire to copy his hair-style. I longed for a fringe like Gilbert's.

Mother didn't approve of fringes for little girls. My hair hung straight and lifeless, tied back with a hair-ribbon, and was only coaxed into some semblance of beauty on Saturday nights when it went into paper curlers for Sunday. A fringe, I thought, would transform me.

I mentioned this one day to Gilbert in the garden. Gilbert's merry eyes twinkled.

'Got any kitchen scissors?' he said. 'I'll cut you a fringe if you like.'

If I liked! I was overjoyed. I stole indoors, knowing well that I'd better not be asked what I wanted scissors for; and opened the drawer of the kitchen table. There it lay, the large pair of scissors that Mother generally used for cutting the string on parcels. I tried the blade, very gingerly, against my finger. It didn't feel at all sharp, but I supposed it would do.

Reaching precariously through the wooden palings between our two gardens — our parents would not let us play in each other's houses, telling us always that we got on much better when kept apart by the garden fence — Gilbert cut me a zigzag fringe while I squatted amongst the wallflowers. The effect seemed to please him, for he sat back on his heels and surveyed his handiwork with pride.

'Your forehead's a funny shape,' he told me, 'but I've done the best I can.'

I was pleased as Punch; but on coming indoors I met with a disappointing reception. The first grown-up who met me was Aunt Jane.

'What on earth — ?' she began, and then hastily snatched me up and ran with me to find Mother. 'Look what this child's done!' she cried. 'Just look! Why, it'll take months to grow out!'

It did; and the grown-ups, I felt, were unjustifiably annoyed. After all, it was my hair, and I liked it. But once more I had to bow to the inevitable. A fringe, apparently, was one of the impossibles upon which childhood can only look sadly from afar. Why Gilbert could wear one and I couldn't, remained a mystery. So many things were a mystery, and no one explained them.

Gilbert's stock went distinctly down with my family after this, and it took a long time for my parents to restore him to favour, though I was uncomfortably aware that it was I who had started the whole thing. Gilbert and I turned our attention to other affairs, and decided to construct a wonderful aerial runway of string and tin cans, which stretched from our respective back yards up to the bedroom windows, and which — so the 'Children's Encyclopaedia' said, and that knew everything — could be used to tap out messages after the manner of a field telephone.

I never remember any messages being tapped out successfully, but the runway gave us hours of anticipatory pleasure.

Secret codes and messages played a large part in our games at this time, and it always gave us a tremendous thrill to be able to transmit correspondence which couldn't be intercepted, or even deciphered, by the grown-ups. It was nice to enjoy a bit of power. Ours was a secret world, jealously guarded against intruders. Behind the palings, on the other side of the garden, I used to exchange these messages with Ethel, who, being older than me by some two years, was rich in experience and a stimulating playmate.

It was Ethel who devised our secret letter-box, hidden under the bushes at the very end of the garden, among the compost heaps, piles of broken flower-pots, and ashes of past fires. Daily — often more than daily — Ethel and I left each other tiny notes folded into tight little crosses with the ends twined together. We slipped these missives discreetly into an old tobacco tin of Father's which served as a post office and collection box at the same time.

There was something indescribably thrilling about this secret place and the routine that went with it. You walked up the garden casually, hands in the pockets of your pinafore, glancing to right and left as though quite unconcerned, and keeping your thoughts on things like liquorice or geography lessons or dolls' dresses — anything but secret letters. And then, when you reached the spot, again casually — for of course there would be nothing there, how could there be? — you drifted over towards the palings, and bent down to slide a hot hand under the coolness of the leaves.

Yes, there it was, the tin tobacco box — hard and angular to the touch. Of course, you told yourself again, there would be nothing in it. Yet when it was opened — wonder of wonders, a tiny letter in familiar slanting writing — big girl's writing — smudgy and damp from contact with earth and rust, but most definitely a letter, and all your own. Nobody else even knew about it, except the sender.

What the letter contained didn't matter in the least; it was the finding that was important. And then in answer, I would write another little note, on a bit of paper torn from the back of an envelope, breathing heavily over the effort as I sat at the writing-table in the window, forming the words laboriously with a pen that kept making blots; it wasn't all that time ago that I had learned to write with a pen.

At last it was finished, and carefully folded, and smuggled up the garden and into the tobacco tin. And the next time I went to the tin, my own letter had magically vanished, and in its place was another in Ethel's superior sloping hand. It was a fascinating game, and I admired Ethel tremendously for thinking of it. It satisfied all my desires for secrecy, privacy and excitement.

Ethel was a sad little person with a long face haunted by worry. She was just like her mother, who was a sad little woman too, and racked with anxiety. I knew why whenever we heard Ethel's father, Jos, shouting through the thin wall that divided our two kitchens. Jos, in one of his tempers, would shout fit to wake the dead.

It would begin with a muffled argument; then a bass voice would rise, above the murmur, and swell to a crescendo, crashing and thundering till we children began to tremble, picturing dire disaster next door. Mother would glance across to Father with a knowing look; Jos was at it again.

In the morning, Mother would commiserate with Ethel's mother over the fence, as one woman to another, listening to her troubles. Mother had her own crosses to bear, for my Welsh father had a true Celtic temper and would fly into rages at the least provocation. But somehow his rages were always rather amusing, like the tantrums of a small boy, and they died in a moment. Nobody took them seriously.

Jos's rages were altogether different, and haunted me with a premonition that all was not well in the grown-up world. What they were about, nobody ever told me, and I dared not ask. It was terrible to hear grown-ups quarrel — really quarrel. The cloud of Jos's anger hung heavily over the household next door, and I would not wonder that Ethel looked sad.

Ethel went to the Council School across the road, and later to something called a Central School where the teachers, she told me, were unkind and frequently 'gave the cane'. I wished she could have come to my school, where nobody was ever cross. I had already discovered, to my bewilderment, that the grownups' classification of 'rough' and 'nice', as regards clothes, manners and schooling, wasn't really any guarantee at all of the essential 'niceness' which lay behind these things. Ethel was kind to me and I loved her, so whatever school she went to, she was 'nice'. Puzzling all this out took a long time, for the grown-ups were so definite about class distinctions, yet in real life those distinctions seemed to mean so little. It was rather like the Vicar telling us to 'sell all we had and give to the poor' when he had no intention of doing it himself. Only Mother was the opposite. She accepted the class distinctions into which she had been born, but her instant sympathy and kindness encompassed all the world, and she would never, I knew, see any distinction between people she liked, however they spoke or wherever they went to school.

I was constantly loyal to Ethel, and on late autumn days we would sit one on each side of our wooden palings and do what we called 'skinning'. We picked a faded leaf from which the flesh had gone, leaving the minute veins delicate as tracery, and with a needle we would 'skin' the leaves till only the skeleton remained — a beautiful fragile piece of work like the decorated windows in an old church, only brown and sere. This simple occupation kept us busy by the hour. We did nothing with the finished leaves; the pleasure was in the skinning of them, the production of these lovely leaf skeletons. I loved the time when autumn came round and gave us an excuse to go up the garden for 'skinning'. We sat in silence, for there was no need for words. Far off we would smell wood-smoke from garden fires, and beneath us feel the crunch of the first autumnal leaves. It was a wonderful place for sitting in companionable silence, dreaming as we skinned the leaves.

There were other children in our road, some of whom I knew from a distance, or met occasionally when our mothers were out walking or shopping. Wally was my hero for a long time. Wally, thin, lanky and dark-haired, with scowling eyes and a perpetual frown, was his mother's pride and joy. Her Walter could do no wrong.

She was fiercely possessive over Wally, and needed to know, from hour to hour, exactly what he was doing. Wally, poor child, couldn't bowl a hoop down the road before a voice from a bay window overlooking the street would call after him 'Walleeee!' And Wally, red-faced and humiliated, would have to leave his games and companions and go sadly indoors. It would be time for his milk and biscuits, or his cup of Oxo, or he needed his hair washed, or had to try on some new boots. Poor Wally, we all thought; they never leave him alone.

Bertie, next door to him, was a different type altogether. Bertie — or Bertram as his parents called him — was the scholar of our neighbourhood. Almost, we all believed, an infant genius. He, like Walter and Gilbert, was an only child, and the apple of his parents' eyes. He was good at his books, and the family, indeed all the families in the yellow-brick houses along the road, rejoiced in Bertie's successes. We all had great ambitions for Bertie, and basked in his reflected glory.

Whenever Bertie, who was a few years older than us, passed an exam or brought home a glowing report from school, the news was relayed from house to house. Bertie's father would casually — oh, so casually — mention it over the garden fence, or Bertie's mother would equally casually let drop a remark or two when she met Mother at Mr Smith's the grocer's. We all had to express our admiration, but there was no doubt at all that we felt it sincerely; we were that sort of community. What Bertie had accomplished was what everybody in the road would have liked to accomplish, given Bertie's opportunities and Bertie's brains.

I longed for the day when I would be privileged to enter Bertie's inner sanctum. This would be an enormous honour, I knew; all my friends would envy me. One fateful day the invitation came. I went in some trepidation, for Bertie was a good deal my senior and of course immeasurably more clever, and I trembled inwardly at the prospect of meeting a real scholar, one who could,

I heard, take things like trigonometry in his stride.

Bertie's father had fitted up the room that corresponded to my attic bedroom as a library for his son. Even the word sounded grand; nobody else, in any house I had ever heard of, not even our rich friends who had the big house and the food-lift in the dining-room, possessed a library. It wasn't even a study; it was a library, lined with books, as Bertie's father dutifully pointed out while I ascended the stairs. My head full of tales about country squires with libraries, like the one in *Little Lord Fauntleroy* that was my favourite reading, I was not a little impressed to find it really was lined with books. They filled all the walls, on neat homemade bookshelves, and left only the necessary gap for a large desk with a leather writing-pad on top, a glass inkstand, and a bust of Shakespeare. Bertie's father had left no stone unturned to provide his son with the accoutrements of learning.

I stepped gingerly inside the door, and within, amongst all this glory, sat Bertie. Bathed in studious splendour, he accepted my homage with a nonchalant smile and waved me to a chair.

Bertie was bright as a young sparrow, talked incessantly with a kind of febrile brilliance, and could never be caught out. He knew he was born for higher things than our modest suburban road could offer him, and already had his foot firmly set on the ladder to success. He told me, with suitable modesty, his hand toying with the pen on the leather writing-pad, that he was writing a play. It would probably be taken by one of the more successful London theatres, he explained seriously, and I could come and see it if I liked.

This prospect, and Bertie's literary pretensions as a whole, dazzled me as I sat trying to reach the carpeted floor with my toes, and I could think of nothing to say in reply. I had done a bit of literary composition myself, but writing — the physical act of it — was as yet quite an effort, spelling wasn't too easy, and most of my stories were still the kind I would spin to myself at nights whilst waiting for sleep. However, Bertie clearly expected some answer, so I swallowed and spoke.

'I — write a bit myself,' I said, wondering at my own daring.

Bertie raised interested eyebrows. His eyebrows, like his hair were sandy, and his eyes a scholarly pale blue; already he had the look of an embryo university don.

'Oh?' he said. 'What about?'

'Fairies,' I told him. It was true.

Bertie stared. Apparently this wasn't, in his eyes, literature. Yet I loved composing fairy stories. I felt a kind of stubbornness setting in. Why shouldn't I write my fairy stories? I liked them, and they were as good as his, any day — of that I now felt sure. My awe of him was rapidly turning to a determination for nobody to get the better of me, not even the scholarly Bertie.

Into this silence came bustling Bertie's mother, and I thankfully accepted her invitation to come down and join them for tea. Tea was rather a silent meal. Bertie's parents obviously imagined I had been overawed by their son's talents; and Bertie kept up an aloofness which I didn't know how to dispel. I left the house, still in silence, with a little less respect for

Bertie but a lot of ideas about having a Library of my own. Even a study would do. At home, I went up to my attic bedroom and looked around. It held a bed, a wooden clothes chest, a table, a tiny bookshelf on which I had stacked my Playbox Annuals and a few 'Books for the Bairns', a shabby green rug on the floor, and that was about all. No, you couldn't call it a study. But still, it had books; and I was determined it should get some more. All my pocket-money now, I decided, was going on books; second-hand ones, it was true, but books just the same. I vaguely regretted that there wasn't a bust of Shakespeare like the one Bertie had. That would have lent the whole room style. But I didn't see my parents being able to afford a bust of Shakespeare, even if they had found a shop that sold one. I would have to do without.

I looked round the little room, at the white frilly curtains at the head of the bed, at the table with its wooden chair, at the window with its lopsided view of the Park if you climbed on the windowsill. It didn't measure up to Bertie's library, still less the one in *Little Lord Fauntleroy*, but it would do. At least it was familiar, and I felt at home in it after Bertie's grandeur. I was glad I was not a scholar.

10

Parties

WE did not go to many parties as children, but those we did go to were remembered for years. An invitation to a party — a proper party as distinct from 'going to tea' — was a rare enough occurrence to make me sick with excitement for a long while ahead.

Party day would be talked about in our family with mounting excitement, my mother planning just what I would wear and putting the finishing touches to the dress of the moment. Mother always made my dresses herself on the little old hand sewing machine that had belonged to her own mother. Before the day, there would be much ironing of hair ribbons and mending of holes in the white open-work socks that were usually kept for Sundays only; and much polishing of shoes and slippers. Nobody went to a party in less than their best.

There were only three girls I knew who ever gave parties; they were expensive affairs, and had to be thought out with care, for food, though it sounds cheap nowadays, was a big item in the budgets of the families who lived round Waller Road, and food, as everyone knew, was the chief ingredient of party success. I would be thinking about the food as soon as I woke up on the day of a party, and wondering whether the jellies would be red or yellow, what the cake would be like — every party table had to have its cake — and whether there would be a murmur round the room as we all sat down to the feast — 'Ice cream!' Ice cream was a delicacy then, and always kept for parties.

After midday dinner, the popping gas fire would be lit in Mother's bedroom; gas fires in bedrooms were a luxury indeed, and Mother was very proud of hers, which had replaced the old open grate 'to save all that carrying up of coals' as she explained. In the gathering dusk of the winter afternoon — parties were always winter affairs — Mother and I would put out my party clothes on her

251

bed. It was far too cold to dress for a party in my own little attic bedroom; there was no fire there at all. Dressing by Mother's gas fire was a treat indeed, for it was only lit when someone was ill in Mother's big bed, or preparing for an 'occasion' like me.

In the bathroom next door, the geyser would be heating up for my bath. It was lit with trembling fingers, and many injunctions to turn off this before turning on that; for it had a nasty habit of exploding if you worked one handle before another. Once, in fact, it really had blown right up through the ceiling; the marks could still be seen on the whitewashed boards.

I remembered that time only too well. I was a baby, having my afternoon nap in Mother's bedroom, and had been rudely snatched from my sleep by my elders when the geyser had burst with a violent explosion, and hustled downstairs to safety. It had been a dreadful moment, and I had never forgotten it. No wonder that we lit the geyser now with trepidation.

The bathroom was freezing cold, and

252

it was always a relief to slide into the welcoming warm water, albeit there was not very much of it, and it was always slightly brown in colour, from the geyser tap. Then a rub with a rough towel, a face polished till it shone like a rosy apple, scrupulous cleaning of the ears, and I would climb on the stool to admire myself in the bathroom mirror, having first wiped off the steam from the glass.

Certainly my face beamed with cleanliness. It was a pity, though, that my hair was so straight; even though Mother would try to conjure up waves with curling papers, nothing ever improved it. I would sigh, and then surrender to the warmth and cosiness of the big bath towel wrapped round me as I was carried into Mother's room.

The first thing I saw on her bed was always a clean pair of combinations. I loathed those combinations, and never so much as at party time. The contrast between filmy party flounces on top, and the wretched tickling combinations below, struck me as worse than incongruous — almost immoral. But Mother and

Aunt Jane, who together ruled over my winter wardrobe, always insisted on the combinations, even to a party. Other girls might catch their deaths in vests, but not me. So I suffered the tickle and scratch of the wool, and the uncomfortable bulkiness beneath my finery. The sleeves of the combinations always showed an inch or two below the puff sleeves of my party frock, and there had to be some deft work with needle and cotton, or as a last resort, safety pins, to ensure that wool-next-the-skin didn't spoil the effect of the new party-dress. This, too, I had to suffer in silence; it was no use complaining when it was two against one, and grown-ups at that; and my mother and Aunt Jane had worn combinations all their lives.

Liberty bodice next; that strangely named garment with even stranger little tabs all round the bottom, which were supposed to hold up the stockings, only I was too young for stockings yet. The Liberty bodice had strappings of wide tape up and down the front, wide shoulder-straps and big ugly white buttons. I hated it, and why they should call it 'Liberty' I could never make out, since its sole purpose seemed to be to weigh down the unfortunate wearer.

Onto the sides of the bodice buttoned the frilly white knickers, with lace insertion round the leg-bands. Nobody thought of using elastic till it got to school-bloomer time. Next the petticoat, white and frilly, also with insertion round the waist, and narrow baby ribbon round the neck; and of course with plenty of tucks round the bottom for letting down; our elders seemed to live in constant fear of our growing out of garments too fast, and 'letting down' was a safe insurance.

Standing in front of the mirror in my petticoat, I brushed my hair till it shone, and took away at least some of its plainness. I put on my white socks, and buttoned the shiny black patent shoes with the strap round the ankle — the latest style in little girls' footwear that Mother had bought at Jonesandhiggins for seven shillings and threepence. Then at last came the grand moment when the billowing party frock went over my head, and I spun slowly round before the long mirror, receiving admiring glances from the womenfolk of the family. For once in my life — and goodness knows it wasn't often — I was conscious of looking nice. I would, as they said, 'do'.

The one thing I longed for, secretly, and never had, was a party cloak. A real cloak, of red or blue velvet, lined with white, that tied round the neck and left the dress beneath all crisp and beautiful and pristine — how perfect that would be! One girl I knew really did have a party cloak. Kathleen was the only child of well-off and elderly parents, and thoroughly spoilt. She was also, I had to admit, pretty in a kittenish sort of way, and a party cloak was just the type of garment to show off her charms. The day we arrived together on the doorstep of a friend's house, she in her party cloak, and me in my old brown corduroy coat that Mother had made me last year, I had a hard time to fight down pangs of envy. Even the newness of my party dress underneath did not compensate for the dark-blue velvet of the cloak, and its collar softly edged with fur.

Kathleen knocked, and then stood simpering on the doorstep, waiting for the admiration she knew would come. It came all right, and I had to listen enviously to 'Kathleen, how pretty you look! Oh, you *do* look nice!'

I crept in behind her, and upstairs to the bedroom, where we laid our respective garments side by side on the bed. I stood about miserably, wondering how I could ever acquire a party cloak, and knowing perfectly well I couldn't. I mentally reviewed the materials at home, trying to work out whether a party cloak could be devised from the velvet curtains in the sitting-room, but I couldn't see Mother or Aunt Jane allowing them to be cut up for a cloak. As for the fur — I had never possessed anything trimmed with fur in my life.

Alone in the bedroom, when the other girls had gone downstairs, I looked in the mirror and considered my appearance. It was the first time I had ever reviewed the situation quite as seriously. Square plump figure, straight hair — eyes, well, they weren't too bad, but they were positively my only redeeming feature. Dark brown like cold tea. I couldn't compete with the glamorous Kathleen, kittenish in her party cloak. No, I would have to concentrate on character. Character, they were always telling me, mattered more than a pretty face; but it would be nice to have both.

However, with party cloaks out of the question, I had to make do with the brown corduroy on party days. It crushed the pretty puff sleeves of the dress beneath it, but still it was warm and comfortable — 'serviceable' as my Aunt Jane was fond of saying when we were buying fabrics for dress-making at Jonesandhiggins. The brown corduroy had certainly proved serviceable.

My indoor slippers I carried in a cotton bag. Nobody went anywhere without indoor slippers. They were the regulation dancing shoes of soft black leather, with thin black elastic to hold them over the instep, and when you went out in your black shiny patent shoes, you carried your slippers in a shoe-bag. And of course I wasn't allowed to forget the brown leather music-case containing 'Scenes at the Farm', laboriously learnt on the piano. We all brought our music as a matter of course, and knew that we should have to produce it, after a show of polite reluctance and a lot of giggling, at the request of our hostess after tea.

'Now can you remember?' Mother would ask anxiously, as I stood at the hall door waiting to go. 'Change into your slippers as soon as you get there; and push your gloves into the sleeves of your coat so that they won't get lost; and don't ask for two helpings of jelly, and say thank-you-for-having-me before you come home.'

'Oh yes, yes,' I would tell her, dancing with impatience on the doorstep. 'Of course I'll remember. I always do.'

Going down the road to the party, I used to pray devoutly that none of the rough boys would be there to cat-call and jeer as I went by in my finery. I never felt quite safe till I had reached the house, and paused, heart beating fast with anticipation, in the gaslit porch waiting for someone to open the door. Then would come the glorious moment when a flood of light spread out over the dark front garden. 'Oh, here you are!' somebody said. 'Come inside' — and the party had begun.

'I hope I'm not too early,' was the

stock greeting to your hostess, though you could see with half an eye the crowds of excited children already peeping over the banisters and round the doors to inspect the latest arrival. There would be balloons tied to the stairpost, streamers festooned from the ceiling, and — sure sign of a party — the gas mantles glimmering in all the passages upstairs and even in the bathroom. Normally, no household would be thriftless enough to use its precious gas to light a mere bathroom or passage out of hours, and you would fumble your way to bathroom or bedroom in the dark. Gaslight in somebody's upstairs passages always seemed to me the height of luxury, and the hallmark of a real party.

When we had left our coats on the beds and changed into the indoor slippers, the business of the party would begin. The guests were mostly girls, but occasionally the odd little brother would come as well. I would look round vainly for Gilbert or Ethel or Bertie or Wally, but none of these went to my school, and our hostesses were usually the mothers of our schoolfriends. The little boys, if there were any, were dressed in best knickerbocker suits, and were suspiciously clean round the ears as though they had been scrubbed for at least five minutes by anxious mums. They wore neat grey socks and house-slippers, and began with ties properly knotted, though towards the end of the party these would usually be skewed round their collars.

In the downstairs room, children would be herded genially together by somebody's benign and red-faced uncle, doing duty as master of ceremonies. You had to have someone with a good voice to announce the games, shout the rules, and settle the arguments about who had won what. In the background usually hovered a bevy of mothers and aunts, enlisted for the occasion, all flutteringly anxious that we should all have a good time and 'join in'. Joining in seemed to be the main purpose of a party, and if you weren't a natural joiner, there could be some pretty tricky moments for you. Hardly a party passed without some small guest sitting in a corner or in a window-seat, dissolved in tears and sobbing 'I want to go home!' We took this for granted, and it didn't worry the party-goers, whatever it did to the party-givers.

The first games were rather formal; we were bidden to 'Form a line now' or 'Make a team' — with many injunctions, 'Now don't be shy, girls', which made the occasional shy one shyer than ever. The ice didn't really break till tea-time, when food became the great leveller. We used to know when the moment was approaching, because of the flurry of aunts and helpers in the background, the clink of lemonade jugs from the kitchen, and the rattle of spoons in bowls and plates which, we knew, would be filled with glorious jellies and blancmanges or even ice-cream. Tea, of course, was the moment we were all waiting for. It would have been bad manners to admit it, but when the hostess put a beaming face round the door of the drawing-room and announced 'Tea's ready', broad smiles would appear on the boys' faces, and excited giggles would come from the girls. A discreet procession would begin, everybody trying to look as though they didn't want to be first in the queue, but desperately anxious for that wonderful glimpse of the food-laden party table in the room next door.

The uncles would have their work cut out at this point, trying not to let the procession turn into a stampede. The party tea, as every party tea was expected to do, started with a long-drawn-out 'A-aah!' breathed from every mouth as we first caught sight of the table. It was not good manners, of course, to gasp at the sight of food, but parties were recognisable exceptions; indeed, most hostesses would have been quite disappointed if you hadn't exclaimed at their tea.

There were so many blancmanges and jellies, wobbly and sparkling in crystal dishes; so many fairy-cakes piled up on plates with paper doyleys; so many trifles heaped with nuts and cream. No savouries; they weren't considered good for children, except for the potted meat sandwiches with which you began. Everything possible would be iced in pink and white, and the centre of interest, of course, was the cake, enormous, taking pride of place at the table, full of dark fruit and almond paste and covered in a snowdrift of icing so hard that it was like cement to chew.

Nobody ever liked the cake, but you had to have it just the same. The plates after the meal were always full of slabs of uneaten almond paste and fragments of rock-like icing, dank as marble. Yet nobody would ever admit to *not* liking party cake. The only cake we all ate greedily was the one baked by May's father, who was a baker and confectioner. May's parties were always a huge success, and an invitation to one of them was eagerly sought after, usually with hints and proddings in the cloakroom at school. At May's parties you knew you were not only going to get cake, but rich swirly meringues topped with whipped cream, and shortbread that melted in the mouth, and crystallised fruit on little plates, and trifle with real sherry in it. Nobody could compete with May's father in the party dining-room behind the confectioner's shop.

There were rarely enough seats to go round, and I usually found myself on a wobbly form, or a plank placed precariously across two chairs to give extra seating. The boys used to love to jog these planks and make them squeak and bounce up and down; and if Gilbert were there, he would always contrive to get on my form and bounce it so that I was in constant terror of falling down into the forest of legs below. I was in terror, too, of those shiny table napkins that we were all given, and that invariably slid off my lap onto the floor, retrieved only by grovelling amidst all those white socks and party slippers under the table.

But all these fears were dispelled by the party tea. We ate and ate, and swallowed huge tall glass-fulls of lemonade, passed over our heads by attentive aunts and hostesses, up and down the table. There were sometimes crackers too, pulled with frightening bangs just by your ear; and mottoes and jokes read out in stentorian voices by the genial uncles, against the deafening noise of twenty excited children verging on riot at the end of the meal. What with all the food and all the excitement, and the inevitable spills of lemonade and consequent mopping-up and apologies, we were all quite glad when the signal came for us to leave the table.

But first, of course, there would be a discreet withdrawal upstairs. 'Would you like to wash your hands?' was the polite euphemism used for the trail up onto the shadowy landing, where gas-lamps flickered and strange draughts blew as you stood about in a long queue waiting your turn. It was always rather frightening in a strange house, up on that landing, with the pop-pop of the gas-mantles and the strange smell of paraffin from the oil-stoves which heated 'upstairs' — for nobody heated passages and bathrooms unless by the occasional stove brought up from the cellars for a party occasion.

The wait on the landing seemed interminable as little girls came and little girls went. (We never knew what happened to the little boys. Uncle, it seemed, saw to them.) The first of the after tea games was always over by the time the last little girl had waited her turn with increasing anxiety and discomfort. So many children, and so few conveniences, in those yellow-brick houses made this aspect of party-giving a trifle difficult.

When everybody was reunited at last,

our hostess would look round with a bright smile and inquire, 'Has anybody brought any music?'

As we knew perfectly well that everybody had brought some music, the question was rhetorical. But it had to be asked. Mothers would have been mortally offended if nobody had invited their children to play the piano; after all, they paid a guinea a term for music lessons. But it was a convention that nobody supposed anybody else had brought their music, or come prepared to do a recitation or two, though we all knew perfectly well that 'Bring your music' had been requested on the invitation card.

'Well — er — yes, I *have* got something here,' one little girl would venture. 'It's out in my music-case in the hall.'

After that, everybody would produce music-cases, and the first performer would trot over to the piano, climb on the horsehair stuffed piano stool, and break gaily into 'Minuet in C'.

We awaited our turns with mixed feelings of uneasiness and pride. The E flat was always a bit tricky at the bottom of the first page; the runs had a way of faltering in the middle; and the stretch of a full octave was quite an achievement for seven-year-old hands that would scarcely span the keys. But we sat and listened, and applauded dutifully as each performer took a turn. We prompted the small boy who got stuck in the middle of 'Marmion', learnt painfully at school; giggled at the duetting brother and sister who could never quite keep time; and caught our breath as somebody's aunt, turning the pages of music at the tinkling drawing-room piano with the candlesticks at each end, missed her cue or turned over two pages at once.

Kathleen, of course, performed with kittenish ease; she usually 'did a recitation' — just to be different, I used to think, still feeling sore about that dark blue velvet party cloak of hers. I didn't mind obliging at the piano; after all I knew plenty of party pieces, and it was just a case of which to choose, 'Scenes at the Farm' or 'The Whispering Glade' or should I, greatly daring, show off with Mendelssohn's 'Spring Song', up and down the piano with fingers flying and only a few false notes?

Sitting through other people's party pieces was much worse than performing; and towards the end we children would scuff our slippers and fidget, to the dismay of the grown-ups determined to hear everybody through to the bitter end. But it did come to an end; and then at last there were games again. This time the fun was more fast and furious.

We all threw ourselves with real abandon into those last party games. 'Puss in the Corner' succeeded 'Blind Man's Buff'; postmen knocked, and tails were pinned on the donkey. Everyone felt slightly sick when we played 'Squeak, Piggy, Squeak' and someone sat down heavily in our laps, with a plump cushion to soften the blow; and everyone was disappointed, or stoic, or both — except the lucky winner — as we finished the party with 'Pass the Parcel'. There were, of course, mutterings of 'Not fair!' That was only to be expected, especially when there were boys at the party. But the uncles soon quelled any incipient riots, as they did those scufflings and squawkings out in the dimly-lit hall, when little boys escaped from the games to roll in mortal combat on the floor. There was always someone to complain 'He punched me first!'

We little girls were more orderly; we might have exchanged a few pinches, but we never fought in the hall. We were all waiting for the grand finale of the evening — Sir Roger de Coverley.

This was only danced in the bigger houses; few of us had enough room for all those dancing couples to take the floor. But at May's the dancing took place in the restaurant adjoining the confectioner's shop, and that was grand indeed. There was a piano; there were two lines of excited party guests; up struck the pianist, and off we went, couple after couple disporting themselves down the middle and back again to the strains of Sir Roger: 'Da-de-da-de-da-de-DAH!' I loved it. Wild with excitement, hair flying and toes twinkling, the girls would romp down the length of the floor (there were never enough boys to provide proper partners) to pass under the arch of hands and jig up and down at the sides as the piano played. The Master of Ceremonies became more and more jovial; the hostesses, aunts and big sisters more and more affectionate, as though they were relieved that the party was nearing its close. Into the shouting and the trilling of the piano and the noise of feet would come the first bang at the door-knocker — a mufflered and overcoated father or heavily-wrapped mother murmuring politely 'I do hope she's been good.' It was like the knocking of Fate, that sound at the door; we knew our time had come, and soon we should be going home.

One by one the pairs would break up, as more knocks came at the door, and more scuffles overhead denoted that coats were being put on and slippers exchanged for boots and shoes. 'Thank-you-for-having-me-I-hope-I've-been-a-good-girl' was duly said, with a swift look round to see if any presents were being handed out to the party-leavers. A draught of frosty air would rush through the gaslit hall as the door opened and shut behind each retreating guest, and yes, there were oranges and apples, a bag of sweets and a coloured balloon for each of us. Something to take home was our crowning joy; something to show admiring relations, envious brothers and sisters, and all the people you passed in the street, that you really *had* been to a party.

The only thing that ever marred, for me, these glorious occasions were the times when I outstayed my welcome, and was left, lone and embarrassed, long after everyone had gone home. I don't think this happened more than twice, and in each case was due to a mistake in the time of being fetched; and since nobody was on the telephone, there was nothing to do but wait. The shame was almost unbearable, and quite spoilt the joy of the party.

'I think they *must* be coming soon,' I faltered to my hostess as she tidied up, as unobtrusively as she could to spare my feelings. 'I'm sure they won't be long now.'

But they didn't come, and I sat, subdued and miserable, in the empty drawing-room, watching the last guest being claimed by the last parent out in the gaslit hall. People were surreptitiously looking at the clock as they came in and out, plumping up the cushions, picking up burst balloons and the gaudy remnants of crackers, and I knew they were thinking 'Hasn't that child gone yet?' The little gilt clock that was invariably on everyone's mantelpiece seemed to be ticking as slowly as it could, to emphasise my shame.

'Would you like to look at a book, dear?' my hostess would offer, trying to put me at my ease while all around me people pushed furniture back into place and swept crumbs from the carpet. So with one ear alert for the door-knocker, I turned the pages of the *Arabian Nights* and wished I could sink through the floor. My coat was brought down from the bedrooms, which were being put to rights upstairs; my music-case and outdoor shoes were laid politely but firmly on a chair. But still no knock; and I would grow hotter and hotter, twirling the hem of my party-dress with nervous fingers. Would I never be rescued?

No sound was more welcome than the rap on the door that announced I had not been forgotten after all. Released from purgatory, nearly in tears, I dashed for my, coat, stuffed my slippers into the bag, and ran to hide my blushes against Father's overcoat or Mother's skirts in the hall.

But this didn't happen often; and at other times it was some other poor child who was last at the party. As I went into the night, I didn't even envy Kathleen in her party cloak. I had all I wanted; the memory of a wonderful tea, the strains of 'Sir Roger' still in my ears, a balloon in one hand and a bag of sweets in the other. I had been to a party, with all the trimmings; and now it was home again.

11

High Days and Holidays

WE children had 'high days' of our own, like the parties we went to in the winter; but the grown-ups, indeed all the family, had high days quite independently of our childish calendar. We joined in all these occasions, as indeed every child did in those days; nobody had heard of babysitting, and if the family were going out for a night or a day, of course we came too. As soon as we were old enough to 'stay out late' now and again, we shared with the grown-ups their own mysterious pleasures. Like the Church Social.

The Church Social was one of the great occasions in our family. It took the place of more expensive jollifications, which we could not afford; and besides, it was a way of meeting people. My parents were sociably inclined, within their own modest limits, and liked nothing more than joining in a church celebration along with all the rest of the families who trooped off on Sundays to the services. Our church had quite a lot of celebrations, especially under our kind old Vicar Mr Crabbe. His successor, indeed, poor Mr Batterby, did his best; but to our childish eyes, he seemed a poor second in jollity to dear Mr Crabbe. Mr Batterby smiled with his face only, and appeared to be wondering how soon he could reasonably get rid of us all and return to the cold Vicarage and his severe book-lined study.

The Church Social was held every few months, and we all looked forward to it for days beforehand. The church was the meeting-point for our little community, the centre of our social lives. Rightly was it called a 'Social'. Rich and poor — at least the not-so-rich, for few really poor people seemed to come to these occasions — young and old mingled here on the heartiest of terms, and we children felt ourselves welcome. On other nights in the week there might be something else to which the church folk

276

went, and to which, very occasionally, we went too; a coloured slide show, usually of a missionary nature, or a talk about Foreign Lands — where these foreign lands were, we were never very sure, but at any rate they provided a diversion. But none of these occasions was enjoyed as much as the Church Social, to which we went with Father and Mother and various other of our friends in the parish, as to some exciting entertainment.

We children, with Mother, arrived early on the evening of the Social. Having been given special dispensation to be 'up late', we were already in a party mood, and looking forward to making the most of it. Our mothers were, of course, to provide the refreshments, and so, at least an hour before the Social was due to begin, we would all tag along to the Church Hall to help, or hinder, and generally join in the fun.

There was a party feel to it all, from the very first moment, when we entered the big hall and found it full of potted plants and aspidistras brought by the families along the road. There was a smell of baking, newly-made bread and scones, and the rich odour of fruit cake; hot sausage rolls were being unwrapped from baskets where they lay covered in white cloths; tea was being brewed in the enormous urns within the church kitchen. Nothing stronger than tea, of course, was ever allowed on church premises, and even if it had been, my parents would have eschewed it. Drink was of the Devil.

We would go into the kitchen, where kettles and urns were on the boil, and there was the hum of voices and the inviting clink of spoons into saucers as the great trays of thick white chinaware were made ready for the evening.

The children would hover in the background, getting under everybody's feet but receiving nothing but smiles and pats on heads; people were all in a good mood on Church Social evenings. We watched our mothers' backs, with the broad white apron-strings hanging down behind, as they bent above the wooden tables, busy with refreshments. Everyone bustled about in a flurry of long skirts and twinkling ankles, setting cakes on plates, spooning jellies into little cardboard cases, and of course cutting sandwiches. Sandwiches were the mainstay of every occasion such as this; the women made piles of them, to feed their hungry menfolk and the children who always had enormous appetites on a Saturday night. Mounds and mounds of sandwiches there were, heaped up on the big white plates, smelling invitingly of fish paste or revealing thin slices of palest pink ham, crowned with tufts of green parsley and topped with white cloths to await the time when they would be served to the company.

Once, indeed, somebody's mother did mention an alternative to the never-ending sandwiches. There was something called a Bridge Roll which was coming into fashion, she told us all, and they were fancy, very fancy indeed, and highly thought of in the best circles of entertainment. But bridge rolls never took on at the Social, as sandwiches did. The men disdained them; the women found them 'finicky'. No, it had to be sandwiches, piles of them, to fill up the company at the appropriate time.

The cakes, to us children, were mouth-watering, like those we got at our own winter parties; great mounds of fruit slabs, gingerbread, butterfly cakes and meringues topped with whirls of cream. We never dared ask for a bite before the Social was due to begin, though sometimes something was popped into an open mouth by a lady in a particularly good temper when the work was finished. No, the best that we could do for ourselves was to filch the crusts cut off from the sandwiches, savouring the taste of sardine or salmon which still adhered to the edges of the bread; or scrape around in an empty jam jar with a spoon, hoping to find a lick of strawberry or raspberry jam left in the bottom.

Preparations over, we children heard with relish, from our posts in the kitchen, the arrival of the first guests at the Social. Fathers came, dressed in near-Sunday best; thankfully, not real Sunday best, I would think, seeing my own father without the hated top-hat, wiping his well-polished boots on the doormat. Mothers — those who hadn't been helping in the kitchen — came flouncing in in long flowery skirts, modesty vests covering any attempt at decolletage — the Vicar wouldn't like it — and daringly strapped black shoes showing beneath their hems. On weekdays they always wore lace-up shoes, but the Church Social demanded something better; and strapped shoes with Louis heels were all the rage.

The two curates — St Mary's was a large parish, and two young men were needed to cope with all the duties — would enter nervously, having left their bicycles round at the back, still wearing their bicycle clips around the bottoms of their thick black trousers. They didn't seem to like these occasions, I would observe; perhaps they were too much the target of the young ladies of the parish, for I noticed them blushing red when they first arrived, as they bent down to unfasten their bicycle clips, and it wasn't only the exertion of bending that brought the flush to their cheeks. All the girls were eyeing them; for a new young curate was what they called, so Ethel told me, 'a catch'. Why they had to be caught at all still remained a mystery to me, for Ethel would enlighten me only so far and no further. Certainly they were soon surrounded by young ladies, and the heat from the church hall, where all the coke boilers were going strong, would bring the beads of perspiration to their foreheads, and they would get out silk handkerchiefs to mop their brows, and run their fingers round the edges of their shiny white dog-collars, which, of course, they were never without, even if it was a Church Social.

The Vicar himself would be early on the scene, in his thick dark suit which looked so different from the flowing white robes he wore on Sundays. These vestments, in my eyes, had always clothed him in majesty as he walked up to the pulpit on Sundays to preach his sermon. Indeed at first I had imagined he was God himself. Surely nobody but the Deity could wear such immaculate robes or command such respect from the congregation? It was only the glimpse, one day, of a pair of heavy boots beneath the robes that dispelled for ever the idea that the Almighty himself had personal charge of our parish. The Deity in boots it was unthinkable. All the same, in some ways the Vicar took the place of God in the eyes of us respectful children. Dear Mr Crabbe could show a human face from time to time, when he patted your head and inquired tenderly about your mother. But straight-laced, hatchet-faced Mr Batterby could be at least as terrible as the Almighty especially in wrath. Poor Mr Batterby seemed to pass his days in eternal conflict with the world, the flesh and the devil, and never relaxed. Had he not vented his wrath at his confirmation class on one poor little girl amongst us who had ventured a remark about St Paul's rather shabby treatment of women: 'Child, do you presume to know better than Saint *Paul*?'

But on the night of the Social, even Mr Batterby relented as much as he could. He shook hands firmly with each of us, gripping our fingers in an iron grasp which left me gasping but honoured. No head-patting for him; he would shake hands with the younger members of his congregation and pass on to the older without a word. As each parishioner arrived at the draughty door of the

Church Hall, and pushed aside the green baize curtain, blinking at the light after the darkness outside, Mr Batterby would pump his hand in that vice-like grip, and manage a lantern-jawed smile as he welcomed him to the Social.

After the preliminary chatter that we took for granted — 'How's Amy?' 'Oh, much the same.' 'And Sidney?' 'Going downhill, I'm afraid' — I always pictured Sidney free-wheeling down a hill on his bicycle, but that clearly wasn't why the grownups were shaking their heads — the business of the evening would begin. We were bidden to take our seats for the Slide Show. Grown-ups and children would scramble for the best places in the front rows of chairs; one of the curates would do mysterious things with the 'lantern' at the back of the hall; the other one would put up the screen and make sure the lights were dimmed and there were no chinks in the curtains. Then, with whispers and giggles and shuffling of feet and hissed admonitions to 'move over, I can't see', we would settle down for our treat. It wasn't as good as the pictures; silent ones, of course, for we never even imagined anything else. But then the real pictures had to be paid for, and at fourpence a time, seats weren't cheap. At the Church Social the slide show was free. It made a difference when you had only twopence a week to spend as your own.

The subject was not very enthralling. It was usually, like the weeknight shows, of a missionary nature; good works among the natives, with dozens of little black boys spooning what appeared to be porridge into their mouths, young black teachers doing sums on the board at native schools — so you couldn't escape sums even in Darkest Africa, I would reflect sadly — and women grinding corn outside thatched huts. In the background was always the inevitable white missionary, in solar topee and baggy shorts, handing out advice and free meals. We didn't care much for the slides of the missionaries; the little black boys were much more interesting.

Nobody in our suburb, of course, had ever set eyes on a black person. We could only imagine them from the Church Social slides, and the pictures in our books, of Little Black Mamba and similar nursery figures. Certainly we hadn't the faintest idea that in years to come the whole of our own suburb would be populated by black people, living in our houses, going to our schools. It was unthinkable. Black people lived in the hot countries and we would never see them unless we were extraordinarily lucky and crossed the seas to the dark continents where they lived; perhaps as missionaries ourselves.

The Vicar, who usually commented on the slides, would plod laboriously through the whole boxful, or several boxfuls if time allowed. They had been sent him by the Missionary Society; square by black-and-white square showing native huts, mission schools, communal meals, baby clinics and mass inoculations. It wasn't exactly heady stuff, but it fascinated us; it also raised a laugh now and again when a slide appeared upside-down, or got jammed and kept coming back onto the screen again, to suppressed whistlings and cheerings from the boys. Some slides had a way of vanishing without comment from the screen when they had scarcely appeared, just as they were getting interesting to the boys in the front row: all those black bosoms, why, they were actually bare! Remarks on these slides were firmly put down, and the Vicar would hastily replace them with another and safer one. We had to leave it till later before whispering and giggling in the corner by the door when the lights went up; 'Did you see that lady? She hadn't got anything on! Nothing at all except a string of beads!'

When at last the Slide Show had hiccupped to an end — no amount of organisation ever ensured that the Vicar's comments should correctly synchronise with the slides — the collection plate would be passed round. This was to make certain that nobody left the Social without contributing his share. Anything from pennies to half-crowns would be dropped in it, and then someone would take the plate away and we would hear the money being counted at the back of the hall. It seemed a dreadful waste to us — all that money, what did they do with it? Send it to the Missionary Society? We could all think of better ways of using it.

But now a clatter from the kitchen regions would proclaim the moment for which we had been waiting all the evening. 'Tea and light refreshments,' announced the Vicar, 'will now be served.' There would be a scraping back of chairs, and a bustling to and from the trestle tables at the back, where the food from the kitchen had been laid out. We children would be enlisted to hand round the sausage rolls and the enormous plates of sandwiches. Tea from the urn was hot, dark and sweet; everybody in those days took sugar, and plenty of it, helping themselves from large china bowls with teaspoons or even dessert spoons. Sugar was good for you, they said; gave you energy.

A few of the men, languishing no doubt for their Saturday pint, would make tentative sallies in the direction of the door, but the ladies of the Social soon got them to heel. None of that tonight, their looks said; the Vicar doesn't like it. We children grabbed as much as we could from the loaded tables and helped ourselves from the lemonade jug; tea was bad for children, they said.

Lemonade was home-made, from juicy lemons bought in the street market, and sweetened with plenty of sugar, like our elders' tea; it was poured from enormous white enamel jugs with blue rims, and seemed inexhaustible, necessitating, during the rest of the evening, frequent trips to the stone-floored lavatories 'round the back'.

Tea cleared away, and everybody in a good frame of mind, we settled down for the best part of the evening. The chairs were scraped back into place again, and all the young people scurried for front seats for the last and most exciting event — the Entertainment. This, we knew, was sure to be good. Hadn't they all been rehearsing it for weeks? Weren't the two curates themselves going to 'give us a turn', to the delight of all the young ladies? Entertainment, our elders knew, would be good, wholesome fun — no doubtful jokes which might be harmful to the children. And everybody in the audience had a husband or a wife or a second-cousin-once-removed taking part, so expectation was high as we settled in our wooden chairs, folded our hands in our laps, and listened to the subdued clatter of washing-up from the kitchen while we waited for the green baize curtains to part.

Each of us had a programme, violently hectographed in purple ink by the children of the Sunday School, and was pre-warned of the events. The Vicar himself trying his best to unbend for the occasion, would come before the curtain and announce the first item, and then, to the shuffling of chairs and scraping of boots, the curtains would part at last, and up on the creaking stage would be revealed — who? We craned forward eagerly to get the first glimpse. Why, wasn't that the chief Sunday School teacher in her unaccustomed best — dark blue satin drawn tightly over ample bust — about to launch into song? Or it might be the fat baldheaded sidesman who handed round the plate at church. Now what was he going to do? Render — they always 'rendered' — a recitation? We would sit through the singing and the recitations, but what we were really waiting for, of course, was the Curates' Comic Turn. No programme would be complete in those days without its Comic Turn.

One by one the singers and reciters laboured through their repertory. It wasn't like the singing round the piano at home. There was something more formal about it, here in the Church Hall; people were singing, not because they wanted to, but because it was expected of them; and success was gauged by the volume of the clapping from all of us down below. We would sigh and wriggle in the front row, waiting for the Comic Turn. We fidgeted through Mr Jones' rendering of that favourite recitation 'Albert and the Lion', and Mrs Smith's tinkling piano solo 'In a Persian Garden', trilled out on keys that got stuck on the high notes.

Large Miss Green, the school-teacher, would launch into a passionate declaration of her love for all things marine: 'I must go Down to the Sea Again, to the Lonely Sea and the Sky'. Funny; we had never associated *her* with a hunger for the ocean. Mr Brown and Miss White would come nervously onto the platform, he creaking in large boots, she swirling in shiny black silk, and stand self-consciously side by side, little pieces of paper clasped in their hands, to give a duet. It was usually 'O——h! that we two were maying' — a song which sent us children into giggles down in the front row, for to picture the pair of them going a-maying in the suburban streets round our home was too much for our self-control. Mr Brown would glare at us, while Miss White shuffled the notes in her hand and tried to decipher the words of the last verse; but they always left the stage to thunderous applause, and various nods and winks from the older members of the audience, who knew that Mr Brown was a bachelor and Miss White, of course, unmarried, and plenty of romances had started, amaying or not, in the Church Hall at a Social. But we were unconcerned with romance; for now at last the Comic Turn was coming.

This might be anything from a Humorous Dialogue between the two curates, to a full-scale Dramatic Performance. The curates usually composed their own turn — vetted, no doubt, by the Vicar, who wouldn't approve of anything, as he put it, 'broad', and had been known to object strongly when one of our more venturesome curates asked permission to impersonate a female ('with cushions, of course, Sir.' 'Cushions? Most certainly NOT!'). All the young ladies in the audience settled back with adoring eyes when the Curates came on. Indeed, it was quite an extraordinary happening, even for us children, to see these two earnest young men, who were usually pedalling about the streets visiting the sick or rounding us up for Sunday School, actually becoming human, exchanging hilarious patter, and calling each other 'mate'.

We often wondered whether the Vicar himself couldn't be persuaded to do a Comic Turn. Laughing ourselves hoarse at the curates, calling them back for encore after encore, seeing what the Cloth could do in its off-moments, we would be all agog to get the Vicar revealed in similar style. But nobody had ever dared suggest such a thing — even to kindly old Mr Crabbe. In those days vicars were vicars, and it would be no less improper to ask the Almighty to do a Comic Turn.

The full-scale Dramatic Performance took in any number of parishioners, and when it was put on, it brought the house down. There would be a part for everybody, of course, and we would all cheer on our respective sides from the body of the hall. 'See, that's my Mum there!' 'Look, there's Dad!' The one I remember best, which was repeated by request at least twice during the years of the Church Social, was 'Life in the Hospital Ward', where any number of our mums and dads lay in serried rows on improvised hospital beds, exchanged juicy dialogue, and ended by pelting each other with breadrolls — thoughtfully supplied by May's baker father for the occasion. By that time, drunk with lemonade and dizzy with excitement and the unusual luxury of 'sitting up late', we children would be pretty well exhausted; and all that remained was to wait about till the grown-ups had changed out of their Comic Turn costumes, stacked the last chairs, collected the last bits of crockery from the kitchen, and were ready to take us home.

The Vicar stood at the door, almost

human this time, congratulating the performers one by one as we wrapped ourselves up in coats and scarves against the cold night air outside. Already the magic of the Social was fading a little. The hall was nearly empty; the two curates were turning out the lights one by one, and packing up the lantern and the screen on which the slides had been shown. We began to feel suddenly very weary, and suppressed great yawns as we waited for our mothers to finish what they were doing. Then at last the Vicar's handshake put a final end to the evening. We went out into the night, full of buns and lemonade and goodwill, singing catches of tunes, giggling over the Comic Turns, pushing and shoving each other like a lot of tired puppies. All we wanted now was home and bed. Tomorrow would be Sunday, and we would see the Vicar again, up there in the pulpit, awesome in his black and white robes. And nobody would really believe that the two curates, solemnly reading the Lessons for the Day, had ever taken part in a Comic Turn.

The best of our high days and holidays

in the winter was, of course, Christmas. Christmas didn't, in those days, begin weeks or months before; it started about the second week in December, when Mother set about making her cakes and puddings, and I would come home from school to smell that wonderful spicy smell of baking from the kitchen, and be commandeered to 'wash and pick over' the currants for the cake and the home-made mincemeat with which she filled the pies.

Christmas was a homely time for us. We hadn't much to spend, and we didn't go out except to family friends; only when the Christmas days were over did we ask the neighbours in to eat and drink, talk and sing. Singing was most important on Christmas Eve. Just before our bedtime, Mother would gather us round the piano, and Father, in jovial mood — it was his birthday too — would launch into the traditional Welsh carol with which we always finished the day.

We stood, a little bemused by all the preparations, in a ring round Mother; my brother and Aunt Jane and myself, with Father, tweaking his whiskers, leaning on the piano ready to lead the singing. Holly was stuck behind all the pictures; ivy trailed along the mantelpiece — though how it had room to do so I cannot imagine, for there were family photographs in elegant curly frames stacked all along it. All through the house was the smell of newly-baked cakes, and we would be looking forward to the mince-pies when the carol was over. We children had already taken a hand in icing the cake, just as we had in stirring the Christmas pudding, with a silent wish. Now we would listen, a little sleepily, to Father's beautiful Welsh voice as he launched into his favourite song:

Fill the mead cup, hang the holly,
Fal-la-la-la de la-la-LAH!

He would sing the ballad and we would all join in the chorus, belting out the final LAH till the ornaments shook along the piano-top. Then it was time for mince-pies and bed — early tonight, for we knew our stockings would be filled if we were asleep in time. Candle in hand we would go up the stairs, and cuddle beneath the bedclothes knowing that tomorrow was the Great Day.

Waking at first light was, I always thought, the best part of Christmas; better even than the present-opening later. No other time of the day — not even the dinner — could match that lovely moment when, rubbing my eyes with sleep, I would reach out in the semi-darkness and feel — yes, there was something lumpy and heavy at the end of the bed. The instant when I clutched the stocking and pulled it up, to feel and fumble in delicious anticipation, was the best in the whole year, I would think; wondering what it would be this time — a penny doll, a new piece of dolls' house furniture, or a painting book rolled up and tied with ribbon? And of course the traditional gifts at the very bottom, that were the essence of Christmas because they never changed; the apple, the orange, the bright new penny, the assurance that all was right with the world.

I kept my simple treasures near me for all the rest of that lovely day; the little china doll in the pocket of my pinafore, the penny wrapped in the corner of my handkerchief, ready to be spent at the Penny Bazaar the next time we went that way. All through church — of course we all went to church that morning, except Mother who cooked the dinner — the little doll would keep me company, to the chant of Christmas hymns and the sharp tang of the greenery decorating pulpit and pews. She would sit by my plate, too, at Christmas dinner, when Father carved the joint of beef — it was seldom we could afford a turkey, and anyhow people in our neighbourhood didn't seem to bother about turkeys at Christmas; and I would clutch her in my hand when Mother brought in the Christmas pudding, decked with a sprig of holly and surrounded by sparklers, carefully kept from the previous 5th November.

We loved the sparklers. Father would draw the green curtains so that we sat, replete with roast meat, potatoes and Yorkshire pudding, waiting in a green gloom. Then suddenly — lo, the gloom would be bright with dazzling glitter, as the spitting lights were sparked off one by one, and we would clap our hands at the magic of it all. As each slice of pudding was dumped on our plates, we children would find our silver sixpences in it — like the orange and the apple and the bright new penny, one of the symbols of Christmas Day. Riches indeed, we thought, munching our unaccustomed dessert of raisins and nuts and succulent dried figs and sticky shiny dates. Christmas dessert was a wonderful affair, and we savoured it to the full.

Last of all, in the contentment of a Christmas afternoon, dinner cleared away and in an atmosphere of oranges and sweets and the unwonted smell of Father's Christmas cigar, we would all open our presents. Each of us had our own pile, carefully stacked on one of the carved oak dining-room chairs, and kept for Christmas afternoon; no opening of presents a moment before, for Father was a stickler for 'patience' and 'waiting', just as he was over opening the mail at breakfast time.

I always hoped for a doll. My doll family was mainly of the Penny Bazaar kind, cosy enough for a pinafore pocket, but oh how I longed each year for a really big doll. The sort you could push out in a dolls' pram — if you had one — and show to admiring friends in the Park, just as the young mothers in our neighbourhood used to show off their new babies, covered in white veiling, in the high perambulators. Quite often my wish for a doll was granted; and one wonderful year, the dolls' pram arrived too. I can't think how my parents had managed to put aside enough money for this expensive item — I suspect Mother went without a lot of purchases at Jonesandhiggins to save up for this fabulous present; but when it was wheeled in after Christmas dinner — it was too big to go on the chair with the rest of the presents — my bliss was complete.

The dolls' pram was large and green, with two seats, one at each end, and a real hood that went up and down. I spent the whole of that Christmas afternoon simply opening and shutting the hood of my new pram; the pram encompassed my whole world, and nothing else mattered, not even Christmas tea with its iced cake. Alas, the pram proved tricky when I got to pushing it out. On Boxing Day, when

I was trying to negotiate the kerb with it on my way to the Park to show it off, the front of the pram tipped forward suddenly and — disaster!, my best doll fell out, breaking her lovely china head into a thousand pieces.

I stood on the pavement and wept with despair. My Christmas wish had been granted, but what Fate had given me with one hand, she had snatched away, all in a moment, with the other — and the very next day. My faith in the goodness of things was sorely tried. People came and comforted me, and the doll was sent away to be mended, but the head that replaced her old one was never quite the same. You could never quite trust the luck that seemed to come your way — not even on Christmas Day.

One present appeared with great regularity every year, on the seat of the dining-room chair; the *Playbox Annual*, given me by my Aunt Jane. As soon as I saw its bright yellow cover, with the date of the New Year blazoned on its front, I knew there would be wonders ahead. A whole year of reading and re-reading; following, again and again, the adventures of Tiger Tim, and Peter and Pauline the Terrible Twins. I loved my *Playbox Annual*, and each Christmas the coming year would be symbolised by that date on the *Playbox Annual*, recurring like punctuation marks along life's way — 1916, 1917, 1918 and on, I thought, for ever.

The rest of Christmas afternoon was always a blur to me; reading my Annual in my secret corner behind the green velvet sofa, dressing, undressing and re-dressing the doll of the moment; shining up with a bit of rag my new penny and my new sixpence. I hardly dared to sample all these pleasures, for fear they would go too soon; the *Playbox Annual* be read too fast, the penny and the sixpence be spent and gone. That was the trouble with Christmas; you had so much, and it went so quickly.

They would sit by me when I was in bed on Christmas night, all those treasures that the day had brought. There would be tissue paper scattered on the floor; the smell of oranges still lingering; the little china doll tucked up on my pillow beside me, so that I could whisper to her before I fell asleep. I would doze happily, my thoughts full of Christmas, the mystery and the magic of it, the glorious once-a-year-ness of it; and, heavy on my feet, whenever I stirred, would lie the yellow bulk of the *Playbox Annual*, waiting to be opened first thing next morning. What more could a child ask?

As winter turned to spring, there were more high days and holidays. In March or April there was Easter — in its way even more religious than Christmas. When I was small, and dear Mr Crabbe conducted the church festivals, Easter simply meant coloured eggs for breakfast, and chocolate ones for after dinner — 'and don't eat them up all at once, dear, just a little at a time and save the rest till later'.

But with the advent of Mr Batterby, Easter became altogether a more serious matter. Besides, I was growing up. Little girls of four could enjoy Easter eggs; but girls of seven or eight had to be made to realise the solemnity of Easter.

It began with Lent — the long, long month when children, like grown-ups,

304

had to 'give up' something; why, I could never quite discover. The Vicar called this self-denial 'mortifying the flesh' but I had no idea what that meant. I only knew that all the little girls at school were asking each other 'What are you giving up for Lent?'

I spent many anxious moments wondering what to give up. You had a choice. Sweets were the obvious answer; the weekend bag of jelly babies or the paper cone of lemon drops we used to suck on Sunday afternoons while Mother read aloud to us. It would be hard to give up those lemon drops, I thought. What other possibilities were there? Through the garden palings I conferred with Gilbert next door.

'I'm giving up jam on bread,' said Gilbert.

Plain bread and butter for tea; that would be boring. 'I'd rather give up the butter,' I told him, 'and just have the jam.'

Gilbert looked doubtful. 'That wouldn't really count. It's giving up something you *like* that matters.'

True. I did like jam. So that would

have to be the thing to go. That or the sweets.

The grown-ups gave up sugar in their tea; or cake on Sundays; or going by tram. Walking, anyway, was good for you, so they walked everywhere instead. Whatever you gave up, it had to be for a whole month, and I used to count the days till Good Friday came. Good Friday was nearly Easter, but it was a gloomy day. Nobody went to work, or to school; instead, they stayed soberly at home, or went to church for long services that went on for hour after hour. We children were exempted from the services, but we had to spend the day soberly; no noisy games, and especially no card-playing on Good Friday. Card-playing, even the cheerful Snap or Happy Families that we so enjoyed, had something especially damning about it when done on Good Friday, the Day of the Passion.

I was puzzled and awed by Good Friday; it was an uneasy day. No children played in the streets, no postman rat-tatted at the door; the shops were closed. Saturday was better; now we would be able to have our jam or our jelly-babies again, and the house had a furtive air as Mother hid our coloured boxes with the Easter eggs inside, the boxes we knew she'd bought at Mrs Evans' sweetshop but were not allowed to see.

But Easter Sunday made up for everything. There was something glorious about waking up on that special Sunday morning, seeing your white dress laid out on the bedroom chair, and knowing you had only to run downstairs to find Father's painted eggs in the egg-cups on the breakfast table. Painting the family eggs was Father's special ritual. Mother boiled them; Father painted them, with funny faces, drooping moustaches, comic hats, put them into the egg-cups and sat back to watch our reactions. It seemed almost a pity to spoil those beautiful eggs by digging into them with a spoon.

You didn't get your chocolate Easter eggs till you had been to church with the family. But though ordinary church services were long and boring, Easter was different. On Easter day the church smelt of flowers and greenery; every corner was decked with foliage, and the font and the pulpit studded with tiny flowerheads set into moss. The hymns were jubilant ones; we sang with zest, thinking all the time of the end of Lent, the end of all that self-denial, and the special Easter dinner that was being cooked at home ready for our return. The choirboys all looked extra clean; there was a special anthem; even the Vicar looked joyous. Of course he was; didn't everyone know that Christ was now Risen? I couldn't puzzle it all out, but I knew I felt fresh and spring-like and the world today was a different place because Christ was Risen.

We went home full of joy, ate our Sunday roast and opened our beautiful chocolate Easter eggs, saving the bright wrappings to take to school the next morning. It was very important to take your Easter-egg wrappings to school, just to show everyone that you really had had a proper Easter egg. And each of us always thought our own special Easter egg was the best one of all.

Soon after Easter came Empire Day, 24th May, a date which all schoolchildren knew by heart. Wasn't it the day when everyone celebrated our glorious Empire, the one marked in red on the map, the one on which the sun never set? On grey asphalted playgrounds and on grassy village greens, children everywhere marched in lines, boys with boys, girls with girls, carrying the flags of the British Empire. All the boys wore best suits, the girls their Sunday white, and as we marched, we sang: 'Rule Britannia, Britannia Rules the Waves.' It was a stirring song; it filled us with a sense of well-being. Somewhere, we knew, a war was going on, but it wasn't here; not on these playgrounds and village greens. Here, all was pride and victory as we marched and sang, rising to a crescendo as we reached 'Britons Never NEVER Will Be Slaves!'

After all the marching we had to salute the flag. This was the part I didn't like so much. You had to march up to a central flagpole in the middle of the playground, where the Union Jack was bravely flying, and as you reached it, bring your hand up in a smart salute. I felt very self-conscious doing this.

It was one thing playing at soldiers and saluting with Gilbert and Wally in

Telegraph Hill Park. That was make-believe, and we knew it. But this was a serious moment; something the grown-ups expected you to do. I wasn't much good at saluting, being small and round and liable to fall over my own feet; and I had a vague feeling that this wasn't something we were doing of our own accord, but something the grown-ups were forcing us to do; making us into patriotic miniatures of themselves. I resented it without knowing why.

My salute to the flag was half-hearted. I didn't think the British flag would gain very much by being saluted by a stout little girl in pigtails. But there it was; they told you to do it, and you did it.

In high summer there were other pleasures for the family; the treats of a 'day out'. They were nothing more, usually, than excursions to the bigger local parks, but we looked forward to them with mounting excitement, watching the sky eagerly in the morning for signs of rain or sun, running round to Mr Smith's to buy slices of pink ham to put in our sandwiches, and filling the new-fangled thermos flasks which everybody was talking about — 'You must get one, they're just the thing for picnics'. By noon the basket would be packed, and we children would be raring to go.

It would mean a long tram ride, of course; but that was fun. We would rush upstairs to try to secure the front seat, that curved round in a bow-shape to give a spectacular view of the streets below. It was funny how different everything looked from the top deck of a tram; especially when you were going on a picnic. All those tiny people down there; the street traders, the barrow boys, the mothers pushing babies in prams, the grannies with their bonnets and their sagging shopping-bags; *they* weren't going on a picnic! We hugged ourselves with delight, there on the top deck of the lurching tram.

The first one to sight the green trees of the Park shouted the glad news back to Mother. The Parks where we went on summer outings were grander affairs altogether than little Telegraph Hill Park where we played on Saturdays. They had immense iron gates, and Park-keepers' lodges beside them; and the paths were straight and bordered with flowers, with never a weed in sight. We walked past the place where it said 'Keep off the Grass' — why have grass if you had to keep off it, I wondered? — past the children's playground, which was a dreary place with desolate stretches of asphalt and forlorn-looking iron swings — on and on, to the far end of the Park, where at last there was space to play games, for my brother to use his cricket-bat (I had to make do with an old tennis racquet) and for running and skipping on the green slopes which were so much bigger than anything we had in the Park at home.

We wandered through the wilder parts of the Park till we came to a seat under big trees, where we could picnic and I could pretend we were in the country. It wasn't anything like the real country, I knew; it didn't look right, or smell right. The paths were too formal, the clumps of azaleas and rhododendrons too well-kept, and worst of all, each plant and bush had a metal name-tab at its foot, which no self-respecting country plant would ever possess; of that I felt sure.

Still, there was a lake with waterfowl; and a bandstand, and if Father came too, he and Mother would sit on little green chairs listening to the band on a summer afternoon, while we children played. Privately I thought the blare of the band and the gesticulations of the conductor, stuck up there in uniform, were over-rated; you couldn't listen to the birds, or watch the sun on the grass, when all the time you were subjected to this oompahoompah of brass bands on their little round bandstand under the trees.

'Nonsense!' Father would say. 'There's no place like London, and nothing like a London park. Why, look around you — all beautifully kept, masses of colours, and — ' I knew what he was going to say next — 'you might be in the country!'

One day we really did go to the country. I think Mother must have guessed something of my longing for things that grew by themselves, and not because the park-keeper told them to. Anyway, one glorious sunny morning in the summer holidays, when only she and I were at home, she suddenly downed tools after breakfast and made the great announcement: 'We're going to the country!'

I could not believe my ears. Here we were, she and I, washing up the breakfast things in our little kitchen, all set for an ordinary day — and next moment, the country. It was really happening at last! And not even a planned day out. Nobody had said, the night before, 'Tomorrow, *if* it's fine enough, and *if* we've time, and *if* nothing else happens, we'll go to the country.' No, Mother just said 'We're going.' She'd never done anything like this before. Nobody did in our road. The week was always a planned one; Monday wash-day, Tuesday ironing; the rest of the week, the cleaning, the shopping and all the rest. You never downed tools on the spur of the moment and just went to the country.

But Mother knew how I felt. In moments I was upstairs finding my hat and shoes — good stout lace-ups, for surely we were going to do miles and miles of walking — and downstairs again, bubbling with excitement, helping to pack up the basket with the sandwiches and the thermos flask with the drinks. It was to be just the two of us, and a whole day in the country, and best of all, we didn't even know where we were going. 'We'll take a train,' Mother said. 'Wherever the train's going, we'll go.' It was just like Heaven opening, and all on a Wednesday morning when everybody else was polishing the brass and dusting the bedrooms and being ordinary. My heart lifted as we started down the steps and I saw the bright blue sky above the rooftops opposite; the flying white clouds over the chimney-pots, the glint of gold and silver on the acacia trees. This was going to be a great day. And mother was breaking the routine of the week — all for me! I couldn't think what had got into her. She seemed to be as happy about it as me.

We walked round the corner, past Mr Smith's, up the hill to the little suburban Nunhead station where the trains ran over the bridge and the noise used to frighten me when I was very small. We scanned the destination board, and Mother chose at random, peering into her old brown leather purse to make sure she had enough money for the return journey. A train was much more expensive than a tram.

Once past the suburbs and there lay the country. I watched it begin, pressing my nose against the glass as the familiar roads and houses and shops jolted by. It seemed like a miracle. Once get clear of all this city jumble, and the country would stretch, wide and beautiful, all the way to the sea! I did not mind where we went, as long as it had cows and fields. There, far below us as the train lolloped along the embankment, were busy little people going to work, midget townsfolk going their midget ways; for them it was just an ordinary day. But for us — ! The train rattled over bridges and puffed towards the fields, and every minute the view from the window was getting greener and greener, the country nearer and nearer.

We got out as the fussy little train stopped at a country station. And at once the smell of it all engulfed me. This was what I wanted, I thought, as we walked out of the open door into the fragrance of a country lane; this was what I was hungry for. There was a smell of crushed grass and hay and growing things; the earthy smell of farm buildings. I made Mother stop while we drank it all in, listening to the silence. It was quieter than I ever remembered.

The porter stood leaning on his trolley, watching us go off down the lane; and I wanted to shout to him, 'Look, we're going to the country!' I wanted everyone to know. Along the hedges the wild roses were out (with no metal labels) and the meadowsweet foamed white on the banks. I walked along, helping Mother with the basket, too happy to talk. No houses, shops or markets; nothing but miles and miles of fields and hedgerows, and a horizon green with trees. Not even a pavement to walk on. You walked, gloriously independent, in the middle of the road! Nothing could have typified the country more. That was what the country was, I told myself a place where you could walk in the road.

We turned off the lane, and stopped by a gate with a stile beside it. I had never seen a stile before. I explored it, wonderingly, climbed to the top, and sat there, dangling my legs. In front of us stretched the meadow where the cows munched, and I listened to them as they moved slowly over the grass; munch, munch as they pulled the tufts and rolled them over their great lolling tongues. It was a lovely sound. Presently one came lumbering up and stood by the gate, lifting an enormous brown head to stare at us. I wasn't used to cows, but I didn't feel afraid. Cows were my friends. On this day everyone was my friend.

We ate our sandwiches that dinner-time on a little sloping bank by a river we had found. It was marshy at the edges, and I stepped carefully over the tussocky grass to where the bank was thick with golden kingcups. The sun shone on them, turning them to glory, and I thought I had never seen anything so wonderful. The Field of the Cloth of Gold, I told myself, remembering history lessons at school. That couldn't have been more magnificent. I bent and picked them, filling my arms with the gold and green of them, burying my nose in them, feeling the juicy stems damp in my hand.

It was like an armful of sunshine. Each little flower looked up at me with a shiny golden face, as different from the flowers in the Park as you could ever imagine. I picked and picked till all my day seemed filled with gold.

In the late afternoon, still clutching our kingcups, we drifted back along the field path and up the lane. We crossed to where a farmhouse stood, sheltered by trees, and stopped by the yard where the cows were filing across for milking-time. It was like being in another world. Five o'clock was the time people at home were hurrying back from the shops, catching the tram from Jonesandhiggins, making their way through crowded streets where the traders shouted their wares and the buses pushed past, roaring beside the pavements. Here, five o'clock was cool and still, smelling of hay and cows; milking-time. When I grow up, I told myself, I'm going to live in the country.

We watched as the great brown beasts came lumbering by, their udders swinging, an occasional tail whisking. We listened to the soft breathing, the muffled snorts; then followed them into the milking shed. We stood by the doorway and heard the milk sing into the metal pails, and I could have stayed there for ever. The evening sun was gold as the kingcups now, as we walked to the station and took the train homewards. It gilded the windows of the houses as they closed in on us; touched the chimney-pots with glory. Even our little suburban streets seemed to hold an aftermath of that wonderful day.

At home, nothing was changed; except that no work had been done. It was as if Mother had forgotten all about the housework, almost as if she had become another person. And I was glad she had forgotten. Glad that nothing had got in the way of that perfect day. It was a rare thing to have a mother like that, who would leave everything, up and go, for a day in the country. For weeks, months, years, it shone in my memory, golden as the kingcups. It shines for me still.

320

12

'Going Away'

'GOING away' — magic words for most families — was a novel thing for us, though all our neighbours used to go regularly to the sea for a week or a fortnight in the summer. We hadn't much money to spend on holidays, so when we did go, it was really an event. I can't remember more than two or three holidays all those years, for in addition to the expense of going away to a boarding-house — nobody went to hotels — there was Father to contend with. Father took holidays hard.

'Gadding about', he called it. In his opinion, nobody in their right minds — and that included the neighbours — ever needed or wanted to budge out of London. He had spent most of his young days plotting and scheming to get to the metropolis, and why we, who had been lucky enough to be born there, should want to move out of it even for a week or so, passed his comprehension.

He was fond of quoting Dr Johnson's dictum that a man who is tired of London is tired of life. Consequently he looked with scorn upon people who made an annual trek to Bognor or Brighton with their families. As to resorts further afield . . . 'Can't see what they get out of it,' he grumbled. 'Least of all, going to outlandish places like Devon and Cornwall. God-forsaken parts — what in the name of all that's sensible do they find to do *there*?'

If you had to go away at all, it might be just tolerable to go somewhere like the big South Coast towns, that were as near as possible little Londons in miniature. So on the rare occasions when Mother managed to persuade him that we children were in need of a change, he would very reluctantly take us somewhere with a big sea front, plenty of shops, a museum or two, and a frequent tram service along the Promenade. As long as the trams were there, the place seemed a little more like home.

Getting Father to go away at all,

however, was such a strain that I think Mother was rather glad we couldn't afford an annual exodus. It was a major operation. As the day of departure approached, the tempo of Father's life would gradually speed up, till he had worked himself into a state bordering on panic. Grumbling ferociously that holidays were all wrong anyway, and who but a fool would take them, that it would be sure to rain, and that we should all catch our deaths, he would be prevailed on, the day before we were due to start, to drag out his old black Gladstone bag from under the bed and put a few things together.

Mother, of course, had long since packed our own possessions into a couple of battered green suitcases for the seaside: a few books to read, a few toys to keep us children quiet, some sewing to do on the beach, and cotton clothes for the family. But when she tentatively suggested to Father that it was time he did some personal packing, she would bring down on her head a veritable barrage of trouble.

It wasn't packing clothes that worried

Father. He would never wear anything else, seaside or town, but his usual garb, except of course for the frock coat and striped trousers and silk hat for Sunday, which he very reluctantly agreed to leave at home. No, days by the sea called for just as formal a costume as days in town; he would never let himself be seen in anything resembling beach wear.

Even when the fashion for short-sleeved open-neck shirts for men was gradually creeping in, Father disdained it; more than this, he fulminated against it. If a fellow couldn't dress decently in a collar and tie, no matter whether he was on the beach or not and wear proper sleeves with cuff-links, he had better not be seen at all.

Father's solitary concession to the blazing sun of Bognor or Brighton was his Panama hat. Wearing this, he considered he had paid quite enough attention to holiday requirements. Everybody could see he was on holiday, surely, if he was wearing a Panama hat. Those blazers and cricket shirts and flannels you saw about were so casual that they seemed almost indecent to him. As for wet weather, he still scorned a mackintosh and clung to the Sherlock Holmes-like Inverness cape which he had worn in his student days, and which, he insisted, kept the rain and the wind out better than any of these new-fangled waterproofs.

No, it wasn't clothes that were going to fill the Gladstone bag, it was Father's precious possessions. If he had to be uprooted and made to spend a week or two wasting time on a beach, at least he would take with him all his usual hobbies.

Into the bag went his old plate camera, the one with the black velvet cloth attached, behind which Father retired, head and shoulders, when he wanted to take a picture; the folding tripod without which you couldn't get a steady photograph had to be strapped on the outside. Taking photographs was a great hobby of his, and many an hour we all had to spend, grouped in statuesque positions in the garden, while he fiddled and fumbled behind his black velvet cloth and exhorted us all to smile nicely.

Then there was the pair of binoculars in the leather case with the strap. Everybody knew you took binoculars to the seaside, so in they had to go. And there was the folding telescope. After all, it *was* a folding one, and nobody could tell you there wasn't room in the Gladstone bag for anything that folded.

Father's telescope, so precious to him, was the bane of all the neighbourhood, though he never guessed and of course we never dared tell him. On a good night when the stars were out, he had a habit of inviting the neighbours to come into our back garden — he disliked using the telescope through the window — and 'have a look at the stars' through it.

'Can you see Mars?' he would whisper excitedly. 'That's Venus over there. Look — the Milky Way. Millions and millions of stars.'

Millions there may have been, but the best nights for stars were usually also the coldest and bitterest ones, and nobody appreciated being dragged out from a warm fireside on a November or January night to shiver in our back garden looking through the telescope, while the frost lay white on the rooftops. But Father loved it; astronomy to him was just another example of the wonder of the universe; he would spend hours gazing at Orion or at Cassiopaea in her chair; and of course he couldn't go on holiday without the telescope. If it wouldn't go into the Gladstone bag, he would stay at home.

Then there were all the books. Books were to him the great comfort of life. If you had enough books around you, nothing could touch you. And what better time than a holiday at Bognor to immerse yourself in reading?

Father never left home without at least a dozen, mostly bulky ones, and if the bag wouldn't hold them, they had to be parcelled up and carried by hand. There was *Einstein the Searcher*, for instance — a good book that, and one which rarely left his bedside, where he would sit up for half the night reading by the light of his little green-shaded oil bedside lamp. There were one or two of Scott's novels, too, nice lengthy ones that would help pass the slow-moving time on the beach; Father grudged every minute spent out of London, but Scott would help to make the ordeal more bearable. There were all those back copies of the

Pharmaceutical Review which he never had time to read; this would be just the chance he needed to catch up on his study of them, so in they went. And naturally he couldn't go anywhere without his Shakespeare.

Shakespeare was the breath of life to Father, and I don't think a night passed in his life when he didn't read at least half a dozen pages from the plays or the Sonnets before going to sleep. When life got hard and disappointments were many, there was always Shakespeare. Nothing you could suffer was unknown to Shakespeare. Father would read for hours — he needed very little sleep — working through the tragedies and the histories and the comedies, turning to the sonnets, and then beginning the whole process over again.

It was unfortunate that he could never make up his mind which volume of Shakespeare to take with him, so that more often than not he ended by bringing the lot. And they were such weighty tomes. By the time Mother had sorted out all these possessions and helped him stuff them into the Gladstone bag, tying onto the outside everything that wouldn't go in, she was exhausted and Father was despairing. What on earth the family had to go away for, when the Park was so near and we had acacia trees growing right outside the door, and a garden back and front — *and* a pond for the children to paddle in at the top of the lawn which was just as good as the sea, if not better — Father failed entirely to comprehend. What was wrong with London anyway? Didn't we have visitors pouring in in their thousands all the summer just to see the sights in the capital that we wanted to get away from?

By the day of departure, Father had usually worked himself into a near-frenzy. He would get up very early, make us all eat an enormous breakfast which we didn't want — 'nothing like travelling on a good substantial meal' — and hurry us around, reminding us of this and that, fussing over last-minute details and grumbling heartily all the time. As according to Father it was a foregone conclusion that we should all miss the train anyway, it didn't seem much good making such frantic efforts to be on time;

but Father rushed and hurried us just the same.

When at last the cases and the Gladstone bag were assembled in the hall, the gas turned off, the windows secured and doubly secured, the back door bolted and barred, and every precaution taken against the burglars who, he assured us, were only awaiting this opportunity to come and ransack the place — he would gaze round the rooms, and suddenly his eye would light upon some treasure that must go to extra-special safety before we could think of leaving at all.

This object and that were sure to tempt the burglars; up they must go, into hiding in the loft above the top landing. Wedding presents, silver photograph frames, precious clocks, cases of cutlery — any of these a burglar might fancy; it wasn't safe to leave them about.

We would all be pressed into service to carry the bric-à-brac up the three flights of stairs and pass it up to Father, who stood, fretting and fuming, on top of the step-ladder ready to stow away the loot in the roof. Hand over hand we passed him up the best silver soup-tureen, wrapped in its green baize cover; the family spoons; the christening mugs that held lime-juice for my brother and myself on Sundays; the entrée dishes that were only used on Christmas Day. All the time Mother would be standing at the top of the stairs, twisting her handkerchief with anxiety and consulting her watch every few minutes lest we should all miss the train.

'There's only ten minutes!' she would tell Father in despair. 'Surely you've got enough up there now?'

'I'm not going to let any burglar make off with my silver brushes!' Father would roar, nearly toppling off the ladder with frenzy. 'If you didn't make all this fuss about going away, we wouldn't be put to such trouble to keep the place safe from burglars!'

Down we would all trail to fetch something else that Father had remembered; and Mother would look anxiously at her watch once more.

'If we don't get off in five minutes now, it's no use going at all,' she would state. 'This is the last time — positively the last time — we're ever going on holiday!'

We children didn't worry. We knew Father's tantrums, and we knew that somehow or other, in spite of all these family arguments on the top landing, in spite of the repeated treks up three flights of stairs with the cutlery and the marble clock, we should all get safely away in the end. And when grown-ups said it was positively the last time they would ever do this or that, we knew quite well that it was nothing of the sort. Grown-ups always said these things.

In the end, of course, we did get away. How, nobody knew; for by this time Father would have decided that it was us who were late and he who had been waiting for us all the time, and couldn't we ever be trusted to be punctual? Nobody in this house ever got away on time except him. When things got to this pitch, we knew that Father was really getting ready to leave; so we picked up our bags and at long last the family procession would move off down the road to catch the tram to the station. Nobody ever thought of taking a cab.

That would be wasteful.

My first ever view of the sea was distinctly disappointing. I had been told so much about its wonders; of the expanse of blue, the dancing waves, the foam, the breakers, the golden sand; and though it all meant nothing as yet, I had gathered the impression that seeing the sea for the first time was something quite momentous.

But when, that first holiday away at Bognor — I was four at the time — we actually got down to the sea, I was not in the least impressed. A grey stretch of water, without a movement, reaching away to an equally grey sky, with no colour, no light and shade, nothing happening to it at all — the sea, if this was it, it hardly seemed worth coming all those miles in the train just to look at.

True, in the bright sunshine the next morning it did look a little bit bluer; but it was still too big to be taken in by a four-year-old. And the sands were a disappointment. For one thing, there was no room to move.

The back of the beach was packed closely with deck chairs in which leaned and lolled fathers and mothers of all descriptions, the men in straw boaters tipped over their eyes against the sun, the women in voluminous cotton dresses, trifling with slim little sunshades of pastel-coloured silk. Little did they know, that careless summer, that in another month the First World War would engulf them all.

Down by the water's edge, the sand was thick with children busy digging castles, filling red tin buckets and hitting each other over the head with wooden spades. The little boys in sailor-suits or belted tunics, the little girls with skirts tucked into their knickers, seemed to be everywhere. There was not an inch of room for me to build my sandcastles. I could only sit down in the shade of somebody's deck chair and wish I were at home again. Privately, I could not see anything to choose between Bognor, with its crowds on the beach, and our own suburb with its crowds of shoppers in Rye Lane leading to Jonesandhiggins on a Saturday afternoon. There was just as much noise, and just as much bustle, and just as little room for a small girl to move about amidst the forest of legs.

Of course, at the sea you had to go bathing. This was done from a bathing machine, of which Bognor still had a few; substantial affairs of wood like garden sheds on wheels, painted in gay stripes, with curtained windows and little doors through which you stepped to descend, gingerly, down the steps into the waves. The beach attendant would push these mighty machines down into the water every morning, and inside them the whole family changed for bathing. Bognor as yet had no beach-huts; they were new-fangled things. All the best people hired a bathing machine.

Inside, they were dim and musty, smelling strongly of sand and seaweed and wet clothes. The grit got between your toes as you stood on duckboards on the bare floor, and I didn't at all fancy changing in there, into my bathing costume of red twill, with short sleeves, respectable legs, and white rickrack braiding round the edges.

My brother too would change into a skinny dark blue bathing suit, also with short sleeves and respectable legs, but he didn't have to put anything on his head. I was made to wear a bathing cap, smelling of wet indiarubber and clinging uncomfortably round my ears. Together we would carefully descend the wooden steps, slippery with wet sand, and put a foot into the uninviting grey water. This was the great moment when we were supposed to enjoy our first taste of sea-bathing. I didn't enjoy mine at all, and began to think Father might be right after all, in not wanting to come to the seaside.

The other attractions, so-called, of the seaside made no more appeal to me than the sea itself. There were the concert-parties with their pianists and pierrots, who every day drew excited crowds of parents and children. I saw nothing funny in the antics of these men in fancy dress, with white baggy trousers and pompoms on their hats. I couldn't understand their jokes at all, and the pianists rattling away at seaside pianos left me cold. The Punch and Judy shows, I was told, were specially meant for small children, but you couldn't get near them on the beach for the crowds, and all a four-year-old could see of Punch or Judy was other children's backs as they pressed forward to get a good view. When at last I was lifted up to look, all I saw was a violent scene where Punch beat his wife around the head with a stick, and I begged, howling, to be put down again.

Elbowed and shouldered to the outer fringes of the crowd, I wandered disconsolately about the sands watching the donkeys taking small girls and boys for rides along the beach. The donkeys looked gentle enough and I would have ridden on them gladly, but the donkey-boys were alarming. They were rough and tousle-haired, and brought back memories of the rough boys at home who, like the Vicar's troops of Midian, prowled and prowled around. To have one of them seizing you and lifting you up would be terrible indeed. Father couldn't understand why I rejected the donkey-rides, and I couldn't tell him I was afraid of the donkey-boys, so we got no further with our seaside pleasures.

Once we went on the pier. Everybody goes on the pier, I was told; you paid your twopence at the little kiosk by the gate, and then walked out, far, far out to sea, till the beach, when you looked back between the white-painted iron railings, seemed like a distant shore seen from a boat. You were sandwiched between ocean and sky, a part of neither, ship-wrecked and lonely. The moment we left the good old terra firma of land, I felt sick with nerves.

'Come along, do, and stop dawdling,' someone would tell me. 'It's lovely at the end of the pier. You'll like it when you get there!'

As these were just the words that, in the past, had always proved that I *didn't* like it, I was not assured. Walking down the length of the pier was terrifying, little though they realised it — and again I had no words to tell them. It was those cracks that worried me; the cracks between the floorboards, through which, as you walked, you could catch a glimpse of grey waves washing underneath; the cracks through which a child might, as I thought, slip to its doom. You could hear the boards creaking as you stepped gingerly over them, dragged along by a

338

grown-up hand; and when you reached a certain point on the pier, you could actually feel the whole structure sagging and swaying. Surely the day would come — it might be today — when the sag and sway would turn to a dreadful ruinous crash, and down you would go to a watery grave. Anything could happen on that dreadful pier; but I couldn't tell the grown-ups; they wouldn't understand.

The only thing I did like at the seaside was the pictures. When it rained, we all made for the cinema, the little silent one in a back street away from the sea front, where they showed horses galloping at impossible speeds over prairies, and maidens constantly being rescued from dreadful fates by good men from bad men, and terrible struggles on the teetering tops of giant cliffs, or in the path of an oncoming express train. The pictures, I thought, were lovely.

True, it always looked as if it was raining inside as well as out. There was so much dazzle on the screen; and periodically the whole picture would unaccountably stop short, and the seaside audience would begin to whistle and cat-call till it came on again. True, there were pictures at home, in the tiny cinema at the bottom of the road, where you could get quite good seats for twopence and very superior ones for fourpence. But at home nobody ever took me to the pictures, whilst now at the seaside there was a reckless abandon about life which made going to the cinema seem necessary and right.

I would sit enthralled at the pictures, watching the snow-dazzled screen and listening to the music from the lady in the low-cut blouse whose flying fingers on the piano keys matched the tempo of the film. And then come out into the sunshine breathless and blinking, wondering at the reality outside. It had stopped raining, and the streets were wet and shiny where the sun caught the puddles on the pavements. But it seemed dull after the excitement of the pictures. After those hair-raising scenes, the ordinary life of a seaside town seemed humdrum and tame.

One terrible day I got lost, and

thought the whole world had come to an end. It was the most frightening moment I had yet known. Knee-high among the swirling crowds passing and repassing along the Promenade, I had got separated from my family as we returned from the beach, and found myself running, breathless and sobbing, between beds of ornamental flowers and in and out of glass shelters, wildly trying to recognise a familiar face among the milling multitudes. But everybody was too busy to notice a little girl.

I got knocked by sunshades and umbrellas and walking sticks, bumped by little boys sucking seaside rock and little girls bouncing balls, elbowed into the gutter by peppery old gentlemen in Panama hats, shoved and pushed by white mufflered men with barrows selling ice-cream and shrimps and balloons and spades. My panic mounted to such a pitch that I accosted a sympathetic-looking lady in a bright orange coat, and poured out my troubles.

'Where do you live, dear?' she asked me.

I resorted to the magic formula that had been taught me as soon as I could talk: '123 Waller Road, New Cross, London SE14', adding for good measure 'England' to make sure she knew I didn't come from overseas. But this time it didn't work. London wasn't Bognor, and I had no idea where we were staying. I clung to her skirts for protection as the crowds knocked and pushed me, but for the life of me I couldn't give her any more information. I was in some strange private hell, where nothing was familiar, nobody knew me, and as far as I could make out, I would never see any of my family again.

Then round the corner of a large ornamental bed of geraniums came a swirl of black — Father's Inverness cape. Nobody else on the whole promenade had an Inverness cape. I blessed it, and rushed off joyfully to hide beneath its protective folds. I never wanted to see the seaside again. It was horrible; just like London, only worse. I wanted to go home.

And yet somehow, I knew at the back of my mind, deeper far than consciousness, that I hadn't really discovered the sea yet at all. There must be something else; something I didn't know. Something different from the Promenade, and the bathing machines, and the crowded sand where little boys jabbed your knees with spades.

It was not until five years later that we had another holiday; and this one was to be in the country. Everybody in our road thought we were quite mad to want to go to the country for a holiday. Nobody ever did; for one thing, you couldn't bring back a stick of rock for the children in the street; for another, there were no picture postcards of the pier, or the promenade, to send back to Aunt Grace or Uncle Henry saying 'Wish you were here'. The country held only cows and fields and sky; Father thought it was madness indeed to think of going there. The seaside was bad enough, but the country was clean crazy.

Father refused pointblank to accompany us to such outlandish parts, and Mother wouldn't budge without him, so it fell to Aunt Jane to take us children to the country. We got the address from one of her fellow teachers who lent her a little blue book of holiday addresses, tried and tested by teachers themselves. It was before the age of holiday guidebooks and travel articles in the papers; if the resorts of England had publicity officers, we had certainly never heard of them.

Aunt Jane decided on a farm and I felt as though the dream of a lifetime was coming true. A real proper holiday in the country, and on a farm as well; what more could life hold?

The farm, when we got there, was only an ordinary country house with a few ducks and chickens and a cow or two. No great barns, no milking sheds, byres or piggeries. It scarcely reckoned itself a farm at all, but it was good enough for me. At last — no streets or trams, no park notices round the flowers; just country, mile after green mile of it, and all growing wild. I walked on air as we carried our suitcases up the lane from the little station. This was going to be a real holiday.

'It's a good five miles from the seaside,' said Aunt Jane, gripping the handle of the suitcase and stepping out firmly.

344

I wouldn't have minded if it were twenty. From the first moment it was heaven. As we walked, I felt the cool air fresh on my cheek; smelled the country tang of cow dung, the heavy scent of the meadowsweet. You could put out your hand and touch the stillness; it lay like a cloud over everything. The crunch of our footsteps on the gravel of the lane was the only sound, except for the birds singing. I revelled in it.

I loved that holiday at the farm. There was nothing to do all day but sit in the sun, watching the fat white ducks paddling through pools of sunshine and shade, through the orchard, down to the pond; the house martins wheeling and swooping over the eaves in low, graceful flight; the cows contentedly munching in the knee-high grass. We went for walks, lazed in the fields, paddled in the stream. We breathed in the peace of the golden days.

At night I would lie awake, too happy to sleep, gazing at the blue-green sky, the colour of a duck's egg, framed in the square of the attic window and criss-crossed with the tracery of trees;

watching the white curtains rise and fall in the little winds of evening; hearing from somewhere the faint bark of a dog, dropping into the stillness like a stone into a well; the call of an owl; then silence, complete and deep. It was the silence that surprised me. I had never realised before how the dull penetrating far-off roar of London traffic had always been a background to life at home. Now I discovered stillness as a beautiful and wonderful thing, akin to the spaciousness outside, the mile upon mile of distance, hill fading into hill, vale into vale. They were new things to me, this stillness and the sense of space. I began at last to perceive that London and the yellow-brick suburbs were not, after all, the whole of life.

There were lanes in this countryside, down which it was a delight to walk. No need to worry about traffic; all the road was free to the traveller. The most we ever saw was a drowsy horse and cart, a dawdling cyclist or a countryman walking home. I felt safe here, enclosed between high hedges thick with meadowsweet.

And the little field-paths fascinated me.

346

With their stiles, where you climbed to sit and view the countryside, they wandered over the fields and through the woods, linking villages as sleepy and quiet as the fields themselves. It was only ordinary Suffolk countryside, but it might have been continents away from the life I knew. I loved the clusters of white and pink cottages bowered in trees; the village greens where dogs lay in the sun, and boys played cricket; the tiny shops, their doors hung with honeysuckle, where you could buy anything from butter to bootlaces, and where the bell jangled as you went in. Even the people were different; they talked in murmurous country voices, unlike the clipped Cockney accent; they moved slowly and with deliberation, lighting up a pipe, scything a field or throwing food to the hens. It was a whole world of quietness.

On Sunday we went to the village church. It was cool and dim and smelt of moss and stone; not of pitch-pine and varnish, like our church at home. We sang:

Fair waved the golden corn
In Canaan's pleasant land,
When full of joy some shining morn
Went forth the reaper band.

And as I gazed from the open church door, I could see the ripened cornfields stretching away into the sunshine. Quite suddenly I knew why the reaper band had been full of joy; in fact, I knew for the first time what religion was all about. It wasn't the Vicar on Sundays, or the choirboys giggling in the front row; or the sidesman passing round the collection plate; it wasn't the troops of Midian, of whom I had been so afraid; it wasn't even the Guardian Angel whom you bribed in prayer to protect you from harm. It was something else, something altogether different; something you didn't search for, for it came to you.

It was here in this cool, dim church; it was the peace, the rightness of things. It was the cornfields outside, that made you want to sing for joy; it was one-ness with God and man. This was what I had been looking for all the time.

On the last day of our holiday we went

348

to the coast. It was a slow, sleepy journey in a little local train, puffing serenely through the summer countryside; only two stops, but the market train stopped at both, collecting enormous countrywomen with baskets covered with white cloths, armfuls of flowers, or squawking chickens in string bags. I had never seen any but sober London passengers on the clanging trams. I was enchanted. But it was a pity, I thought, that we were going to the sea. The sea meant piers and promenades and bathing machines and crowds. Why spoil this wonderful, blissful, perfect holiday by going to the sea?

But when we got to the sea, it was entirely different. We left the little town behind us, and climbed up onto the cliffs, where the sky was riotous with larksong, and where the great clouds billowed up over a green horizon. The cliff path dipped and mounted; we were going away from the town, away over the sweet-smelling turf where sheep bleated thinly and the air seemed high and rare. But still all I could see was the cliffs and the clouds and the grass; there was no sea.

And then, with a twist of the path, it was there. The sea lay wide at our feet, far, far below — a great stretch of shimmering blues and greens and violets, lit with sunshine, shadowed with cloud. Little white flecks of foam danced on it; gulls wheeled above it; waves broke at the foot of the cliff and echoed hollowly in the caves. And there was not a soul in sight. No pier, no people; just the immensity of ocean and sky.

So this, after all, was the sea. I had always known I should find it some day.

13

Kindergarten

I WAS six when they took me to kindergarten at the Haberdashers' Ashe's Girls' School in Erningham Road, and the knob of the classroom door-handle came just about the level of my chin. I had had so many illnesses and bad dreams and childish fevers that they had kept me at home for a year; but now the day had come, and I was face to face with this door-handle, all black and ridged and forbidding, that I had to turn to go inside — away from the comfortable little world of home, into the new and strange one of school. It was rather like drawing a deep breath; you were suspended in emptiness midway between the things you knew and the things you didn't; the familiar and the unpredictable. I was not exactly afraid; I drew my deep breath and went in. All the same, school looked dreadfully big when you were only doorknob high.

I shut the door behind me, and a teacher at least twenty feet tall took my hand and was kind. But even her kindness didn't bring her down to my level. My gaze travelled wonderingly up her from shoes to skirt, from skirt to neat belt, from belt to blouse and collar, right up to the face at the top; and it was a face I didn't know. And the faces of the children were all faces I didn't know; ten thousand of them, it seemed, and all chattering, all unknown. This then, was school.

And suddenly, on the second day, I had been at school for years and years. Here was the world itself reflected small and neat and crystal-clear as in a concave mirror; the world in miniature, with its events and personalities, its hierarchies and its conventions. To a little girl fresh from the cloistered world of home, it seemed strangely exhilarating, and I threw myself into it all with vigour. It was wonderful to be part of a community, a little society so different from everything I had known at home.

Kindergarten, I soon discovered, had

352

a rigid social scale. There were the Babies, and the Lower Transition, and the Upper Transition. Nobody knew what a Transition was, but it had a grand sound, and we repeated the word with relish. Being already turned six, I was allowed to skip the Babies and start straight away in the Lower Transition.

To us tiny ones the Upper Transition ruled the kindergarten rather like Eton's 'Pop'. They were a race apart, the lordly ones, not even to be approached directly. At prayers, when we stood in three lines, they lounged against the wall at the back with careless grace, like infant undergraduates; and we worshipped from afar. Such a gulf was fixed between us that it seemed quite impossible we lower ones would one day join those illustrious ranks ourselves.

The kindergarten was taught by two ladies, Miss Bradfield and Miss Kemp. Miss Bradfield provided the brains, and Miss Kemp the love. We respected and admired Miss Bradfield, who taught us pot-hooks and read to us out of books, but we adored Miss Kemp, who mothered and cuddled us, did up our shoe-laces, bathed cut knees and blew our noses for us when they needed blowing. Dear Miss Kemp, with her sweet smile and her comfortable lap; she bridged the gap between school and home, and we took her to our hearts.

But for Miss Bradfield we worked and concentrated, bending over our copy books with tongue between teeth and breathing heavily as we pushed the pencil to make the top of an 'I' or the tail of a 'g'. Miss Bradfield knew everything; the world was her oyster. Whether she had ever been to those far lands she told us about in Scripture or Geography we never knew; but nothing, not a detail, about them escaped her. No sum was ever too hard for her; no word but that she didn't know its derivation and meaning. Nobody ever caught her out at spelling. She was rather like an archangel to the Headmistress's God; second in command, but only just.

The personalities of other children filled me with excitement. After the quiet years at home, these brave new contacts were like a kaleidoscope, changing and challenging. I soon had my heroes, all of them in the Upper Transition, all of them boys.

Martin was seven, and, tall and handsome, topped the rest of the Upper Transition when we lined up in our serried ranks for prayers. He wore a brilliant red jersey; and since I was at an age when jingles and rhymes ran constantly through my head, the sound of his name reminded me of tomato soup in a tin — lovely tomato soup, which matched the colour of his red jersey, and which I adored. Consequently it was easy to adore Martin too.

I gazed from a distance, never daring to go near him in person, but waiting for those moments when Martin dropped a handkerchief or a pencil, which I could, by darting forward, retrieve for him and return through the medium of his round, fat little brother in the Babies — the perfect foil for Martin's godlike grace. I lived for moments like these.

Raymond, too, soon came to fascinate me. Raymond had fair hair, a long angelic-looking face, and a blue jersey the translucent colour of the early morning summer sky. With the wordless affinity that certain small children have for each other, I realised that there was something appealing about Raymond; something slightly fey. He would stand lost in dreams, or shine out suddenly with a reflective secret smile, as though some memory had caught up with him from the heaven which, after all, he had left only a brief seven years before.

It was through Raymond that I first came to know pity, the compassion of the child for his like, helpless and humiliated among the grown-ups. One day, during a game in which we were all bidden to be trees and sway in the wind, Raymond's newly learned physical control had suddenly left him, and he had disgraced himself upon the kindergarten floor. People had run for mops and cloths, and Raymond had been hustled away. Kind Miss Kemp hadn't been cross; but from that moment Raymond's stock had gone down in kindergarten circles; those who could do better scorned him. From that time on, Raymond's troubles became mine, and I suffered daily with him, feeling the pang of one child for another, small and desolate in a disapproving world.

Then there was Neville. Drama came into our little group with the brothers Neville and Granville, about whom from the first there hung, in my mind, an aura of the sinister. Neville and Granville had short-cropped heads and scowling faces, and were dressed alike in grey jerseys with polo necks — rough, hairy jerseys which chilled me with revulsion when I had to get close to them.

With my own persistent habit of associating names with sounds and jingles, Neville seemed to me reminiscent of the Devil, about whom I heard so much from the Vicar on Sundays. Just as Martin borrowed reflected glory from the tomato soup, so Neville was complemented by his Mephistophelian partner. I was not at all surprised when one day a cloud of disapproval descended on the kindergarten, emanating — needless to say — from Neville.

With a child's uncanny way of scenting trouble, we knew as we came in that morning that something was dreadfully wrong. Neville's parents had come to See the School about him. Wild were the rumours and black the shadow that blotted out for us the usual joys of plasticine and paint, coloured pictures and absorbing story and song. The fact that Neville's parents had actually come to the school, and were even now closeted with Miss Bradfield in secret, weighed upon our consciences almost as if the sin were our own.

Afterwards I discovered with surprise that the misdeed had only consisted of coming home late from school, and the parents had been, not wrath with anger, but merely concerned as to their little boy's safety. But to us the awful sight of grown-ups in conclave — especially teachers and parents in conclave — had meant only one thing, trouble.

Poor Neville, much maligned; but what could you expect with a name like that?

The child most akin to my heart was Conrad, and it was Conrad too who brought me my first bitter humiliation at school. Conrad came from a far country — I didn't know which — and was marked out from the others by his jet-black hair, small peaked face, and the fact that he wore an iron brace on one leg.

I was drawn towards him, feeling then, as I have so often since, an irresistible attraction towards the lame, the halt and the blind — probably because I too was a plain child with no charm, who envied the social ease of others. For Conrad I soon conceived a deep, if dumb, passion.

One day a band of little girls came running up to me in the playground. 'Conrad's brought you some flowers, Eileen.'

My heart leaped; I was no longer a plain child with no charm; someone desired me. Somebody had brought me flowers. I flew to find him, glowing with gratitude and pride; but as I advanced, Conrad backed away and hobbled off down the playground path, the flowers clutched in his hand. They were meant for somebody else; I had forgotten there was another Eileen in the kindergarten.

In bitter shame I longed to hide myself away and never be seen again. I had been so sure the flowers were for me, and had let everybody see my eagerness. The hurt now seemed quite unbearable. Instead I pretended gaily that of course I'd known all along the flowers were meant for another child, and went into school with head held high but an aching heart.

It did not take long, fortunately, to make the useful discovery that you could always turn from the disappointment of People to the comfort of Things. There were many things of wonder and delight in kindergarten. Colours and shapes were exciting; even more, the elemental sensual pleasures of feel and smell. Who could ever explain to a grown-up (indeed, they almost seemed to shrink from the stuff) the peculiar charm of plasticine, with its faint sickly aroma? Plasticine that you could squeeze into sausages, punch and pummel, roll into balls, crumble or squash flat with all the strength of a six-year-old palm. Out of it would come birds, eggs and nests; baskets with wobbly handles and plasticine apples inside; snakes and monsters, flowers and fruit and strange little dumpy, hunchbacked people. It was magic stuff plasticine; the raw material of creation. I would sit on the little kindergarten chair and imagine myself God, doing his creation. Since he made everything in the world, this is how he must have felt. I made animals, two by two like the ones in the Ark; flowers and wobbly trees; and finally, Man himself. It was a wonderful feeling to create a plasticine world in miniature.

There were so many other raw materials, too, with which to make things, and I mastered them slowly, one by one, always with a feeling of pride. It was a wonderful thing to create, with your fingers, your eyes, your hands. Dear Miss Kemp brought us canvas and wool, with which we darned geometrical patterns up and down the squares; the wool came in lovely rainbow colours, and the patterns obeyed our commands. It was exhilarating. Then there was sticky paper and scissors. Miss Kemp brought us those too, and we cut clumsily round the shapes, and stuck them onto big friezes of paper which went round the walls; flowers and grass in springtime, Palestinian palm trees with long fringed leaves for our Scripture lessons; Easter eggs for Easter, and snowballs and snowflakes for Christmas. It was wonderful what you could do with sticky paper and scissors. The only thing about the scissors was that you were so tempted to go on cutting; round the edge of the check tablecloth that covered the kindergarten tables, round the bottom of your skirt. It was a real effort not to keep snipping, and only Miss Bradfield's eagle eye stopped me from scissoring everything within sight.

Best of all were paints and brushes. You had to be careful with these, for spilling paint was a major sin, and spilling water only slightly less of a crime. The little round paint pots and water pots wobbled on the boards we painted on; and it was a temptation, like the temptation of the scissors, not to paint everything within sight. Especially red; red had a life of its own, that could barely be contained within the limits of the paint pot and the brush.

With red we produced sunsets and fireworks and Guy Fawkes bonfires; with blue, endless seas and summer skies; with yellow, many-beamed suns that shone from the page. They were mysterious things, those paintings, that shaped themselves from your inmost mind and were more akin to feelings than pictures. You took up the brush, dipped it in colour, and you never knew what would result; the paint itself took over. Red was excitement, and passion, and anger, and joy; yellow, dreams and songs and fancies; blue, contentment and peace and the continuity of things.

In all these things you were truly creating; like God. And then, all in a moment, something would happen. The scissors would suddenly bite your hand, or the needle prick, or the chalk squeak on the slate, or the bristles of the paintbrush flatten out into nothingness against the paper; and you were not God after all, but only a six-year-old with tools you couldn't manage. Then you turned to kind Miss Kemp, and buried yourself in her motherly lap, and smelt her nice smell of camphor and sweets, and everything was all right again.

We played games in kindergarten; games in which we had to turn into trees, or be rabbits skipping around, or horses galloping. These were wonderful at first; but soon the wonder of them was spoilt by other children knocking into you as you swayed like one of the delicate acacia trees down our road, or tripping you up just as you were galloping at full speed across the prairie. There was no room in our little kindergarten for physical make-believe. I preferred the mental kind, the kind where nobody could spoil your joy. And this was where the magic of words came in.

Words, leaping from a page or chanted in dreamy unison, brought another dimension into the flat pattern of kindergarten days. They opened up new vistas, intriguing and disturbing by turns.

'Little brown seed, O little brown brother' we chanted; or 'O where are you going to, all you big steamers?' and though the words were nothing special, they held a hint of mysteries still to be discovered — the seed secretly growing in the darkness of earth, the lands far away across the uncharted seas. I felt they were in some way a key; and what wonders can be unlocked if you are only given the key?

Most enthralling of all was to listen to the Upper Transition reciting on Friday mornings behind the green baize curtains that divided our classes. I used to sit enthralled with my plasticine, while the chant came dully from behind the curtains: 'The Inchcape Rock'.

No stir in the air, no stir in the
    sea;
The ship was still as she could be.

I listened enchanted, my fingers idle,
waiting for the terrible moment when
'Down sank the bell with a gurgling
sound' and ready to gloat with the
moralists when wicked Sir Ralph the
Rover

    . . . tore his hair;
He curst himself in his despair.

Fascinated, I would wait for the final
climax, when, the chanting voices rising
to a crescendo as the Upper Transition
swung triumphantly into the last few
verses, we would hear how

    The fiends below were ringing his
        knell.

After this, plasticine would seem banal,
and I would long for words, words, bright
words. It was as if a spark from heaven
had touched the Lower Transition where
we sat with our handwork at the little

tables; and I knew suddenly that there was more to learning than pushing a needle through canvas to make a penwiper, or a hair-tidy to hang on the corner of the dressingtable mirror; more even than sorting beans into bags, or matchsticks into bundles of ten. There was all the bright beauty of words that could spirit you away from the battered little kindergarten tables to realms undreamed-of, realms of gold.

Fridays were memorable in other ways, besides the morning chanting of 'The Inchcape Rock' behind the green curtains. The rest of the week went by at a jog-trot pace, but Fridays were different. Friday morning, perhaps, was not so distinguishable from other mornings, except for the odour of fish drifting in from the Big School kitchens about midday; Fry-day, I knew of course, was so called after the frying.

But as soon as dinner-break was over, the blessedness of Friday afternoon enveloped the kindergarten. We were relaxed and happy; it was the end of the week, and a sense of ease and wellbeing lay over us all. Books were stacked away; slates and pencils piled on the shelves; we played instead with bricks and toy animals, or brought our dolls from home; and at the end there were special hymns to sing and illustrated Bible texts, hectographed in alarming purple ink onto paper, for us to take home and colour. We all felt very holy on Friday afternoons.

The Headmistress herself, Miss Young, would come down from the Big School to be present at our Friday hymn-singing. Two of us would be deputed to go upstairs and fetch her. This was a thrilling and awful moment, and you waited in trepidation for weeks for your turn to come; yet with a certain precarious pleasure. You tiptoed out of kindergarten, clutching your partner's hand, up the wide stone staircase where you seldom ventured, up into strange territory where it was all closed doors, and unseen humming voices, and echoing passages. There would be the sound of trills and chords from the music practice rooms, where the big girls were 'doing their piano'; it all sounded most wonderful to us. Occasionally we would pass someone on the stairs, all navy blue and white in unaccustomed school uniform, on which we looked with awe. It was a different world from the gentle familiar one of kindergarten.

Outside the Headmistress's room we would knock and wait, trembling; and then, out she would sail, rather like God himself making a condescending appearance to a six-year-old; white hair, piercing eyes, noiseless step, gliding without seeming to touch the ground, like Deity upon the clouds. Her smiling, pontifical presence at the hymn-singing made us all feel doubly blessed. 'All things bright and beautiful' we would pipe, knowing our weekend would be filled with gladness.

Afterwards we trooped into the cloak-room for hats and coats in a daze of pious happiness; our texts for colouring were clutched tightly in our hands, the echoes of the last hymn still rang in our ears; all the golden weekend stretched before us, and soon there would be our mothers' arms around us and toast for tea.

Only once was I alarmed or unhappy about what the grownups at kindergarten would say or do. Mostly they were kindness itself but conscience can be unkinder than any teacher. I had been playing in the glass porch of the school entrance with the little Scottish boy Angus, the local doctor's son, whom everyone called Bunny. Bunny, with his freckles and his Scots accent, was a great friend of mine, and we never lost an opportunity of chasing each other about.

'Race you to the window,' called Bunny, and headed for the glass panels. I did the same, but in my headlong flight put my hand straight through one of the panes. There was a sudden awful crash of glass, splinters showered around us, and there was I standing staring at the terrible, gaping hole — the hole that I had made, that nobody could possibly hide, that couldn't be covered up or put right again. It was like standing on a comfortable substantial floor, and suddenly finding the boards give way and reveal all hell yawning at your feet.

I was ordered to go and confess my misdeed to the Headmistress. If I had been ordered to my execution

I couldn't have been more terrified. Trembling and cold with fear, I toiled all alone up the stone steps to the Big School, and stood waiting, too fearful to knock, outside her study door. But to my utter bewilderment, when at last she came out and found me, there was not a word of scolding; instead she tenderly examined my hand for cuts.

I was amazed, dumbfounded. Feeling like a reprieved murderer, I went downstairs on shaky legs, wondering at the ways of grown-ups. You expected them to be angry, and they weren't. And all too often, you expected them to be pleased, and they were angry. Truly they were an inscrutable race.

But by and large, our kindergarten was an extension of the family; a lovely, warm, friendly place where you lived untroubled by the formalities of the Big School upstairs. In the two little rooms divided by their green curtain, next door to the Dining Hall which smelled so invitingly at a quarter to twelve each morning when they were preparing dinner, we were a race apart;

370

a little community of fives-to-sevens who knew few cares.

Dear Miss Bradfield and dearer Miss Kemp were like substitute mothers; or nice amiable aunts with so many ideas for things to do, songs to sing, stories to listen to. I never wanted to leave kindergarten and venture up those big stone stairs to where the Headmistress had her awe-inspiring study and classrooms rang to the chant of tables and corridors to the marching of feet.

It would come one day, I knew. The worst part seemed to me that I would leave all the boys. Bunny with his Scottish accent and his freckles; and dreamy Raymond, and Neville and Granville with their grey jerseys and cropped heads; and Martin, the god-like Martin whom I worshipped from afar. All these would be lost to me. Martin had already gone. He had vanished to the Boys' School up the road where there were columns of marching boys; classrooms full of boys; masters, and a Headmaster. It was only us little girls who would join the Big School upstairs. It seemed very unfair.

It was rather like a kind of dying, I

thought sometimes. All the familiar life you knew would suddenly end. The days would be different; everything would be different. The future lay unknown.

In bed at nights I tried to picture that world of the big upstairs; the echoing corridors, the vast classrooms, all that space I had never explored, all those hundreds and hundreds of girls, amongst whom I would be the least, the smallest, the most insignificant.

But, like dying, I knew, the time had to come. It came; and one day, trembling, I changed into gym shoes in the echoing cloakroom and walked, for the first time as a schoolgirl, up the stone stairs.

14

Big School

THERE were so many girls. Hundreds and thousands and millions of them, it seemed to me. Girls marching everywhere, waiting at strategic points along the corridors, stepping forward at a signal, halting at another signal. It reminded me, that first day, of the ants in the garden at home; a whole world of purposeful marching, with everything regulated to some mysterious end which I couldn't understand. Yes, it was just like the ants I used to watch at their comings and goings, spread-eagled on the summer lawn on a Sunday afternoon.

I marched with the rest, the smallest ant of all. When they asked me my name, I answered desperately with the old ritual that made me feel safe and wanted; Eileen Elias, 123 Waller Road, New Cross SE14, adding 'London' as an afterthought. They seemed surprised; the school was only just around the corner; but at any rate that was something to cling to in the frightening anonymity of my new world.

The girls, after the first few days of panic, began to take on form and intrigue me. I viewed them from afar, as you would view some strange race of natives in faraway jungle forests. They came in so many shapes and sizes. The biggest ones seemed hardly distinguishable from the teachers, in their blouses and serge skirts, their black stockings and their ties. When they got to the heights of the Sixth they put up their hair, and passed once for all out of the world of little girls into the world of young women. I used to long for the time, far distant, when I too would 'put up my hair', never imagining that fashions would change and the time wouldn't come.

As for the rest, they were a motley crowd; big, small, fat, thin, cheerful, sad, beautiful, plain — a world of bewildering variety passing me by like figures in a pageant. And I was part of the crowd; now that I had gone into school uniform, and Mother had turned me out, like all the rest, in an outfit of blue serge tunic and white blouse.

The uniform that we wore twice a week on 'drill days' was both exciting and alarming. Alarming, because the heavy blue serge 'drill' tunic was so different from the comfortable jersey I had worn, like all the other little girls, in the kindergarten; exciting because anything at all in the way of new clothes was a thrill to me. Clothes, after all, played a very big part in the business of being a little girl.

Mother made my tunics and blouses for 'drill days' on the little old black sewing machine she had used for all my dresses. The house, at weekends, would be full of the soft whirr of the sewing machine running up seams, gathering and tucking. It only did chain stitch, an inadequacy about which she would often warn us. If the sewing wasn't securely fastened off or if you pulled the end of an inviting thread, the whole seam would rip itself undone.

Once this had actually happened. Mother had made my brother a pair of long white sailor trousers to go with the white sailor top with its square collar, of which he was so proud. In church the next Sunday, fidgeting through the Vicar's interminable sermon, he pulled the end of a thread with each hand, and in moments the two long legs of his trousers were flapping helplessly. Mother, recalled from higher thoughts by his persistent tugging at her arm, looked down and saw the disaster. She spent the rest of the sermon-time trying to think how best to smuggle him out. Finally she managed to wait until most of the congregation had dispersed, under the excuse of looking beneath the pew for a lost glove, then wrapped her long skirts as fully as possible around her errant child and progressed, albeit rather slowly, out of church and home along the tree-lined streets. Their gait was something like the progression of a pantomime horse, with two pairs of legs getting entangled now and then, and my brother's flapping white trousers protruding beneath Mother's skirts of modest grey. It was an embarrassing scene.

Still it did teach us children not to

tamper with the seams on our home-made clothes. I used to watch with interest while Mother and Aunt Jane bought the fabric for my dresses at Jonesandhiggins, and particularly when they went to choose the navy blue serge for my very first school tunic. It was a great moment when I saw the length of it being spread out upon the dining-room table, and the paper pattern being pinned into place.

The pattern for the tunic looked deceptively simple; mostly a huge width of serge cut into an oblong and folded concertina wise into three enormous box pleats back and front. I thought I might even manage to do the cutting-out myself. Those scissors always tempted me. But whenever I suggested having a go, I was firmly discouraged. A friend of Mother's had recently recounted how her little girl, cutting out for her small brother an unauthorised pair of school trousers from a piece of stair-carpet ('I thought it would be hard-wearing, Mummy') had cut out the dining-room carpet as well, upon which the pattern had been laid, and left a permanent trouser-shape in front of the fireplace. Touching Mother's cutting-out scissors since then had become a heinous crime.

I watched while the serge was cut into. Snip, snap went the bright scissors, and soon the garment was being assembled on the table. The next part of the dressmaking process, though, wasn't so good. It was 'trying on'.

How I always hated 'trying on'! It entailed standing on the table in my stocking-feet, and keeping perfectly still like a statue while Mother stood on one side measuring, and Aunt Jane on the other, turning up the hem. It couldn't have been more than ten minutes at the outside, but to me the process seemed to go on for hours. Even on the day they tried on my school uniform, it was an agony. Outside the sun was shining brightly and all I wanted to do was to run out into the garden and climb the pear tree. The novelty of watching the serge tunic being cut out and the pleats pinned into place had worn off now; I wriggled and grumbled while pins stuck into me right and left and Aunt Jane complained because I wouldn't stand still.

Eventually the tunic was finished, and the blouse to go with it, and I tried the whole thing on in front of Mother's long mirror. It was impressive, but I didn't like what I saw. If this was Big School I was under a disadvantage from the first; for I was short and round, and the heavy tunic with its huge box-pleats hung on me, making me look shorter and rounder still. Around my waist I had to wear a coarsely-woven 'girdle' in some material which was scratchy to the touch. Only the white blouse looked becoming.

Still, this was what everybody else wore for 'drill days', uncomfortable as it was for gymnastics, and I did at least look the same as the others. One thing I could at least be thankful for; I was at last released from the agony of wearing my cousin's handed-down dresses, those hateful affairs from the Hampstead Garden Suburb.

It took me a day or two to settle down in my new classroom, a place of desks and ink-wells and blackboards, so different from the cosy child-sized chairs and low tables of kindergarten. Here you were expected to learn to write in ink, and only to use pencil for 'notes'; something that was new to me. The ink made great blots on the paper, the nibs 'crossed' at awkward moments, and my fingers were usually stained a dark blue by the end of the day. However, there was one joy about using ink. Two of us each week were deputed to be 'ink monitors', staying in the classroom during lunch-break and pouring ink from an enormous long spouted jug into the inkwells on the desks. This was great fun, and I longed for the day when it would be my turn to fill the ink-wells. When it came, it was not an unqualified success. I managed to tip too much ink into the inkwells, so that they overflowed like dark blue lakes and had to be hastily mopped up with a rag. I also got more ink on my fingers and clothes than went into the appropriate place, and was scolded for clumsiness. I was subdued and miserable. Handling those great cans with their long spouts had been a difficult operation, and it had never occurred to me that people would be cross in the Big School for something you couldn't do because you were too young and your fingers unskilled. I longed for the comfortable bosom of Miss Kemp, downstairs in the kindergarten. If this was Big School, I wasn't sure if I liked it.

Lessons were a mixed blessing. Gone were the days when we played blissfully with coloured beads, waved our arms like trees, and sang of 'Little brown seed, O little brown brother'. Now we were up against the hard world of sum books and satchels and homework. We had proper teachers, who never tired of reminding us that 'life is real, life is earnest'; and our school motto, we learnt, was 'Serve and Obey'; we were expected to do it. We spent a lot of time trying to gain 'marks', those mysterious things that appeared to matter so much, or 'ticks' or 'stars'. My books became covered with marks, occasionally ticks or stars, but far more often ugly blue crosses which meant someone was angry with me. The kind of marks I was supposed to get were the sort that did you credit — something they called 'ten out of ten'. It was all very bewildering. I felt I was trying to thread my way through a maze of knowledge, out of which I was expected to emerge at the other end with the answer they wanted. It was a precarious affair.

I didn't mind the English lessons, which came easily and filled my mind continually with fresh wonder and magic; or the history, or the geography, which did after all deal with real things and people and make sense. The lessons that filled my days with dread were the sewing lessons and the arithmetic.

Sewing was considered an essential part of our education, even if we were, as the prospectus had it, being prepared for careers as worthy as those of our brothers in the Haberdashers' Aske's Boys' School up the road. I couldn't make out why the girls had to learn to sew, whilst their brothers most certainly didn't. Who ever saw a boy mending his own socks, or heard of a man making his own suit? Yet we had all the ordinary lessons, and these terrible sewing lessons as well. It wasn't fair.

My fingers were all thumbs when it came to the sewing class. The nice clean white thread with which we were all provided became in five minutes grubby and dirty; the seams wouldn't go straight;

the stitches wouldn't keep the same size; and worst of all, it took me longer than anybody else to begin, for I could never thread the needle.

Time and again I watched other little girls stitching gaily away and earning smiles and approval, whilst I had not even got started. The harder I tried, screwing up my eyes to will the thread to go through, the longer the job would take.

'Haven't you started *yet*?' someone would say accusingly, and feeling an eagle eye upon me I would redouble my efforts with needle and thread, and my fingers, tenser than ever, would fail me altogether. The entire affair of the sewing lesson seemed to me infinitely ridiculous. I thought longingly of Mother running up dresses on her little old sewing machine, but nobody mentioned sewing machines here; you were expected to learn to sew by hand. It was part of your education.

We started with felt, and big stitches, and made penwipers and needlebooks for mothers, bookmarks for aunts and uncles, and 'hair tidies' that consisted of cardboard cones covered in felt, meant to hang on the corner of a dressingtable to hold pieces of hair that had 'come out' in the brushing. I thought this a horrid idea but everybody was busy making hair tidies, so I followed suit. Later we made handkerchiefs, hemmed and initialled, and embroidered handkerchief sachets like envelopes. But worse was to come. Soon we were promoted to the making of babies' clothes; and not only clothes, but patterns.

I struggled miserably week after week with pencil and squared paper, trying to make my own pattern for a baby's matinee coat. Why matinee, I wondered? Surely you didn't take a young baby to the theatre, and that was the only place I knew where they had things called matinees. Our patterns had to be copied onto the paper from a diagram marked in chalk on the blackboard. It was entirely incomprehensible to me; I couldn't count the requisite number of squares, and I couldn't draw the tidy curves and straight lines that the others did so easily, so that my drawing looked more like some crazy piece of patchwork than a respectable pattern

384

from which to cut a coat. Anyway, I thought, why can't they buy their patterns from Jonesandhiggins like my mother does? Just one more example of the mysterious ways of the grown-ups, who seemed bent upon making the simplest process more difficult.

My pattern never came out the same size as anybody else's, though I was assured that if I'd done my calculations right, it would. The teacher seemed more worried than I did about this; after all, I argued, babies came in all shapes and sizes, and if it didn't fit one baby, it would be sure to fit another. But again the grown-ups wouldn't listen to reason. I had to go over and over the exercise, till I produced something the right size.

I would do my best to use this pattern for the cutting out of a matinee coat in white flannel, and at the end of it all would feel quite sure that no self-respecting baby would ever be seen out in a thing like that. We did feather-stitching round the edges — blue for a boy and pink for a girl. All the others did neat rows of feather-stitching, but mine went in crazy curves round sleeves and neck, with the stitches never the same size. Tears would fill my eyes as I pushed the needle with the blue or pink thread in and out of the grubby bit of flannel; the thread had started such a lovely colour, and the flannel had been so white; now everything was a dirty grey. I privately decided that should I have any babies of my own, they would never wear matinee jackets designed and sewn by me. I would go straight to Jonesandhiggins and buy their outfits from the babywear department.

Even more of a torture than those dreadful sewing lessons were the arithmetic ones. I had quite enjoyed the days in kindergarten when we sorted matchsticks into little bundles and tied them up with elastic bands, or played with coloured counters at little tables. Up here in Big School arithmetic didn't seem to concern itself with sensible things you could see and handle, like matchsticks and counters; it was a matter of blackboard and chalk and sums, ticks and crosses in our books, and mysterious measurings with rulers, which were so much black magic to me.

I had even been quite happy with old friends like Tens and Units. Now there were things called Remainders and Carrying, and 'Goes-into' — so much mumbo-jumbo in my mind. 'Two goes-into Ten' and 'Three goes-into Nine' they chanted, and I had not the remotest idea of what was going into where. I saw marching numbers 'going into' lines, forming and re-forming like my brother's toy soldiers when he was marshalling them on the kitchen table, but why and how they went-into certain numbers and not into others, I couldn't imagine.

There was a dreadful thing on Monday mornings called 'Mental'. This maniac game — when anybody used the word at home, it did indeed signify the madhouse — consisted of short sharp-fire questions which we had to answer like the rattle of machine-guns, out of our heads.

My whole body used to tense up for 'Mental'. You never knew who would be picked to answer, and the pace was so fast. My head would spin and all thought would freeze up like water in a pond in wintertime. No sensible answer could ever be expected to come out. I was dumb.

'Nine twelves!' someone would shout, and round and round went the horrible figures in my head, making no sense but a jumble: nine twelves, nine twelves. I was so paralysed by fear that I couldn't open my mouth, let alone produce an answer.

Then there were the Problems. These came later, and when they came, they were the worst of the lot. They began in a promising way with baths filling or express trains running or people going on a walking tour; all quite probable and possible events, and interesting to think about. But just as your mind was pleasantly filled with an image of the nice homely bathroom on a Friday night, with the taps running and Mother ready with a warmed towel, you would find that water was going into the bath at the same time as it was flowing out through the plug-hole or through some mysterious hole which nobody had noticed, and be asked to calculate the number of gallons a minute which were going in, or out, or something else equally ridiculous. Who in their right minds, I would think, would try to fill a bath when the water was pouring out, or having done so, would stop to do calculations instead of running for help? Just another example of the strange ways of the grown-ups.

And there were the express trains, those thunderous engines that roared along at so many miles an hour to destinations A, B or C. The very thought of an express train rushing along brought back my early panic about going under a railway arch or standing on a station platform; and my mind was too befogged with fear to begin to work out the sum.

Then there were the walkers, those strenuously active people who spent their lives tramping from one place to the other at one rate, while their counterparts tramped from another place to somewhere else at a different rate. They didn't seem concerned about getting anywhere, but only about comparing their different speeds per hour. Or even more foolishly, I thought, they would set out to walk towards each other at different rates. Why they had to walk so far and so often, I couldn't make out; or why they should choose to walk in opposite directions and get so concerned about where they were likely to meet each other. I could readily understand the necessity for walking; probably, like ourselves, they couldn't afford to take the tram to somewhere like Jonesandhiggins. But they were so anxious to calculate their positions all the time, and so taken up with the rate per hour. What a lot of sights they must miss, I would think, plodding along like that with numbers and times revolving about inside their heads, instead of looking at the scenery. It seemed such a waste.

The rooms to be papered, at so much a roll, missing out so much for windows and so much for doors, filled me with sheer panic. I was sure I would never be able to undertake such a thing as papering our kitchen at home if I had to go through all these preliminaries first. If only they would set about it the sensible way, buying some wallpaper and sticking it on, and running out to buy some more when the supply failed. Surely that would be simpler?

As for the eternal Mr A, Mr B and Mr C, who were continually deciding to set up in business together, dividing out their capital, buying and selling, and generally making nuisances of themselves, I pictured them as something in the City; bowler-hatted and twirling furled umbrellas, and carrying little black bags like the Gladstone bag that Father had at home. I would get so carried away imagining these three gentlemen (there were always just three and no more) transacting their business in the City that I would be quite surprised when somebody interrupted my dreams to ask sharply some question about the amount of money Mr A had put into the business, or Mr B had taken out of it, or Mr C decided to invest. I didn't in any case understand what the word 'invest' meant; except that it might have something to do with the vests I was always trying to persuade Mother to buy instead of combinations. Did Mr C really walk about the City in his vest? All these speculations were so interesting that I was brought sadly down to earth when someone demanded an answer and I had none. Then they would ask me, trying to keep the impatience out of their voices, what it was I didn't understand.

Since what I didn't understand embraced just about everything we had been told throughout the lesson, I couldn't make any reply at all, and was scolded for wasting the teacher's time.

'If you can't even tell me what it is that you don't understand, then I can't help you,' would come the answer; leaving me in despair so absolute that it seemed there was no hope of my ever learning arithmetic at all.

We were frequently reminded that all we were learning now in mathematics would be immense material benefit to us when we grew up. 'How will all you girls ever manage a house and home', the teacher would say accusingly, 'if you don't know how to calculate?'

I was quite sure that the duties of a house and home wouldn't include anything like the knowledge we had been painfully trying to acquire over the term. We would all manage perfectly well without knowing any arithmetic at all. After all, who would be so silly as to run the children's bath without first putting in the plug? Household shopping just meant running round to Mr Smith's the grocer's; kind Miss Hobbs would, I am sure, add all my bills up for me in her usual comforting way, and I knew she wouldn't cheat. And if I couldn't marry a man rich enough to afford a decorator to do his papering for him, or at least calculate how much paper he would need for the job, then I wouldn't marry at all. Altogether I found the grown-ups had the oddest ideas about what was going to be useful to you in your future life as wife and mother.

Another subject was soon added to our syllabus, and another enormous room in the school opened up to us, terrifying in its proportions. This was the gym. Gymnastics — strange word, I thought, having no idea what it meant — were to take place twice a week, on Tuesdays and Fridays. We were all to come to school in our 'drill' dresses on those days, and troop along the corridor downstairs to the gym.

The gym was enormous. I stood, my first morning, by the open door and caught my breath at the sheer size of it. It seemed to stretch away for ever, and rise to immeasurable heights above my eight-year-old head. It looked even bigger than the school hall; for the hall was filled with familiar-looking forms, and this was just a bare space, seemingly acres upon acres of naked floor upon which we walked nervously in gym shoes, feeling as antlike as we had on that first day in the Big School.

There were strange things ranged round the walls and hanging from the beams overhead, which resembled nothing so much as instruments of torture, and I wondered whatever we were expected to do with them. Along one wall was a row of wooden rails, called, I was to learn, 'the ribs' — which suggested the bones of some prehistoric monster. On this we were to climb and hang, like mountaineers suspended on a precipice, but without the comfort of a rope for safety. Then there were mysterious square things called 'windows', suspended in mid-air, through which we had to wriggle and squirm like monkeys in a cage. There were parallel bars which let down on a pulley, and had to be swung along by the hands — again like monkeys. There were forms which were inverted on the floor, so that you had to walk gingerly along them, balancing on a two-inch wide bar. And there was a 'horse' over which you vaulted, or tried to, flying through the air onto a prickly mat on the further side. I could do none of these things, and at every turn I seemed destined to suffer like the victims of the torture-chamber I was imagining in my mind.

When we weren't doing exercises on what they called 'the apparatus' we were marching round the gym in long lines, or standing one behind the other and 'numbering off'. This, like mental arithmetic, took place at such a machine-gun fire pace that I could never answer quickly enough, and was scolded for my slowness. How we stood, apparently, was of great importance, and the gym teacher would come along the lines, prodding out a chest here, prodding in a stomach there, till we stood like pouter pigeons too scared to move. I was sure this was a most unnatural position, and longed to be free and lithe, climbing the pear-tree in the garden or running on the grass in the Park — anything but standing like this, wooden and paralysed, being prodded by a grown-up finger in all the most uncomfortable places. If this was how you were supposed to stand for 'poise' and 'health', as they kept telling us, I would rather not be poised or healthy at all.

Sometimes they would make us play a game to sharpen up our wits and exercise our limbs; 'general alertness' it was called. It terrified me. We would stand in a circle, whilst someone stood in the middle, wielding a long rope like an instrument of torture, with a bean-bag attached to the end. The bean-bag whipped round the circle at enormous speed, aimed at your toes, and you had to jump smartly when it came at you, to avoid a sharp rap on the foot. As with the 'numbering off', anything that required speed paralysed me completely, and I would retreat from this fearful game with a throbbing foot and a sense of utter desolation. 'Drill' seemed designed to do nothing but personally hurt and humiliate me. What made it all worse was that most of the other little girls seemed to be enjoying it, and I was almost the only one to find it difficult. They swarmed up the 'ribs', wriggled in and out of the 'windows', swung on the bars, and vaulted the horse with ease and agility, and were rewarded with smiles and encouragement, while I was left, lumpy and miserable, in my serge gym tunic, standing on the sidelines and trying not to cry.

The only thing I found I could succeed at was the ropes. Climbing the ropes came naturally to me, and as soon as I saw them being let down by pulley from the roof I would forget my misery in the joy of finding something I could do, at least reasonably well. I would imagine myself climbing the old peartree at home, wriggling my way up with elbows and knees, waiting to catch that glorious view of the whole world from the top. The view in the gym wasn't anything like as interesting as the view at home, but nevertheless, up there at the top, away from the crowd, I could feel joy in my own strength like a bird in the sky. At last, blessed relief there was something I could do. It was exhilarating, and I loved it. But 'ropes' didn't come very

often in our drill lessons; so for most of
the weeks in the term I was left miserable
and awkward, trying hopelessly to follow
the others in strange contortions which
to me seemed to have no meaning at all.
It was a relief on Saturdays, to get away
to the Park to enjoy the strength and
vitality of my own limbs; to run down
the hillsides, balance on the railings by
the Pond, swarm up trees and feel the
sun and the fresh air on my body. It was
all so different from 'drill'.

15

'The Extras'

LESSONS were fairly wide-ranging at the Aske's Girls' School, but there were certain 'extras' which most of us coveted. Some were free; for others you paid. Swimming was an 'extra' for which you had to get your parents' consent, but it cost only four pence a week, so when I was eight, along I went with the others — a troop of little girls clutching their 'swimming things' in mackintosh bags.

The local Baths at Laurie Grove were within walking distance of our school. They were huge ugly buildings, with forbidding marble portals, through which we went, in an orderly queue, sniffing the peculiar smell of chlorine. I was wary of the Baths. I didn't like the muffled shouting and screaming that you heard on the way to the changing cubicles; I didn't like the claustrophobic feeling of undressing on slippery wet duckboards in a little wooden cubicle with curtains over a stable-door; most of all I didn't like the first moment of coming out onto the tiled verge and catching a glimpse of all that expanse of water below, grey-green and faintly rippling, and cold, cold, cold like the North Sea.

'Come on in, it's warm!' someone would cry; but it didn't feel warm as you stood on the side, divested of Liberty bodice and knickers, clad in a red twill bathing suit, with short sleeves, hair hitched up under a floppy white bathing-cap that smelled, like the water, of chlorine.

It didn't feel warm when you stood shivering on the wet tiles, being bombarded with cold spray from the bathers; and it certainly felt icy cold as you stepped gingerly in from the shallow end, watching the black and white wavy lines glimmering up from the bottom, and holding onto the brass rail as the water came higher and higher up your legs, step by slippery step.

The shallow end came just about up to my chest, and I stood there miserably, while children jumped and splashed and shouted around me, wondering what to do next. There was, of all people, Miss Bradfield from the kindergarten, already in the water amongst us non-swimmers. A great wave of nostalgia for the kindergarten filled me, and I wanted to be back again with her and dear Miss Kemp, as I had so often wanted to be, these last few terms. I waded to her side, and was filled with amazement at her garb: a long black outfit with legs like combinations, sleeves reaching demurely to her elbows, and a pair of long black stockings which, in the green water, appeared to wiggle like black worms as she moved soundlessly about in the shallow end. Even to my eyes the dress looked incredibly old-fashioned. But Miss Bradfield valued her modesty; on the days she helped in the Big School with the swimming lessons, nothing would induce her to dress like the other swimming teachers in a short red twill bathing suit.

'Over to me!' she called, and over I went, to have a noose-like harness of wet leather slipped over head and shoulders, and be pulled by a rope towards the side, where another teacher was waiting with words of encouragement.

I clung to dear Miss Bradfield's black-sleeved arm, but nothing, not even the memory of kindergarten could save me now. I waited for the pull on the rope; then my legs silently slid from under me and I was suspended, flailing madly, on top of the water swallowing great gulps of it in panic. Now I was pulled taut against the rail at the side of the bath, scrabbling for a foothold on the slippery bottom, and spouting water like a whale. The face above me didn't look too pleased with my prowess, and I was made to wade back again and repeat the process. More chokes and struggles; was this the way you learned to swim? When it came for another child's turn on the wretched rope, I escaped from the horrid sight of Miss Bradfield with her black bathing suit and wobbly black legs, like a huge wet spider in the water; this couldn't be the Miss Bradfield I knew. I climbed the steps and sat on the edge, teeth chattering, arms clasped across my chest to keep warm. Were they really enjoying it, all those girls splashing each other at the deep end, flailing through water with graceful movements, kicking fountains of spray as they back-stroked happily like young seals?

Some of them, I noticed, were actually trying that monstrous invention at the deep end — the chute. This was a wooden contraption to which you climbed up twisted steps, to spread yourself at the top and shoot downwards with a splash into the water. It looked horrifying to me, and I prayed I would never have to dare it. It was nearly as bad as the diving-board, which, suspended above the deep end, dipped and swayed as swimmer after swimmer bounced off it and sank into the green glassy depths, from which I was quite sure they wouldn't emerge. But emerge they did, laughing and triumphant, to swim the length of the bath, cheered on by girls and teachers, and climb out at the shallow end, pushing me where I sat dangling chilly legs in the water. Would I ever, I wondered, learn to swim?

I did in the end; but it took a long time.

Another 'extra' we were allowed when we were eight was the dancing class after school, which cost half a guinea a term. This was a great moment; something to look forward to for a whole term beforehand, provided you had managed to persuade your parents to pay for it. I still don't know how they did it; they were hard put to find the £2. 9s. which they paid for normal tuition, but my parents somehow scraped up the extra fee, and on the first morning of the dancing class I was able to come skipping into the school cloakroom and chant with the rest of the lucky little girls — '*I*'m going to dancing class! *I*'m going to dancing class!' It was the first time I had ever felt the joy of scoring off other children, and I was going to savour it to the full. It was wonderful to be doing something that was special.

At intervals, all that day, I twirled around the classroom in my navy-blue tunic, showing yards of navy bloomer, and doing highkicks towards the ceiling. All the other children stood around envious, as we, the chosen few, rubbed in our superiority. At last someone gave me a sharp pinch on the arm which brought me to my senses and made me stop my twirling for the moment; but inside I was still bubbling with happiness. Was not my dancing outfit safely stowed away down there in the cloakroom, just waiting for four o'clock?

The dancing outfit consisted of a green cotton tunic, with a full skirt coming well above the knee, green cotton knickers to match — it wouldn't do to show your knickers if they didn't match — and a pair of bronze dancing shoes which fastened with crossed elastic over the ankles. I was entranced with them. Mother had made the tunic and knickers on the sewing machine, and these were exciting enough, but to go to Jonesandhiggins and buy a pair of dancing shoes as well was the height of bliss. More times than I could remember, this past week, I had donned the shoes and pranced before Mother's long mirror, twirling and whirling till the skirt flew up waist-high in a halo round my middle. I slept with the shoes on the chair beside me, so that I could wake up in the morning and feel the softness of the bronze leather, the suppleness of the soles, and the delicacy of the tiny metal rose that adorned the toe. I had never had any shoes as grand as these before. Wearing them, you could forget you ever had buttonboots, and trip, light as a feather, round the room like a miniature ballerina. In fact I had serious thoughts about becoming a ballerina in future.

Hitherto, when I thought about the future, which wasn't often, I had imagined myself as a vet, caring for sick animals, or just possibly — on Sundays mostly — a lady clergyman. Both careers seemed to me eminently suitable. A Florence Nightingale of the animal creation; what could be nobler than that? Except, of course, being a lady clergyman and delivering sermons, clothed in white, from the pulpit at St Mary's.

But today, being a ballerina seemed at least a viable alternative. You only had to learn to dance; that was easy. Then off you went, pirouetting and swirling and whirling and drifting, on the stage with the spotlight upon you, and the sighs of an admiring audience following every movement. In addition, I would score off all those of my teachers and fellow-pupils who had ever thought badly of me in sewing lessons, swimming lessons, arithmetic lessons. I'd had the talent, the wonderful talent, all the time, and nobody had ever guessed. Now they would all be put to shame and I would graciously forgive them and offer them presentation tickets for my next performance. My thoughts ran ahead as the classroom clock ticked on towards a quarter to four, and we raced down to the Dining Hall where, for the dancing pupils, places had been laid out on the scrubbed wooden table with bread and jam and currant buns to stave off hunger.

We little girls sank into our chairs and started gaily on the bread and jam. The school cooks made weak tea for us and handed it round in thick white china cups which we downed gratefully. We didn't feel quite so light and fairylike by the time we had eaten two thick currant buns apiece, but no doubt that feeling of fullness would go, once we got onto the dance floor. We had changed into our beautiful green tunics and were eager to go upstairs again, into the Big Hall where the classes were held, and start our pirouetting in earnest. But the buns did lie heavy.

Miss Perrett, our new dancing mistress, who had been specially engaged for the class, was standing at the top of the stairs looking us over as we came up, in our green tunics and bronze dancing shoes. We must have looked a pretty sorry lot to her; round and fat, dumpy-legged and freckled, but each of us was sure of being a budding Pavlova. Apart from Tina, who was blonde and fairy-like, there was nobody in the class who looked anything like a dancer. Most of us were decidedly heavy on the feet.

Nevertheless, we were told smilingly to go and sit on the chairs at the back of the hall, while Miss Perrett sorted us all out. The hall looked different, somehow, with the forms stacked away, and the great space of the floor waiting to be danced upon. Miss Peskett, who was the school secretary, and usually stamped envelopes and returned lost plimsolls, was seated at the piano — much to our surprise — with hands poised above the keys.

Nobody knew she could play at all, and her stock immediately rose. We eyed each other in our green dancing tunics, pirouetted around on one leg, and fidgeted with our skirts. When would the dancing begin? I could hardly wait.

At length it was really dancing time. We gazed at our new teacher in awe. She was much the most sophisticated person we had ever seen, with a lissom figure clothed in total black, and patent leather shoes with Louis heels, like the fashion plates. Her hair, which was blonde and smooth, was piled up on top of her head in a style never seen amongst our ordinary teachers. Her voice, when she spoke, was tuneful in the extreme. We were impressed.

'Now I want all you little girls to form up in a row. That's right. Next, when the music starts, you are all to begin walking round the hall. As beautifully as you can — understand? *Really* beautifully.' My heart swelled; I was determined to make my walk the most beautiful she had ever seen. 'Hold your heads high and point your toes — like this — ' and Miss Perrett imitated a mincing gait which I had never tried in my life, but which I was determined to master, or die in the attempt. Miss Perrett would soon see what an exceptional pupil she had in me. Better by far than the odious Tina.

Off we went, to stirring music from Miss Peskett at the piano. Round and round we paced, holding our heads as high as royalty, pointing our toes in their bronze dancing shoes in the daintiest of poses. *Now* she's going to look at me, I told myself; *now* she's going to single me out as the best. The most beautiful dancer in the whole hall.

Then a waving hand went up in the air. 'Please may I leave the room?' It was Tina, the little blonde, just ahead of me. Miss Perrett's thin eyebrows lifted, and the faintest trace of annoyance passed over her features. 'Well, if you must, dear — ' she offered.

Two minutes later, just as I was trying again, and certain that this time she would notice me, there was another hand waving in the air. 'Please may I leave the room?' The eyebrows went a shade higher, but such a request, politely made, could scarcely be refused. It was another death-blow to my hopes; how could I launch myself on the inspiring career of dancing if people kept asking to leave the room?

It was at the third time of asking that Miss Perrett's patience snapped. 'Really, children, couldn't you have thought of all this before?'

The hand that had been waving in the air was hesitantly dropped, and its owner, abashed, fell out of line and began screwing up her eyes and twisting her knees in agony. Soon nearly everybody in the class was doing the same; the complaint was infectious, and even I wasn't immune.

Miss Perrett signalled to the pianist to stop playing. 'We can't have this, you know. Why didn't you all take the opportunity of — er — going, before class began?'

We looked at each other miserably. It was all that weak tea that the kitchen staff had given us to accompany our currant buns.

'Well.' Miss Perrett looked anything but pleased. 'You'd better put an end to all this nonsense by going down to the cloakroom, the whole lot of you. And please be *Quick*!' She snapped out the word as the mass exodus began. We flew out of the hall and returned as fast as we could; but for me the magic spell had been broken. I had been waiting, in a rapt world of my own, for recognition of my talent as a dancer. Now, nature had supervened, and here we all were scrambling up and down to the cloakroom, and Miss Perrett was cross. My spirits began to sink.

When order was restored, Miss Perrett began to put us through a series of movements which I tried, not very successfully, to follow. They seemed to consist of commands to do something which sounded like 'chassy to the left' and 'chassy to the right,' involving much sliding about on the well-polished floor. If this was dancing, it wasn't very creative, I thought. The waving hands and mass exodus to the cloakroom had taken most of the romance out of it, and now it simply meant doing exercises like those we did in drill.

But things got better, when Miss Perrett smartly divided us into two groups, the Elves and the Fairies. This was something like it, I told myself; this was going to be truly imaginative dancing, and I would get my chance to shine after all. We'd done Elves and Fairies in the kindergarten, and I knew exactly how to sway around with wings and hop behind imaginary toadstools and all the rest. Now she would see what stuff I was really made of.

'You.' She pointed a decisive finger at me. 'You can be a Wood Fairy.'

A Wood Fairy. Wonderful! Soon I was skipping round with the rest of the Wood Fairies, 'interpreting', as Miss Perrett put it, the music coming from Miss Peskett's vigorous piano behind us. I interpreted as hard as I could. I swayed and writhed, dipped and circled in wild fantasy. If I was going to be a Wood Fairy, I would do it with all my might and main. It wasn't till I kept bumping into other children circling in a completely opposite direction that it occurred to me that perhaps we were all supposed to be doing our interpreting together, in one long sinuous movement instead of prancing all over the place as the fancy took us.

413

Miss Perrett was advancing ominously in my direction. 'You,' she said. 'You over there. You're distracting all the other Wood Fairies. You'd better come over here and be one of the Elves instead.'

I came out reluctantly, blushing with shame. To be singled out was bad enough; to be seen as disruptive instead of talented. But to be an Elf all you could do to the music was to crouch behind your toadstool.

The dancing lesson dragged to an end; by this time most of us were breathless, our green tunics were sagging, the thin elastic of our bronze dancing shoes was cutting unkindly into our ankles, and to be a dancer no longer seemed the very top of my ambition. When at last it was time to go home, and Miss Perrett bade us curtsey as she dismissed us, dancing had lost its magic. It was simply another of the things I couldn't do.

Miss Perrett smiled us goodbye, trying to be encouraging, whilst Tina, whom she had praised, smirked in the background. 'Next time,' Miss Perrett said as we trooped downstairs, 'try and remember to "go" before you come into the class, will you?'

The hall was empty now. Miss Peskett was already stacking her music together on top of the piano, and the cleaners were waiting with brushes and brooms and wooden boxes of sawdust to scatter on the floor before sweeping. It was the end of the dancing class; and the end of my dreams.

Nobody, I was sure, ever reminded Pavlova to 'go' before she went on the stage.

Walking home, trying to put a brave face on it so that Mother shouldn't see I was disappointed, I took stock of the situation. It was navy-blue serge for me now; not green cotton and bronze dancing shoes. I'd never make a ballerina. Still, perhaps there were compensations, even if I had to settle for being a vet or a lady clergyman after all.

There was one day in the year, however, on which all these troubles melted, and I was glad I went to school. It was Prize Day — the one day of the year on which everything always went right. It didn't matter if you didn't have a prize, either; this was a day of bounty, a day of special dispensation, and every child in the school was caught up in it somehow. It gleamed like a jewel in the calendar of our school days, somewhere around the second week in October, when the leaves were turning gold and the first fires were being lit and there was a crispness in the air. Prize Day was coming.

On the great day, the whole school took on a gala atmosphere. Early in the morning, before we little ones were even awake, the senior girls — the ones with their hair up — had been, greatly daring, to Covent Garden market and brought back box after wonderful box of our token school flower, the red rose. Red roses were the symbol to us of Prize Day; every child in the school, from the highest to the lowest, wore one pinned to her dress. Every child, too, wore a white frock on this day of days; of course we wore white, for it was a special day like Sunday.

In our clean white dresses, with the dewy red roses smelling faintly beneath our chins as we walked up the stone steps to the Big Hall, we felt different children altogether; blessed ones, lucky ones. No matter if we couldn't do sums or sew matinee jackets or swim; we were all lucky, all sharing in the sense of exhilaration that came from Prize Day when the whole community, teachers, parents, girls, got together in rejoicing. If I had been excited before entering the Big Hall, I was doubly so when we got inside, as I caught my first glimpse of it, packed with visitors, massed with bronze and yellow chrysanthemums, purple Michaelmas daisies, and sprays of shining beech leaves, which everyone had worked for hours to arrange.

It was all so different from the everyday school hall that it felt like walking into fairyland. There on the platform were the Governors — I wasn't too sure what Governors were, but they were always there on Prize Day — headed by the bearded and venerable Chairman, who told us every year without fail that 'Education is a drawing-out and not a putting-in'. There, in unaccustomed glory of black gown and brilliant university hood, were our staff unrecognisable, till at last you sighted the familiar personalities behind the scarlet or yellow silk and the black drapery.

Voices rang up to the rafters with the school hymn, practised again and again over the previous weeks: 'Praise my soul, the king of Hea-ven'. How we sang! Speakers droned on and on, while we gazed at the stained-glass window behind their heads, bearing in colours like jewels the arms of the school; girls in white frocks tripped onto the platform to receive their piles of books tied with red ribbon, and tripped down again to applause. I listened and watched, not minding that I hadn't got a prize; I was mesmerised by what they were telling me. That we were the pupils of the best school in the world, that this was the most wonderful age ever to be born into, that these were the happiest years of our lives, that we were privileged to receive the same education as our brothers at last. I marched out with the rest, at the end of it all, feeling exalted, almost too good to live. It was the climax to the whole of your school life, when you walked out through the bowers of chrysanthemums and potted palms, in your white dress, the red rose still faintly fragrant against your shoulder. All those struggles with Subject and Object, all that mumbo-jumbo of ten-sixty-six, all those pricks with the sewing needle, even the crazy antics of Mr A and Mr B and Mr C, and the water pouring madly into the bath and as madly out of the plug-hole — all were worth it on that day of days. In your white frock you felt only a little lower than the angels.

School Prize Days started me thinking about the world and its possibilities. We heard so much on Prize Day about the future which lay before us all, like the blank pages of a book on which anything might be written. It was a thrilling prospect, but also a trifle alarming. In the days after Prize Day I began to be troubled by thoughts of the future.

'What are you going to be when you're grown up?' was a question we were always being asked by visiting aunts and uncles. At four I had already been attracted by literature, and was surprised at the amused glances from the grown-ups when I answered 'A book-maker'. It seemed a reasonable enough ambition to me. The making of books certainly sounded attractive, but there were so many other things you could do in the world besides write books. I considered them one by one.

My brother was expected to become a doctor like Father; there was no doubt about that. What the family wanted of me I wasn't quite sure. I could teach, like Aunt Jane, but somehow that didn't sound very exciting. There must be some more romantic way of using up those glorious empty years ahead.

I used to think about them, on hot summer afternoons after school, squatting in the long grass under the gooseberry bushes, the hairy fruit hanging above me in appetising globes, with tight skins stretched to bursting, green and yellow and amber. The gooseberry bushes had a smell all their own, a tart tang which was somehow conducive to thought. Besides, nobody could see you here, so you didn't get interrupted. Nobody cut into important affairs of the mind by asking you to 'run round to Mr Smith's' for mundane things like half a pound of butter or a bar of Sunlight soap. I would idly reach up a hand, and picking the most luscious of the berries, bite slowly till the cool juice ran down my chin, and meditate about the future.

The obvious thing to do seemed to become a poet. Poetry was much the most exhilarating of the many things we learned at school; and besides it was so easy to write. You shut your eyes and the poems just came. I had already written dozens of poems, both in my mind and on bits of paper. One of them, about Scotland, I considered especially grand. It began:

The lofty crags of Scotland
Rise towering to the sky.

'Sky' was an easy word to find rhymes for, fortunately; so from the first the going was good. It was different when you got landed with a word like 'bird', for which there were only about four rhymes, and when you had exhausted the possibilities of 'heard' and 'third' and 'word' you had to fall back on 'absurd', which sounded all wrong.

I had never been to Scotland, and the

nearest I had ever got to seeing a lofty crag was looking at a picture postcard of Beachy Head, which you could hardly call a mountain; but never mind, you only had to add a few hundred feet onto Beachy Head and there you were with something recognisably like Ben Nevis. Anyway, Scotland was a good subject to write a poem about, I reflected. The sort of adjectives I had heard applied to it were 'grand', 'majestic', 'lonely' — all mysterious words with mysterious implications, worthy of poetry.

'Lofty', I thought, was a particularly noble word, and I was glad I had used it in my poem; it sounded so much better than 'high', just as 'crags' sounded worlds better than mere 'mountains'. I was very pleased, too, about 'towering'; that certainly was a word fit for a poet.

In fact, that was precisely what made writing poetry so wonderful; you could travel out of this world altogether and use magnificent remote words that nobody would dream of using in the yellow-brick suburb where we lived. Yes, it was a good thing to be a poet; so long, that is, as nobody called you a poetess, which had a slightly pejorative ring, as though a woman poet could never be quite as good as a man.

Could you make money out of poetry, I wondered? Well, Shakespeare and Milton obviously had; look at all the copies of their books in the school library, though what became of all the money after the poets died I could never imagine. Longfellow must have made millions out of his 'Hiawatha', for every child along our road learned Hiawatha at school, and acted it in end-of-term plays for proud parents to watch. That must mean hundreds and hundreds of copies of Hiawatha sold to schools all over the world, and think what that would bring the author so long as he wasn't dead. I was not quite sure whether Longfellow was dead or not, but if he was alive, surely he must be a millionaire by this time.

It was easy to be as good as Shakespeare and Longfellow, I told myself, chewing another gooseberry. You didn't even have to make the words rhyme at the end of the lines, which everybody knew was the most difficult thing about poetry. Privately I thought

Shakespeare and Longfellow had won their reputations somewhat irregularly, if they hadn't even had to put themselves out to write stuff that rhymed.

Of course I could be an artist instead. Art sounded mysterious and exciting as an occupation, and I loved art at school. We went upstairs to a large airy studio right at the top of the building, looking out over rooftops, and painted and splashed away, mixing glorious colours and letting them run down the white sheets of paper till they somehow turned themselves into ideas. Yes, art was good, and an artist would be a fine thing to be.

When you thought of an artist, you imagined him — only it would be her, of course — different from other people. Men artists had beards and wore smocks. I wondered about the lady ones; you could scarcely grow a beard if you were a lady; and smocks well, we wore them as children, so it wouldn't be much of a change to go on wearing them once you were grown-up.

I had been taken to visit an artist once. He was a real artist, and had had pictures hung in the Royal Academy, whatever that was; one of them actually adorned the wall of our dining-room, above the green plush couch, and we thought it was beautiful. It showed a waterfall splashing over a high cliff with lots of shadowy trees in dark greens and greys, and a heavy bronze-coloured sky. Rather peculiar for a sky, I always thought; we did our skies at school the most brilliant blue in the paintbox, and everyone knew they weren't yellow; but perhaps real artists saw them differently. Anyway the picture was worth a lot of money, my parents told me, and one day they actually took me to see the artist himself. He lived in a gloomy Victorian house with many dark passages and no garden, just a courtyard outside, which I thought very poor living compared with our suburban greenery.

There had been oil paints and palettes, long brushes stuck in tall jars, bits of rag covered with blotches of colour, canvases stacked against walls, and lengths of glowing velvet and satin draped over chairs. I was overcome by the grandeur of it all, and brought home a confused impression of colour and muddle.

But what a wonderful life to lead! Nothing to do but paint all day, and not mind whether it got on to your clothes, and arrange things like jugs of marigolds and plates of silvery herrings and tables spread with vivid cloths, and paint them all as 'Still Life'. Or better even than that, take your easel and spend whole days in the country — the real country, not the Park — painting and painting till the colours swam before you. It was all very well to write about the lofty crags of Scotland, but if I became an artist I could actually go and visit them and paint them too. It was an artist's life for me.

Or what about being a musician? I had lately started proper piano lessons on the old upright piano in the dining-room, and once I got used to the slippery black American cloth of the piano stool and could keep from sliding off it, music seemed to me a good profession.

All the little girls at school compared notes about the pieces they played. Everybody learned Czerny's exercises; we didn't much care for them, but there were plenty of others which would do for concert pieces if I became a musician.

'What are you learning?' someone had asked me; and when I told them 'Scenes at the Farm' they had retorted that 'Woodland Melodies' was much better, *and* it went into flats too. Pieces that went into flats could certainly be used on a concert platform, I thought. Anybody could make a living from playing those, and how exciting to have an audience that really listened, instead of scuffling and eating sweets surreptitiously, as our child audiences did when we played our pieces at parties, or talking about their rheumatism, as the grown-ups did when they asked us to 'play something nice' for them and then went on with their interminable conversations. Perhaps I could learn the violin, like my brother, who went to weekly lessons with a Mr Valentine Hemery, at half a guinea a term. 'Mr Valentine Hemery' sounded a lovely name, and surely he could teach me enough to go on a concert platform.

Gradually, however, my ambitions underwent a subtle change. It was all very well being a poet or a painter or a musician; but these were very lonely occupations, things you did by yourself all day. As I grew older and more sociable, it became increasingly important to do things with other people, or at least other creatures. At one time I was obsessed with the idea of caring for animals, being a vet. Healing sick animals seemed the most noble and rewarding of all careers. How invaluable you would be to the pet-loving community, how beloved of all creatures great and small, rather like Saint Francis, only with a surgery attached.

Our own pet family consisted of a dog, old Gelert; a cat, or rather cats, for the cat population seemed to change from year to year; and some guinea-pigs, which my brother kept in a hutch outside the kitchen door. But of course you could learn how to care for any animal, not just the ordinary ones. I imagined myself binding up the broken limbs of rabbits, bandaging poor grateful-eyed dogs, putting match-stick splints on canaries, so that they could turn from broken limping things to creatures of joy. These were all pretty small, to be sure; but I could easily graduate to horses, if only I could persuade the milkman to let me practise on his, which always stopped at our door for a lump of sugar in the mornings, hauling the cart with its clanking milk cans and ladies.

I mentioned my veterinary ambitions to Mother one morning, whilst helping her to make the beds. I half expected to be met with disapproval: it wasn't very often that the grown-ups' ideas coincided with ours, and it was perhaps flying in the face of Providence to let them in on our secret thoughts. But this thought was such an exciting one that I was bursting to share it with someone.

'I'm going to be a vet,' I told her. 'People for miles around are going to bring me their sick animals for me to heal.'

To my relief she took the news quite calmly. She even suggested that I could tie a bit of white tape round my arm, and using her John Bond's marking ink with the special little nib attached, designate myself on the tape 'Animal Doctor' and wait for custom. (Grown-ups could be surprisingly co-operative at times.) It was a grand idea. I hastened to find some tape in the workbox, and the marking ink, then sewed the two ends of the tape carefully together, proudly put on my official armlet, and established myself on an upturned sugar box in the garden to wait for the sick animals to come and be cured.

I had to wait a long time. During the day I managed to capture the family cat, and after examining it meticulously for thorns or battle-scars or even burrs — for want of a better ailment to treat — had to let it go. But the horses, the donkeys, the monkeys just didn't come. Not even a sick canary flew my way. At length the next-door dog came in sight, and I at once took a firm grasp of his collar, hoping to find some symptoms of disease. But I received a bite so sharp that my enthusiasm for being a vet was severely damped, and I ran indoors complaining. Somebody else, I decided, could treat the sick animals if that was how they were going to behave.

It wasn't long before I turned to something more spiritual — in fact, towards the Cloth. Lady clergymen had been in the news lately; especially one very famous lady minister who happened to be remotely known to my family and was the subject of a good deal of conversation over the teacups. What one woman had done, I decided, another could do; and the profession had a great deal to recommend it.

Upstairs in the privacy of the bedroom I put on my white nightgown over my cotton frock, and going down, nearly tripping over its folds, surveyed myself in Mother's long mirror. The effect was quite impressive.

How good to stand in the pulpit at St Mary's on a Sunday, with the whole congregation hushed and still, waiting upon your words — except, of course, the younger choirboys; I knew only too well what they got up to as soon as the preacher mounted the pulpit and had his back to them. I imagined the silence, the expectancy all round; all those important ladies and gentlemen in the front pews — the expensive ones — listening to me; the portly sidesman with the bald head; the Scouts every fourth Sunday; all reverently hanging upon my words. I would clear my throat and begin . . .

Certainly it would be a fine thing to

be a clergyman, much better than being a vet, and I was puzzled that so few ladies had been fired with this ambition before. To me it seemed the most noble of all callings, and for a long time I cherished the idea in private. I even composed a sermon or two.

Then, when I was twelve, a new curate came to our parish, and I fell in love with him. Being a lady clergyman didn't seem half as wonderful as being a clergyman's wife and opening all the Church Bazaars.

But that was much later. Now it was summer, serene and bright; the gooseberries fell deliciously into my mouth; the golden years stretched end-lessly ahead; and there was plenty of time to decide about the future, this year, next year, some time — never . . . .

16

Saturday Night

SCHOOL ended for the week at half-past three on Friday afternoons, and the glorious weekend began. Saturday teatime was the favourite visiting-time amongst our friends and relations. Other people exchanged visits on a Sunday too, but this Father would not allow. Sunday, he insisted, was a family day; none but our own little circle should partake of it. So the caller who happened to look in on a Sunday afternoon sometimes received a chilly welcome.

But on Saturday, around five o'clock, when we had got back from shopping at Jonesandhiggins, there was nearly always a visitor at the tea table. Saturday tea, with the second-best cups and saucers — the best were reserved for Sundays, the damask tablecloth with the vase of flowers in the middle, the huge fruit cake made by Mother, and the piles of bread and butter and the jam in its glass dish, was an open-house affair.

We children always hoped the Saturday visitor would be Uncle Robert. Uncle Robert, by age and general seniority, was the head of the family on Mother's side. He held, to us, an exalted position in the Civil Service, was cheery, authoritarian and thorough-going, and with his white whiskers and craggy countenance typified to us children the idea of the Family. He seemed to us a creature from another world; rather like God, or at least the Archangel Gabriel, coming down from above to hobnob with the lesser fry. His own ideas about the Deity were robust, to say the least. Darwin's Theory of Evolution roused him to positive fury. '*You* may be descended from a monkey if you like,' he would rap out with eyes blazing, 'but *I'm* not!'

Our eagerness to see him on Saturdays was not, I am ashamed to say, wholly disinterested. He might assume the dignity of the Archangel Gabriel, but he also kept wonderful things in his pockets. Like half-crowns. Uncle Robert could be counted on to give what seemed to us the most fantastic tips. Other people occasionally slipped the odd penny into our palms, but when Uncle Robert said goodbye at the front door — whither we were careful to accompany him — his hearty handshake would incorporate something cold and hard pressed into our palms, and when, with a quiver of excitement, we looked down at our hands later on, there lay a shining new half-crown, the equivalent of no less than fifteen whole weeks' pocket-money! These were indeed momentous occasions, and it was hard not to think about them when we came in from shopping at Jonesandhiggins to find Uncle Robert's black hat hanging on the hall stand.

Uncle Robert lived in a house in south-west London that was like a museum to us. It was crammed with treasures from a lifetime of travel, and here in the midst of bric-à-brac from the East and relics of medieval London, Uncle Robert lived contentedly and energetically, cared for by a devoted housekeeper whom we always knew as Aunt Susan.

'How on earth poor Aunt Susan keeps those treasures all dusted, goodness only knows,' Mother would sigh. Dusting Uncle Robert's museum-like drawing-room must have been ten times more difficult than dusting our monumental oak sideboard, I would reflect, and silently sympathise with Aunt Susan and all who had to do the dusting of the ornaments and furniture grownups were always so proud of.

Uncle Robert, even in extreme old-age — and he lived to his nineties — was a vigorous walker, and would often turn up at our house on a summer Saturday, having travelled on no tram or train at all.

'Walked all the way,' he would announce, stripping off his overcoat and flexing his muscles proudly. 'Nothing like a good walk to keep up the health and the spirits.' And he would peer at me with a quizzical gaze, as though guessing that I had been grumbling that very afternoon at the two miles I had tramped from Jonesandhiggins, when he thought nothing of tramping ten. But then, I thought, his legs were longer than mine.

He was eccentric in his habits, and astonished me one cold day in winter by suddenly peeling off his coat before Mother and inviting her to put her hand on his shirt at the back. It crackled strangely; and turned out to be stuffed with layer on layer of, of all things, brown paper!

'Brown paper,' he told us, 'is the best way of keeping out the cold. Wear it under your clothes. Capital!' Then, glancing at me, '*That* child ought to wear it!' And I had a sinking feeling at the thought of going to school crackling with brown paper under my navy blue serge tunic.

Another of Uncle Robert's eccentricities — one most welcome to us children, though slightly disconcerting to Mother — was his way of appearing, quite without warning for of course we had no telephone, at ten o'clock in the morning, and ordering anybody he found at home to put on their hats and coats; he was taking us all out for the day. He never said where until we were well on our way, which again was exciting. We adored these surprise outings. What would Uncle

Robert do today? Hire a boat and go down the Thames? Ride on an open bus to Epping Forest? Go dashing off to Richmond or Hampstead or Windsor? Mother must have found this spur-of-the-moment benevolence rather difficult to cope with, for she might be in the middle of spring-cleaning, or about to turn out the bedrooms, or expecting the sweep. But Uncle Robert would brook no delay; off we all had to go, and there was nothing for it but to give ourselves up to the wonder and glory of the moment.

Another frequent visitor was Cousin Prissie. Cousin Prissie was a sad little person who led what seemed to me a colourless life, eternal companion to various ladies in different parts of the country. She never seemed to be allowed to develop any personality of her own, and I used to feel vaguely sorry for her, and do my best to cheer up her shadowy existence by making fancy kettle-holders for her out of multi-coloured wool, or penwipers for her birthday.

Cousin Prissie was an enthusiast for tracts, and always, after her visits, we would find the house littered with little pamphlets and envelopes about the Lepers or the Africans. They would pop up in the most unexpected places, lying on a corner of the green plush couch, propped against a picture frame on the piano, or tucked into the bowl of the aspidistra. Cousin Prissie was generous to a fault, and out of her slender resources, often pressed tips into our hands as she left with her sad, sweet smile; but as she also pressed so many tracts and envelopes, I felt in honour bound to give my precious tip to the cause of the moment, and regretfully put it into the envelope and sealed it up for the post, wishing my conscience didn't prick me at such awkward times.

My father's relatives rarely came to see us, for they lived far away in Wales. But on one never-to-be-forgotten occasion — it was a Saturday teatime, too — I had come home from Jonesandhiggins to find two handsome young boys in officers' uniforms ensconced on the couch, very much on their best behaviour, and with strong Welsh lilts which sounded strange to our ears, for Father's accent had disappeared with the years. They were my cousins from Anglesey who had journeyed south to join their first ships with the Merchant Navy, and had come to pay their respects to their uncle and aunt.

I was impressed to think that two boys to whom I was talking here in our homely dining-room in a London suburb would soon be on the high seas adventuring, for I had never travelled far from home, and to go to sea seemed the pinnacle of experience. Those boys took on a glamour that stayed with me for weeks, and when we sang at kindergarten 'O where are you going to, all you big steamers?' I would think of the two young cousins and feel a prick of family pride.

Adventuring to foreign parts was always attractive to us stay-at-home children, and I used particularly to enjoy the Saturday visits of one of Aunt Jane's teaching colleagues. Lucy, as they called her, had been to foreign parts. I was always profoundly puzzled by my parents' attitude to the wonderful Lucy, who had travelled so far and seen so much, and who would sit on our couch by the hour, her ample figure shaking with mirth and enthusiasm as she talked and gesticulated about Californian beaches, prairie fires and skyscrapers. I thought she was fascinating, but I rapidly sensed some hint of disapproval in my Aunt Jane's cautious attitude.

Aunt Jane, it was easy to see, didn't hold with all these gallivantings. Once I asked her why.

'You'll understand when you're older,' she told me. 'Throwing up a nice safe pension and a promising teaching career to go cavorting around like that! She never did know the meaning of caution.'

But caution to me also, was a meaningless word although I looked it up in Father's dictionary to discover its implications. Who in their senses would worry about a pension, or saving up for their old age, when the world held so many delights that could be yours for the asking?

I privately thought the audacious Lucy had been sensible enough to forget about pensions and travel the world. Besides, did not the Bible tell you to take no thought for the morrow? I couldn't understand why grown-ups so rarely did what the Bible so clearly said. So I would sit entranced, listening to her stories about lands across the seas, and only afterwards feel faintly uneasy because I had obviously been disloyal to my family's avowed principles of caution, common sense and a safe pension at sixty-five.

Aunt Jane's teaching colleagues had a language all their own. I was accustomed from earliest years to hear this strange esoteric tongue spoken when any fellow-teachers dropped in to Saturday tea. Nickie and Aunt Jane would sit by the hour throwing out dark references to the Eltee Ay and the Guinea Girls. These two mysterious subjects haunted my thoughts for years.

At first they were sounds. Then they acquired significance — not meaning, for the Eltee Ay I imagined as a strange sort of bogey-like creature, and the Guinea Girls I associated in a vague way with my brother's pet guinea-pigs, dressed naively in skirts like Beatrix Potter animals. Finally, the Eltee Ay turned out to be the London Teachers' Association, a

442

worthy body to which my aunt and most of her professional friends belonged. Its doings were a source of constant interest to them all; but I pictured it still as some fantastic animal, living in a distant lair in Central London, and from time to time giving forth pronouncements of awful significance. 'The Eltee Ay' says this and 'The Eltee Ay' says that.

The Guinea Girls baffled me for years. I came to picture them, first as guinea-pigs, later as elegant young ladies tripping along the corridors of some unspecified school, clasping golden guineas in their hands. I knew what guineas were like, from the one that Father dangled on his watch-chain, though as coins they had gone out of currency long ago.

Apparently the Guinea Girls owed their curious name to the shortage of teachers in the elementary schools at the end of the First World War, when girls without proper training were recruited to cope with London's enormous classes, presumably at a wage of a guinea a week. The iniquities of the Guinea Girls seemed to form the subject of countless animated conversations between Aunt Jane and her friends, and my imagination was whetted accordingly. I tried to imagine the unspeakable things they did, these golden ladies who had invaded London's schools. Did they, for instance, talk with their mouths full, or walk about with dirty boots, or keep their hats on in class, or make faces in Prayers? There was no end to the fascinating possibilities of girls who were talked about with such disapproval.

By contrast, the conversations of our relatives, dropping in to Saturday tea, seemed dull and tame. They consisted, as far as I could make out, of a series of pointless inquiries about various members of the family, most of them unknown to me, and equally pointless answers.

I would listen thoughtfully, busy with pencil and paper, drawing pictures in the bay window, or curled behind the couch with the Playbox Annual.

'How's Tom?' someone would ask; and there would be a pause, a scarcely perceptible sigh. 'Much the same; much the same.'

'And Nellie?' Another pause, fraught

444

with significance that escaped me. 'Well — she gets along, you know.'

I wondered what they meant by Nellie getting along. Was she a cripple or something, walking laboriously with irons on her leg?

'Tell me about Frank, now . . . ' and they would go on interminably about Frank, whom I had never heard of but whose doings seemed as vague and pointless as Tom's and Nellie's.

Complaints of all kinds were a fruitful source of conversation with the grown-ups. They delighted in describing their symptoms, and inquiring about the symptoms of others.

'How's Jack's rheumatism these days?'

'Oh, terrible; terrible . . . ' Another pregnant silence; and all the grown-ups would sigh in unison.

Or 'Ernest; does he get those headaches still?' No answer at all this time, but a great deal of head-shaking and eyebrow-raising, through which the conversationalists, I gathered, derived as much information as they would from words.

Another topic they never tired of was the doings of the various younger members of our large and far-flung family.

'Amy; now what's *she* doing?'

'Oh, she's teaching, of course.' (Why 'of course', I would wonder?)

'And John?'

'John's doing very well; very well indeed.' A pause, during which I could almost feel the warm glow of approbation surrounding John. But they never told you any more. What was John doing? The conversation would flag for a moment; then burn up again brightly with a new inquiry. 'What about Ethel these days?'

How they went on, I would think! So many names; so many people; and who cared, after all, what Ethel and John were doing, or how Jack's rheumatism was, or Ernest's headaches either? The world was so full of exciting things to talk about; really absorbing things like pet rabbits and jelly-babies and dolls' clothes and circuses. Why didn't the grown-ups talk about these, instead of wasting time discussing illnesses?

But sometimes on Saturday nights, when we had visitors and the tea things had been cleared away and everyone was feeling relaxed and happy, they would gather round the piano and sing. Singing was something that most grown-ups were ready to join in; and then I knew the evening would be a magical one. I would sit on the green velvet-topped hassock beside Mother's rosewood piano, and listen entranced.

Singing was nothing new in our family; everyone sang. Father, with his lovely Welsh tenor; Mother with her warm contralto, my brother and myself with our piping trebles. Singing was something everybody could enjoy. It didn't cost anything, either. Not everyone in our suburb had money to spare for musical instruments; indeed not all homes boasted a piano; but we all sang.

On Sunday evenings, hymns rose up from many a home; hymns the grown-ups knew by heart, and that we children sang with straight backs and open mouths, making as much noise as we could. I could quite understand the Bible's always telling people to sing aloud, praise the Lord with gladness, come before His presence with a song, make a joyful noise and all the rest. People sang on weekdays, too, as they went about their daily tasks. You could hear our neighbours singing any day; Gilbert's mother as she went about her dusting and polishing; Wally's mother as she pegged out the sheets on Mondays, even Bertie's mother as she pottered about the long back garden. Everybody sang. So of course, on sociable Saturday evenings, the time seldom passed without a song or two.

I loved the ballads they sang, especially the sad ones with a dying fall, that brought tears to my eyes when sung by a highbusted aunt with hands clasped fervently together. Though I liked some of the robust ones too; full-blooded, swinging songs rolling from the open mouths of energetic uncles, who invariably finished on a grand note, with chest fully expanded, and then sank blandly into their armchairs to mop their brows and pretend they were surprised at the resultant clapping.

I used to long for the moment when the best-acclaimed singer amongst our aunts — had she not taken proper singing lessons? — would rise and take up her position by Mother's piano to begin 'Pale hands I loved'. The words of the song were quite incomprehensible to me; not because the singer didn't give them full voice, but because I could never make out what they were about. Nevertheless I listened enthralled:

Pale hands I loved, beside the
    Shalimar,
Where Ah — ah you now?
Where Ah-hah-you now?

Where indeed, I used to wonder? Who in their right minds would compose a song, not to a person but merely to a pair of hands? And why were they pale? And what, and where, was the mysterious Shalimar? Nobody ever gave me the answers, so I listened, with vague visions floating before me of disembodied hands, pale like corpses, wafting through the air of our cosy little room on Saturday nights. As the last notes died away, I would gaze on the singer through a mist of tears. The image she invoked was so remote, so dream-like; what could one do but listen and cry?

Sometimes, in his clear treble, my brother would sing the lullaby he had learnt at school:

Sweet and low, sweet and low,
Wind of the western sea:
Low, low, breathe and blow,
Blow him again to me.
Over the rolling waters go,
Come from the dying moon and blow,
Blow him again to me,
While my little one,
while my pretty one, sleeps.

I didn't know yet that this was by Tennyson, but the music, as well as the words, filled me with a vague, sweet sorrow; the melodies were exquisite, almost too painful to be borne. I not only pictured the fisherman's wife, gazing out across the ocean, her babe in her arms; I *was* the fisherman's wife, and waited and sighed and suffered with her. My tear-filled eyes used to embarrass my brother, who hated singing it; the song was bad enough, but to have a little sister sniffling through it was intolerable, and when he had duly sung it and sat down, he would glare at me on my green velvet hassock as if it was all my fault.

Uncles and other male visitors would often 'oblige', as they called it, with rousing songs of their own, usually a sea-shanty or two, or one of the rollicking songs which went so well with a manly figure and a good chest. Chief of these on Saturdays was 'Devon, glorious Devon', which many an uncle roared out with full enthusiasm. It had a grand finale which gave full rein to the male voice, and when he reached the last three words, the singer would throw back his head, fix his rolling eyes on our ceiling as if his audience no longer existed, and with bulging Adam's apple give vent to the last ringing phrase:

Devon, Glaw-haw-haw-rious DEVON!

When he sat down, the applause was always deafening. It had to be; the singer would have taken it very much amiss if the clapping had not kept on for at least a full minute.

Best of all, I liked to hear my father sing. Father sang with rich abandon, and a wide repertory of song covering, for the most part, the days of his young manhood when every man-about-town would be humming the latest Gilbert and Sullivan or a snatch from the fashionable operettas of the time. His favourite was 'I dreamt that I dwelt in marble halls,' closely followed by 'Take a pair of sparkling eyes,' and the light-hearted 'I love a lovely girl, I do' — often with his eye on Mother as she sat at the piano. I would wonder if he was really addressing these passionate songs to the Mother I knew — the one with the comforting smile and the hands worn with Monday's washday and Tuesday's ironing. Had she been the lovely girl, the one with the sparkling eyes? She was lovely to me, but I couldn't picture her as a girl, any more than I could picture the marble halls, or even Father dreaming that he dwelt in them. These songs were far removed from the fisherwife singing with her baby in her arms, with whom I could easily identify.

The one which did touch my heart, though, was the one which Father would usually finish the evening with — 'Just a song at twilight'. When Father's eye alighted on Mother while he was singing this song, I knew his feelings were true:

Just a song at twilight,
When the lights are low,
And the flickering shadows
Softly come and go . . .

He would sing it with such sincerity that I knew that, however different Mother was now from the girl with sparkling eyes, all was right with their world. And so it was.

Going up to bed on Saturdays, I would beg Mother to stay and sing me one more song; one to go to sleep with. She would sit on the end of my bed in the attic bedroom, and softly sing the one her mother used to sing to her, that nobody knew nowadays except ourselves:

A dear little girl sat under a tree,
Sewing as long as her eyes could
    see.
Then she smoothed her work, and
    folded it right,
And said 'Dear work, goodnight,
    goodnight'.

I was sleepy now, and her voice came more remotely, as I lay in bed at the contented close of a child's day:

A covey of rooks flew over her
    head,
Saying 'caw, caw' on their way to
    bed . . .

Dimly I saw the little girl, the spreading tree, the sewing, the covey of rooks in the evening sky. As I drifted into sleep on a Saturday night, I could still hear Mother softly singing; the loveliest voice in the world.

17

Sunday

IF I had to pick out one feature which made our childhood so very different from today's, it would be the wearing of white on Sundays. To me as a child, Sunday was the great day of all the week. No matter that it was, technically, the first; to me it was still the seventh day of the Bible, the climax to which the whole week worked up. 'Monday, Tuesday, Wednesday', you said, rolling it off your lips like a chant, 'Thursday, Friday, Saturday' rising to a crescendo — and then in a burst of triumph, 'Sunday!' the day of days.

The white frock which I always wore on Sundays, starched and ironed and spotless, typified for me the nature of this day. Sunday was pure white like the dress. You would no more think of wearing a coloured frock than you would think of flying. On this solemn, awe-inspiring, breath-taking, altogether different day, it was white dress, white petticoat, white knickers with frilled edges, white coat and hat, white hair-ribbon, white socks and shoes, white gloves — and for going to church, the very special white bead bag with the flowers worked in blue beads and the shiny chain handle to carry it by. You never used a bag like this except on Sundays.

It was the family's great pride to have everyone well turned out on Sundays. Nowadays people put on the oldest possible clothes for Sundays; but then, few of them go to church any more, and Sunday is the day for the lie in bed, for doing the garden, for catching up on the housework or the laundry when you are out all the week. But the Sunday we kept at home was the day nobody worked. Six days shalt thou labour.

We got up an hour later on Sunday; breakfast was at nine, with hot yeast rolls which Mother had baked the day before, setting the dough to prove by the kitchen fire while we watched, fascinated, the bulgings and quakings of the mysterious substance under the white cloth. On

Saturday nights we were allowed one roll each from the trayful on the larder shelf; but the rest was to be put into the oven for Sunday's breakfast, and came hot to table, to be eaten with butter melting deliciously on the crumbly broken surfaces.

Sunday breakfast was different, too; for there were no letters to be opened. Father had an invariable rule, which we dared not disregard, that no correspondence was ever to be opened until breakfast was completely finished.

'If it's bad news,' he would say, eyeing with a stony stare the pile of letters by his plate, 'it'll spoil the breakfast anyway; and if it's good news, it'll wait. Nothing like a square meal inside you to meet difficulties with.' And he would attack his bacon and eggs with relish while we fretted and squirmed with impatience as some long-awaited missive lay beside our bowls of bread-and-milk, not to be opened till the last napkin was folded, the last crumb brushed away.

But on Sundays there was no post, and everyone could relax. Father would spread out the *Sunday Dispatch* across the toast and marmalade, so that we all had to dive under its sheets to get what we wanted, and would proceed to read through the news of the week, whilst my brother and I tried, not very successfully, to read the headlines upside down as he folded the pages over. They didn't convey much to us anyway; breakfast was much more important than anything that happened in Westminster or the Empire; still it was fun to make out the headlines and mouth them silently at each other under Father's nose.

When Mother had cleared the table — Frances the 'girl' never came on Sundays, and Aunt Jane had breakfast in bed — and the washing up had been disposed of, the entire household would be marshalled upstairs to get ready for the day's great occasion, the family procession to church. Everywhere else, in similar yellowbrick houses and behind similar lace curtains, in front of similar spotted dressingtable mirrors and in similar cold marbled bathrooms, other families were making the same preparations. It was the token that you belonged to the respectable middle classes if you went to church. Church of England, of course; there were other churches about which we dimly heard, Baptist and Methodist and all the rest; our own Aunt Jane went to the Unitarian chapel in Peckham, a mile away; but this defection Father viewed with unmistakeable, if unspoken, disapproval. He escorted his family to St Mary's Parish Church, week in, week out, at precisely a quarter to eleven on a Sunday morning, reaching the door just as the chiming bells broke into the steady rhythmic single note that announced that Morning Service was about to begin.

Hair nicely brushed, face scrubbed with the harsh bathroom flannel till it shone, hatted and coated, dressed in white from head to toe, I would survey myself in Mother's long mirror before going downstairs. Hats were a necessity for little girls — indeed for every female, didn't St Paul say so? — in church, and nobody would think of going without one. I would view my own hat with approval, or occasionally with doubt. The Leghorn hats, of fine cream straw with dipping brims and daisies round the crown, were uncomfortable to wear, slippery as eels, and, so I thought, definitely unbecoming. Money being short in our household, the Leghorn hat of the moment was all too often last year's outgrown one, and perched on the top of my head like an acorn cup, giving me an air of astonishment which I didn't like.

Sometimes the hat would be a legacy from an older cousin. This was all right when it was a sensible affair, but my cousin's parents lived in the very new and fashionable Garden Suburb at Hampstead, where tastes tended to the William Morris, Liberty's, Kate Greenaway — in fact, the generally arty. Most of these country dresses and hats may have looked delightful in the Garden Suburb, but they definitely didn't suit a little girl with a tubby figure and uncompromisingly straight hair.

My favourite of all Sunday hats was one Mother made herself, following with loving care the pattern in one of the women's magazines. It was of spotted muslin, and resembled nothing so much as a couple of pancakes, one placed airily upon the other, the bottom layer flopping round my ears in billowing curves, and the whole thing prettied up with blue satin bows. I would stand before the mirror in this Sunday confection, imagining myself a milkmaid or a princess, or some other creature set apart from the world of yellow-brick houses and suburban streets. What a difference, I thought fondly, a hat made — especially to someone plain like me. And I hoped most sincerely that someone in church would notice the latest fashion in little girls' hats, and forget I had ever worn those hateful Leghorns.

The white frocks were a uniform pattern for little girls then — high round necks, lace-edged and threaded with narrow ribbon; bodices tucked with many tucks or decorated with insertion or broderie anglaise; wide skirts tucked once again, in case they had to be let down; and a slotted waist-line to take whatever sash the wearer might fancy.

What sash to wear for Sundays was a great subject for concentrated thought in that half-hour before we departed for church. Should it be the pink, or the blue, or the white — the satin one that looked as if it had come off somebody's birthday cake? Whatever was chosen had to be threaded through the slots and tied at the back in a bow, as I stood wriggling before Mother or Aunt Jane. The ends had to fall just so, which was a tiresome business that you had to suffer in silence. Then the white openwork socks had to be pulled up and secured by garters made from white elastic. Sometimes the white shoes were so new that the buttonholes were mere slits, and there would be another frantic hunt for a button-hook to do them up. Then the white coat — cashmere or shantung, with white pearly buttons, which I used to suck when everybody knelt down in church; they tasted cool and smooth. The white bead bag had to be found, and a white handkerchief put in it, with the penny for the collection; and when all this was done, in summer I would run out to the garden and pick myself a buttonhole from the rose-bush by the fence — the little moss rose bush that had tiny buds just the right size for little girls' Sunday coats. But I had to be quick over this, for there was something else that I had to do before we assembled for church.

462

I would go into the hall, open the drawer in the carved oak hall-stand of which Father was so proud — it matched the carved oak desk in his study, and the enormous carved oak sideboard in the dining-room — carefully take out the soft brush with the faded green velvet back, and lift Father's silk hat from its cupboard. Then, holding the hat reverently with my left hand inside its white satin interior, I would brush it gently round and round with the soft brush until the nap lay gleaming like sealskin, black and smooth, every tiny hair in place. Brushing a silk hat was a work of art as well as a Sunday ritual. You acquired the knack over the years, but it took time. I brushed it, one eye on the hands of the grandfather clock in the hall, lest we should be late; not that there was any need to worry, for we were always on time as our family procession entered the church door.

Father's silk hat was itself something of a ritual. Not many fathers in those suburbs still wore silk hats — or top hats as the uninitiated called them. But Father, a stickler for etiquette, never failed to put on his silk hat every Sunday. The curly bowler was for weekdays, but Sunday would not be the same without the silk hat, the black coat, the striped trousers without turn-ups — 'a ridiculous fashion' Father called the trouser turn-ups that everybody else wore.

Father, indeed, would make no concession at all to modern fashion. The silk hat, the black coat, the trousers, had all been correct formal wear in his student days, and correct wear they would still be for him, even if everybody else had abandoned them. 'People are getting slacker and slacker in dress,' Father would declare roundly. 'Slack in dress, slack in morals. Thank goodness I know better.'

As we grew older, my brother and I grew more and more uncomfortable about Father's silk hat. It was embarrassing to walk the suburban streets alongside a father dressed so uniquely. The climax to my own discomfiture came when a nasty little girl at school called Ruby dared to criticise Father's hat.

'He's short, so he only wears it to make him look taller,' announced this horrid child one day in the school cloakroom;

and though my wrath rose and family loyalty made me take suitable vengeance on Ruby, the hurt remained.

Actually, though his shortness may have had something to do with it, Father kept to his old-fashioned conventions more from a love of the past than from any other motive. To him the past always set the standards; it was invariably better, by far, than the present. Long after everyone else had gone into soft collars, Father kept to his stiff cutaways that pressed uncomfortably into the chin. Long after everyone else had taken to mackintoshes, he clung to his old Inverness cape with its voluminous black folds and shapeless sleeves, as worn by Sherlock Holmes. (He was fond of reminding us that the creator of Sherlock Holmes had been his predecessor in one of the country practices where he had worked as doctor's assistant in the old days.)

He was a stickler for correct, precise, almost pedantic speech, too, and scolded us roundly if we dared to say 'bus' for omnibus, 'bike' for bicycle, or 'pram' for perambulator. And again I suffered untold humiliation at school when unkind friends teased me about my queer vocabulary.

But the silk hat, like it or not, had to be worn every Sunday, and had to be brushed by me. When I had got it gleaming to my satisfaction, I would balance it carefully on the hall stand, next to Father's gloves and prayer-book, and wait obediently by the grandfather clock, watching the hands slowly creep towards the quarter-to.

Promptly at quarter to eleven, the family set off for church. Father was invariably the last to appear, but did so in such a way that he seemed to be the first to lead forth his little brood, and chided the rest of us for keeping him waiting. 'Look at me!' he would say, stepping confidently out of the front door, with us at his heels. 'Always the first out. I don't know what you all find to do that makes you so late!' And Mother would catch my eye as I was about to remonstrate, reminding me silently that peace at all costs was the rule on Sundays. Mother bore with Father as one would with the vagaries of a little boy; and we children dared not argue. Father was always right.

We set off down the steps and turned into the road, Father and Mother in front, my brother and myself bringing up the rear. My brother was dressed in a Norfolk suit or else in blue serge with his school cap crammed firmly on his head, but ready to raise whenever we encountered a neighbouring family also churchbound: boots shining so that you could see your face in them, clean handkerchief, clean finger-nails; and I was in all the glory of my Sunday white.

All down the road, similar families were emerging from doorways and joining the procession to church just as the bells began ringing. Mothers nodded sedately to mothers; fathers allowed themselves a discreet smile of recognition at other fathers leading their broods in the same direction, and I noticed thankfully that there was at least one other father also wearing a silk hat. Round the corner, along the street, past Mr Smith's the grocer's, bolted, shuttered and barred; past the public house where you averted your gaze and tried not to breathe in the beery smell that emerged as they were sweeping out the bar, and on to where the houses became bigger and grander, until finally, as the bells changed to a single peal, you turned solemnly in at the church door and climbed the stairs to the gallery. A cold chill of stone, and a smell of wooden pews and hassocks met you here; the sunshine was left behind. Don't fuss; don't look at the ladies' hats you are in church now, and must behave accordingly.

Our gallery seats were a continual thorn in the flesh to me. I would have liked to sit in the body of the church, which I could just see far below, amongst the grand ladies in feather boas and flowery headgear, where there was a view of the chancel and the altar, and you could watch the mischievous choirboys misbehaving when the sermon got too boring.

The gallery, where we sat, was altogether more humble; probably it cost less, for you paid for your seats at St Mary's then, if not openly, at least tacitly in the form of pew-rent every so often in a little yellow envelope. To make matters worse, we were not in the front row of the gallery, but back in the second row, where you couldn't even have the fun of leaning over the front rail and watching what went on below.

The only good view we had was of the Vicar when he mounted the pulpit to deliver his sermon. Here he was just on a level with us, and you could follow every movement, every gesture, every expression, and notice when he was going to cough or clear his throat or sneeze or get out his handkerchief. Looking at the Vicar was fun, but it wasn't quite as much fun when he looked at you, and you remembered that he — like God — had an all-seeing eye and could detect it if you had holes in the fingers of your gloves where you had chewed them during the litany. The gallery ran round three sides of the church, but the side opposite afforded no pleasure; it was full of dull people, except for the boy and girl at the end of the front row — the boy who wore an Eton jacket and had once exchanged a wink with me during the sermon.

We proceeded in an orderly fashion to our allotted seats, my brother first, myself second, Mother third and Father last. His was the task of passing the collection plate to the row behind when we had all put in our offerings. I was glad I didn't have to do this, as the Sunday gloves when new were so slippery, and it was the easiest thing in the world to drop either your penny or the whole collection plate.

We settled in our pews; Father reached backwards to place his silk hat carefully on the empty seat behind, which nobody rented; we bowed our heads, and then, as the clergy and choir trooped in far below, raised our voices in a mighty chorus for the opening hymn. The service had begun.

At first I was so small that I couldn't even see over the top of the pew without standing on a hassock, and when I knelt down amidst all the legs and skirts, it was like being buried underground in some great sepulchre smelling of pitch-pine and camphor balls. The service seemed to go on for ever, and the only part of it in which I could join at all was the singing of the Amens. Even this seemed to me very unreasonable: why Ah-men and never Ah-women? were we really such a negligible sex? For the sermon, which lasted a full twenty minutes — more if the Vicar forgot to look at his watch — I was allowed to take a Sunday picture-book to keep me quiet. The usual one was *Daniel in the Lions' Den*, which had gaudy but fascinating pictures of Daniel being miraculously preserved from the most ferocious-looking lions. After a time I knew the book so well that the lions lost their ferocity and became old friends, so that I would mentally pat their heads when I got to the pages with the pictures, and wonder how Daniel could possibly be afraid of them.

When the sermon ended and the collection came round, you had to have your money ready in your gloved hand. As soon as the plate appeared, you discreetly opened the little bead bag and extracted your penny, watching out of the corner of your eye as the plate approached nearer and nearer, till the fat sidesman with the bald head and the twinkle in his eye that belied his solemn Sunday expression, was holding it right under your nose. Quick, pass it on and pray you wouldn't drop it. There were sixpences and shillings in the plate, sometimes even half-a-crown, occasionally and unbelievably, a ten shilling note, more money than we had ever seen except for the golden guinea that Father used to keep on his watch-chain and dangle before us when we played on his knee. How we could have spent all that money at Mrs Evans' sweetshop, on sugared almonds, and hundreds-and-thousands to eat on bread and butter, and lemon drops, and Van Houten's chocolate bars! But on went the plate on its remorseless rounds, and left us with only our Saturday coppers.

We used to long for something to happen to break the tedium of that service. It went on such a long time; the lengthy prayers were mostly incomprehensible; the responses were always just the same, intoned on just the same notes. Only the hymns were ever different, and most of these I couldn't understand.

When the Vicar called the banns,

ending with 'If any of you know just cause or impediment . . . ye are to declare it,' I used to pray that someone would come running up the aisle to stop the forthcoming marriage, and at least enliven the proceedings; but no one ever did. Once Mother was afflicted with cramp, just as the Vicar was giving out the text for his sermon, and was forced to writhe in agony till Father could lead her out into the passage. The Vicar saw all this and assumed an expression of grieved dismay, which I resented strongly: hadn't *he* ever had the cramp?

Once at a Scout service, which we had every month, some twelve-year-old Scouts were put in the vacant pew behind us, and sat down heavily on Father's new silk hat, which he had placed as usual on the empty seat. Father's language was anything but reverent, and the Scoutmaster had to do some explaining.

Once a dog got into church, and caused disruption amongst the ladies, who wanted to scream and couldn't, and the choirboys, who wanted to giggle and daren't. The organist came to the rescue here, and led us all into a loud paean of

'Onward Christian Soldiers' under cover of which someone discreetly led out the dog. I often used to try to induce our old collie to come to church with us to break the monotony at a suitable moment, but I could never solve the difficulty of his joining the solemn Sunday procession to church.

When the organ at last pealed out the voluntary, we shook off the drowsiness of the sermon and the last hymn, and filed out into the sunshine. After-church was an occasion of its own. Families met and mingled; mothers inquired about Clara's cough and Grandma's rheumatism, and wondered whether the good weather would hold for the choirboys' outing. Fathers exchanged greetings, and commented solemnly on the sermon; they were great judges of sermons in those days. Boys furtively watched out for the girls, seeing a chance of walking home with a pretty neighbour under cover of family conversation about the new curate or the Church Hall Building Fund. Little girls admired each other's frocks and Sunday bags, and compared the celluloid bookmarks which we delighted to keep in our prayer books. The road home was full of contented people, Sunday worship over and the prospect of a good meal and an afternoon nap before them. From every house wafted the aromas of the Sunday joint being basted, Sunday vegetables being cooked. The 'rough' boys seemed to keep off the streets on a Sunday; where they played, or whether they ever went to church, nobody seemed to know. Certainly there was no poverty in the congregation we saw around us at St Mary's; they were all well-fed, well-dressed, uncontrovertibly 'nice'. Even the Park, where my brother and I used to walk with Father and the dog after church while Mother was putting the finishing touches to the dinner, seemed full of little girls in white and little boys in sailor suits or Eton jackets; there were no children with tousled hair or holes in their elbows, positively no boys with bare feet such as I had seen calling at our house with the manure buckets. Sunday had cast its spell over the whole suburb, and everything was serene and bright.

Sunday dinner, cooked by Aunt Jane who went to chapel in the evenings, was the dinner of the week. In every house along the road the pattern was the same, at least as regards the meat and drink. With great to-do, Mother dished up the roast meat and vegetables. There were all the trimmings; sauces, Yorkshire pudding, stuffing or whatever Mrs Beeton recommended; Mrs Beeton's heavy red tome was prominent on Mother's kitchen mantelpiece, and when I was in bed with a cold it was a treat to leaf through her monumental pages and amuse myself with coloured pictures of luscious jellies and blancmanges, calves' heads, cold meat shapes and bridal cakes.

We always had a white damask cloth for Sundays, immaculately laundered, and immaculately laundered table napkins to match, which crackled with starch as you spread them on your knee. The table was laid in full glory, mostly with Mother's wedding presents — the cut-glass tumblers, the cut-glass water-jug, the cut-glass supports where Father rested his carving knife and fork, the best silver, the best dishes. A bottle of Rose's Lime Juice stood demurely at the corner — nothing stronger than lime juice ever entered our house, for both my parents were strict teetotallers and believed you only had to take one sip from the Devil's bottle to be on the way to alcoholism.

There would be a heavy hot pudding with plenty of custard, and of course a big rice pudding for Father, who never had anything else for a sweet during the whole of his life. There was dessert to follow, which was kept for a special Sunday treat — nuts and grapes and raisins in a blue dish — and when all was eaten, and the table cleared, we would pester Father to play his game with the musical glasses.

Father would reach for the used tumblers, just as they were being whisked off to the kitchen, fill them to varying heights with water, then place them in a row, and, wetting his finger, run it round the rims, producing a low musical hum like that of a spinning top in motion, each one different. 'Let us try too!' we would shout, but our glasses were never so musical as his. Up and down the scale he would play, with Mother and Aunt Jane hovering impatiently in the background waiting to finish the table-clearing and washing up, so that they might enjoy a Sunday afternoon nap. But Father would be busy explaining to us the scientific reasons for his musical glasses, and the womenfolk's beseeching glances would go quite unnoticed.

Sunday afternoons were a mystery to me. I couldn't understand why everyone retired to the bedrooms just as the afternoon sun was at its brightest, and the whole glorious day at its fairest — just to lie down on their beds in darkened rooms and sleep. But that is what they liked to do. To me the entire golden afternoon was wasted — time, full of precious moments and wonderful things to do, spent in merely lying down. What fools the grown-ups were! How much they missed!

I would dance with impatience as the hours sped by and still nobody was stirring, nobody would come downstairs to play or read or sit in the garden with me. Upstairs the rooms were hushed and still, the Venetian blinds tight-drawn, as though someone were dead. Downstairs in his padded old armchair, Father slept

— stretched out in abandonment, his brown velvet smoking-cap pushed to the back of his head — another outmoded piece of costume to which he clung, yet which Mother religiously provided for him on every one of his birthdays, cutting out the brown velvet to some pattern of her own and stitching away on the little old chain-stitch sewing-machine.

I would creep in to watch him, fascinated and awed; it wasn't often that we got the chance to see authority relaxed and defenceless. His shoulders would heave rhythmically, his breathing become more and more stertorous, till suddenly his whole body would twitch and contort in a sonorous snore ending in a grunt, which woke him up to stare at me with accusing eyes. Of course he hadn't been asleep; of course he never snored; and indeed, though I had only just heard him with my own ears, I would never dream of contradicting him.

After wandering up and down the garden in bored impatience, kicking the edge of the little stone pond with my white Sunday shoe, knocking off the heads of a few dandelions out of sheer spite, staring up at the curtained and shrouded windows of all the other houses where other parents slumbered and snored the golden afternoon away, I would go into the house again and regretfully decide to learn the Collect for the week. We always had to repeat the Collect for the week to Mother on Sunday afternoons when she came downstairs, and get it word-perfect too. I would take my prayer book, the red leather one that had been mine since I was first taken to church at four years old, and sit down on the bottom stair, within listening distance of the bedrooms, to learn it.

Most of the Collects seemed to me very wordy, and I could not get much sense out of them: but just here and there a light shone out, and I knew that I was reading something precious, dimly apprehended. 'Pour down upon us the abundance of Thy mercy . . . the author and giver of all good things . . . unto whom all hearts be opened, all desires known, and from whom no secrets are hid . . . ' I thought of the all-seeing eye that knew even if I only told the smallest fib, filched the greenest gooseberry. How well the people who wrote the Collects seemed to know the mind of a small child!

At last there would come a creak from the bedroom, as of someone getting up from the bed. Soft sounds and movements, that betokened the world would soon go on again. Mother would come downstairs looking wonderful in her best black silk; Father would heave himself from his chair and deny he had ever been to sleep; life would resume. And then, for me, once the Collect was repeated, Sunday afternoon — glorious, relaxed Sunday afternoon — would really begin.

Mother didn't wish us to go to Sunday school, preferring to keep us with her at home on Sunday afternoons; so, whilst other children ran down the road with hymn books tucked under their arms, hair brushed and faces shining, we spent our time peacefully at home. In summer we would sit out in the garden; in winter, gather before the fire. Mother would give up all the afternoon to reading aloud to the family.

We loved winter Sundays. My brother and I would settle ourselves, he with a bit of machinery, a clock he was taking to pieces, or something else to satisfy his craving for scientific experiment; I with a brush and paintbox, intent on colouring the text we used to bring home from kindergarten on Fridays: 'God is Love' or 'The Lord is my Shepherd', in large hectographed purple letters, with an accompanying picture of fruit or flowers to blossom gorgeously into paintbox reds and blues, greens and yellows. These we would take back with pride on Monday mornings and get the best of them pinned to the wall, and great was our joy if our own text was chosen for display.

There would be a bag of sweets at our elbow, for each of us, on Sunday; a quarter of a pound of toffees, or acid drops, costing fourpence (the cheap ones) and fivepence-halfpenny (better quality). These had to last us all the week, but we invariably ate them all while Mother read, and Father half-slumbered in his leather chair. And what books we got through!

Mother loved them all, and made us

love them too. Children's books there were of all kinds, from *Little Lord Fauntleroy* to *Alice*; and as we grew older, the girls' classics Mother had saved from her own youth — *Daisy*, *The Dove in the Eagle's Nest*, *What Katy Did* or the boys' books, *Masterman Ready*, *Swiss Family Robinson*, *Five Weeks in a Balloon*; and later still, most of the classics, Dickens, Scott, Thackeray, with the dull bits tactfully skipped and the whole narrative brought to life through Mother's vivid voice.

Then we would try books from the Lewisham Public Library: Conan Doyle, Stephen Mackenna, Galsworthy, Philip Gibbs. Much of these I couldn't understand, but it was pleasant merely to sit and listen, watching my purple irises and yellow crocuses, the green and crimson apples and the golden beech leaves burgeon under my brush as I painted my Sunday text. We never even wanted to stop for tea, but promptly at a quarter to five Aunt Jane would descend from the bedroom and we would scramble to get the tea in time for her to go to chapel.

After tea, with an enormous Sunday

fruit cake taking pride of place, and the best gold and red tea-service brought out, Mother would begin reading again. This time she would read special requests from me, and I would come into my own with the old favourites — the nursery stories I already knew by heart, or a tale out of *Little Folks*, the big thick American-type annual we children loved.

Sunday evening would always finish in the same way, with hymns as we gathered round the piano — the little old tinkly piano that was Mother's cherished possession. Our evening hymn-singing put the seal on the day. Mother would play, Father would join in with his beautiful Welsh tenor, my brother and I, craning our necks to see the words in the hymn book, would sing as lustily as we could, whilst through the bay window we watched the sun go down behind the chimney-pots in a blaze of gold and red.

The last hymn was always the same — 'The day Thou gavest, Lord, is ended' — and as the gentle melody sank into my drowsy mind, it seemed as though there were some special benediction about those dim and quiet Sunday evenings. Especially in summer. Outside, the golden sunset would transform even our ordinary little road; the brick houses would be ruddy with evening light, the roofs silhouetted against the shining west; birds would be flying homeward; the streets would be quiet, with only the odd footstep falling into the silence. Soon we would be going up to bed, the last bars of our evening hymn-singing in our ears; the house barely stilled from the tinkling piano and Father's rich tones, the voice of a Welshman to whom singing was as natural as breathing.

Now all that remained was bed. We took our candles from the top of the kitchen dresser, my brother and I, filched an apple each from the sideboard, and munching silently, went up the stairs. One flight, two flights, three flights — and the little top room under the roof where you could lie in bed, hair brushed, teeth cleaned, prayers said, and watch the first stars twinkle out from the night sky over the chimney-pots.

The white dress and its accessories had

been tidily put away; tomorrow it would be back to ordinary clothes again. But at least for this one day of the week, I had been resplendent in glory. I had worn white on Sunday.

486

18

Endings

IT was when I was twelve that I think my childhood ended. Three things happened then that seemed to close one chapter and open the next. A young Scottish minister came to Aunt Jane's Unitarian chapel; I had an argument with Father; and a new headmistress was appointed to our school.

The young Scottish minister was rawboned, raven-haired and luminous-eyed. He was a true Celt from one of the remoter islands, and had all the Celtic fervour for learning that marked his race. He came as a kind of unqualified lay pastor, and was a frequent visitor to our house, calling my mother Mistress in the traditional old Scots way, and communicating to us something of his own unappeased hunger of the mind. After a time he managed to get a place at a theological college at Oxford to complete his training; and it was while he was there as a student that he invited Aunt Jane and me up for the day.

It was an unbelievable day. It had something of the quality of that perfect day with Mother in the country, when we picked the kingcups; but in addition a fascination of its own, a revelation of something quite new to me. I felt as though the heavens had opened, and shafts of sunlight were pouring into the dusty recesses of my mind.

For one thing, the city itself was such a perfect, lovely place. I had never been very far from home, and Bognor and Brighton, and even Suffolk, bore no resemblance whatever to this entrancing city of spires and pinnacles, green lawns, dim cloisters and everlasting bells. It seemed as remote from the clanging trams and yellow-brick streets of our suburb as some fair city on an unknown shore.

I drank in its beauty, and more than its beauty, its spell; the spell cast by a whole tradition of learning, built up by saint and sage, poet and scholar through centuries of time. Now at last

I began dimly to perceive what the world could hold of wonder and beauty. There were things of the mind, beyond the narrow confines of text-books and school homework; things of the spirit, beyond the banality of city streets. Walking in the quietness of New College Gardens, I suddenly saw quite clearly a new horizon — far off but attainable. It was so very distant; nevertheless I knew now that you didn't stay a child for ever; that you moved on; could it be to places like this?

The second event happened in our own home, over the breakfast table — a most unlikely time and place for anything so significant, but that is the way things happen. Father had finished his breakfast, and, pushing aside the marmalade and toast, was opening his paper.

Something in the day's news turned his mind to the question of peace and war. 'These pacifists — ' he said.

Immediately we were clashing in argument. Somehow I had never realised before that Father stood for the old school, King, Country and Empire. Where else indeed could he stand, brought up in the Victorian tradition? the most peaceable of men, yet prepared to fight to the death in defence of what he saw as the Right.

I hadn't thought about pacifists before; but now I suddenly knew what the word meant, and why it was important. More important, somehow, than anything had ever been to me before. I found myself blurting out passionately that if pacifists were people who refused to kill, then I was one of them. All the stored up emotions of years seemed to come and choke me; all the dim memories of the war in which I had grown up; things I barely remembered, like the burning Zeppelin, yet which were a part of me; and it became the most urgent thing in life to convince him that he was wrong. I knew that I hadn't really changed since those early days when I had stood in the kitchen and asked Mother 'Why don't they stop fighting?' It was — it could be — as simple as that; a personal thing, something I knew instinctively as right. I leaned across the table and argued with Father till the tears came with the sudden surge of feeling.

Father just could not believe he was hearing a child of his say such things; even — as he thought — for argument's sake. When I burst into tears he was aghast. He rose from the table, scattering the sheets of the paper and knocking over the marmalade; and his expression was one of utter disbelief.

'Well,' he exclaimed, 'I'd never in my wildest dreams — '

I did not wait to hear more, but rushed from the room and up to my little attic, where I lay on the iron bedstead and cried. And I knew I was crying, not merely for an argument I wanted to win and couldn't; but for the end of a childhood. The serenity, the acceptance, had gone. Father no longer knew best; I could no longer obey him implicitly. I was beginning to perceive that in the things of the mind, one has to go forward quite alone.

The third event happened about the same time. Our dear old headmistress Miss Young, with the snowy hair and the Jehovah like presence, was to go; the one who had examined my hand for cuts when I broke the window with

Bunny in the kindergarten; the one who had presided at those wonderful Prize Days, for years and years and years; the one who *was* my school. Her place was taken by a vigorous woman from one of the Oxford colleges, hockey-playing and modern. She wanted to bring the whole place up to date. And the first thing she did was to decree that henceforth there should be no more white dresses for Prize Day. We were to wear our ordinary school uniforms of navy blue. Nobody wore white any more, she said.

Not wear our white dresses! I could scarcely believe it. As long as I could remember, we had worn white on Sundays and special occasions — white as a mark of respect, as a token of something very precious, and utterly, utterly different from every day. Lately, it was true, things had subtly changed; even I now wore shantung dresses for church, and fawn coats. But still at least once every year, on Prize Day, we could wear the lovely white frocks, so immaculate and virginal, so special and beloved, against which our red roses glowed like jewels.

Now, with the white dresses, the glory of those Prize Days, with their chrysanthemums and beech leaves, their hymns and their long, unintelligible but oddly exalting speeches, would be past for ever. And a lot of other things would be past for ever, too. Nothing would be quite the same again. Nothing at all.

Slowly I folded my white dress, wrapped it in tissue paper, and laid it away in the drawer.

THE END

THE WILDERNESS WALK
Sheila Bishop

Stifling unpleasant memories of a misbegotten romance in Cleave with Lord Francis Aubrey, Lavinia goes on holiday there with her sister. The two women are thrust into a romantic intrigue involving none other than Lord Francis.

THE RELUCTANT GUEST
Rosalind Brett

Ann Calvert went to spend a month on a South African farm with Theo Borland and his sister. They both proved to be different from her first idea of them, and there was Storr Peterson — the most disturbing man she had ever met.

ONE ENCHANTED SUMMER
Anne Tedlock Brooks

A tale of mystery and romance and a girl who found both during one enchanted summer.

CLOUD OVER MALVERTON
Nancy Buckingham

Dulcie soon realises that something is seriously wrong at Malverton, and when violence strikes she is horrified to find herself under suspicion of murder.

AFTER THOUGHTS
Max Bygraves

The Cockney entertainer tells stories of his East End childhood, of his RAF days, and his post-war showbusiness successes and friendships with fellow comedians.

MOONLIGHT
AND MARCH ROSES
D. Y. Cameron

Lynn's search to trace a missing girl takes her to Spain, where she meets Clive Hendon. While untangling the situation, she untangles her emotions and decides on her own future.

NURSE ALICE IN LOVE
Theresa Charles

Accepting the post of nurse to little Fernie Sherrod, Alice Everton could not guess at the romance, suspense and danger which lay ahead at the Sherrod's isolated estate.

POIROT INVESTIGATES
Agatha Christie

Two things bind these eleven stories together — the brilliance and uncanny skill of the diminutive Belgian detective, and the stupidity of his Watson-like partner, Captain Hastings.

LET LOOSE THE TIGERS
Josephine Cox

Queenie promised to find the long-lost son of the frail, elderly murderess, Hannah Jason. But her enquiries threatened to unlock the cage where crucial secrets had long been held captive.

THE TWILIGHT MAN
Frank Gruber

Jim Rand lives alone in the California desert awaiting death. Into his hermit existence comes a teenage girl who blows both his past and his brief future wide open.

DOG IN THE DARK
Gerald Hammond

Jim Cunningham breeds and trains gun dogs, and his antagonism towards the devotees of show spaniels earns him many enemies. So when one of them is found murdered, the police are on his doorstep within hours.

THE RED KNIGHT
Geoffrey Moxon

When he finds himself a pawn on the chessboard of international espionage with his family in constant danger, Guy Trent becomes embroiled in moves and countermoves which may mean life or death for Western scientists.

TIGER TIGER
Frank Ryan

A young man involved in drugs is found murdered. This is the first event which will draw Detective Inspector Sandy Woodings into a whirlpool of murder and deceit.

CAROLINE MINUSCULE
Andrew Taylor

Caroline Minuscule, a medieval script, is the first clue to the whereabouts of a cache of diamonds. The search becomes a deadly kind of fairy story in which several murders have an other-worldly quality.

LONG CHAIN OF DEATH
Sarah Wolf

During the Second World War four American teenagers from the same town join the Army together. Forty-two years later, the son of one of the soldiers realises that someone is systematically wiping out the families of the four men.

THE LISTERDALE MYSTERY
Agatha Christie

Twelve short stories ranging from the light-hearted to the macabre, diverse mysteries ingeniously and plausibly contrived and convincingly unravelled.

TO BE LOVED
Lynne Collins

Andrew married the woman he had always loved despite the knowledge that Sarah married him for reasons of her own. So much heartache could have been avoided if only he had known how vital it was to be loved.

ACCUSED NURSE
Jane Converse

Paula found herself accused of a crime which could cost her her job, her nurse's reputation, and even the man she loved, unless the truth came to light.

CHATEAU OF FLOWERS
Margaret Rome

Alain, Comte de Treville needed a wife to look after him, and Fleur went into marriage on a business basis only, hoping that eventually he would come to trust and care for her.

CRISS-CROSS
Alan Scholefield

As her ex-husband had succeeded in kidnapping their young daughter once, Jane was determined to take her safely back to England. But all too soon Jane is caught up in a new web of intrigue.

DEAD BY MORNING
Dorothy Simpson

Leo Martindale's body was discovered outside the gates of his ancestral home. Is it, as Inspector Thanet begins to suspect, murder?

A GREAT DELIVERANCE
Elizabeth George

Into the web of old houses and secrets of Keldale Valley comes Scotland Yard Inspector Thomas Lynley and his assistant to solve a particularly savage murder.

'E' IS FOR EVIDENCE
Sue Grafton

Kinsey Millhone was bogged down on a warehouse fire claim. It came as something of a shock when she was accused of being on the take. She'd been set up. Now she had a new client — herself.

A FAMILY OUTING IN AFRICA
Charles Hampton and Janie Hampton

A tale of a young family's journey through Central Africa by bus, train, river boat, lorry, wooden bicycle and foot.

THE PLEASURES OF AGE
Robert Morley

The author, British stage and screen star, now eighty, is enjoying the pleasures of age. He has drawn on his experiences to write this witty, entertaining and informative book.

THE VINEGAR SEED
Maureen Peters

The first book in a trilogy which follows the exploits of two sisters who leave Ireland in 1861 to seek their fortune in England.

A VERY PAROCHIAL MURDER
John Wainwright

A mugging in the genteel seaside town turned to murder when the victim died. Then the body of a young tearaway is washed ashore and Detective Inspector Lyle is determined that a second killing will not go unpunished.

DEATH ON A HOT SUMMER NIGHT
Anne Infante

Micky Douglas is either accident-prone or someone is trying to kill him. He finds himself caught in a desperate race to save his ex-wife and others from a ruthless gang.

HOLD DOWN A SHADOW
Geoffrey Jenkins

Maluti Rider, with the help of four of the world's most wanted men, is determined to destroy the Katse Dam and release a killer flood.

THAT NICE MISS SMITH
Nigel Morland

A reconstruction and reassessment of the trial in 1857 of Madeleine Smith, who was acquitted by a verdict of Not Proven of poisoning her lover, Emile L'Angelier.

7/13/22 JR
8-14 23